Parenting in Poor Environments

of related interest

Imprisoned Fathers and their Children
Gwyneth Boswell and Peter Wedge
ISBN 1 85302 972 6

Supporting Parents of Teenagers
A Handbook for Professionals
Edited by John Coleman and Debi Roker
ISBN 1 85302 944 0

The Child's World
Assessing Children in Need
Edited by Jan Horwath
ISBN 1 85302 957 2

Approaches to Needs Assessment in Children's Services
Edited by Harriet Ward and Wendy Rose
Foreword by Professor Al Aynsley-Green
ISBN 1 85302 780 4

A Multidisciplinary Handbook of Child and Adolescent Mental Health for Front-line Professionals
Nisha Dogra, Andrew Parkin, Fiona Gale and Clay Frake
Foreword by Panos Vostanis
ISBN 1 85302 929 7

Engaging with Fathers
Practice Issues for Health and Social Care
Brigid Daniel and Julie Taylor
IBSN 1 85302 794

Child Development for Child Care and Protection Workers
Brigid Daniel, Sally Wassell and Robbie Gilligan
Foreword by Jim Ennis
ISBN 1 85302 633 6

Social Work with Children and Families
Getting into Practice
Ian Butler and Gwenda Roberts
ISBN 1 85302 365 5

POLICY ● RESEARCH ┃UREAU

Parenting in Poor Environments

Stress, Support and Coping

Deborah Ghate and Neal Hazel

Jessica Kingsley Publishers
London and Philadelphia

The right of Deborah Ghate and Neal Hazel to be identified as authors of this work has been asserted by them in accordance with the Copyright, Designs and Patents Act 1988.

First published in the United Kingdom in 2002
by Jessica Kingsley Publishers Ltd
116 Pentonville Road
London N1 9JB, England
and
325 Chestnut Street
Philadelphia, PA 19106, USA

www.jkp.com

Copyright © 2002 Policy Research Bureau

Library of Congress Cataloging-in-Publication Data
Ghate, Deborah.
Parenting in poor environments : stress, support, and coping / Deborah Ghate and Neal Hazel.
p. cm.
Includes bibliographical material references and index.
ISBN 1-84310-069-X (alk. Paper)
1. Poor families--Great Britain. 2. Poor parents--Great Britain. 3. Poor parents--Social networks--Great Britain. 4. Stress (Psychology)--Great Britain. 5. Family social work--Great Britain. 6. Family life surveys--Great Britain. I.Hazel, Neal. II. Title.

HV700.G7 G435 2002
362.82'53'0941--dc21

2002025466

British Library Cataloguing in Publication Data
A CIP catalogue record for this book is available from the British Library

ISBN 1 84310 069 X

Printed and Bound in Great Britain by
Athenaeum Press, Gateshead, Tyne and Wear

Contents

Acknowledgements

Many people contributed to this book and the study it describes. The Policy Research Bureau team were responsible for the initial conception and overall design of the research, including sampling, questionnaire development, qualitative interviewing and all analysis. Data collection was carried out on our behalf by a team at MORI Social Research, directed by Andy Cubie and Mark Speed, and over a hundred interviewers worked very hard to screen households and interview parents. Statistical consultancy for the sample design was provided by Simon Hearn at Hearn Taylor. Anna Thomas, former Research Fellow at PSI, made a major contribution to the development of the questionnaire and to gathering data for the construction of the PPE-Index. At the Policy Research Bureau, Rebekah Kops worked on the graphics for the book, and Patricia Moran and Ann Hagell made helpful comments on the text. We are also grateful to Caroline Thomas and Carolyn Davies at the Department of Health for their support throughout the entire project, and to the Department's Research Liaison Group who made helpful comments on early drafts of the book. Last, thanks are due to all the parents who gave so generously of their time to participate in the study interviews.

Deborah Ghate and Neal Hazel
Policy Research Bureau, January 2002

Preface

This book documents the findings and conclusions of a large national study of parents living in poor environments which was conducted by the Policy Research Bureau between 1997 and 1999 under the Department of Health's children's research initiative, 'Supporting Parents'. The study involved face-to-face survey interviews with over 1700 parents or main carers of children aged up to 16 years and in-depth qualitative follow-up interviews with a subsample of 40 parents. The initiative of which this study was a part built upon a previous research programme which focused primarily on the workings of the formal child protection system. The research produced under that programme led to the publication of an influential report (Department of Health, 1995) that showed that effective and sensitive child protection systems need to be buttressed by well-targeted support services for families, some of which may well exist outside the remit of formal helping agencies. Our study set out to explore issues of stress, support and coping with parenting from the perspectives of parents themselves, looking not just at the issues for families in difficulties (such at the families who typically make up the case load of child protection agencies) but also at parents who, despite having less than optimal social circumstances, were coping well with the challenging job of raising children in contemporary Britain.

Since the study was commissioned, there has been a rising tide of policy interest and practice innovation in the field of family support, and a broadening of the departmental base within central government in terms of the number of departments involved in developing services. To pick just a few of the key developments, in 1997 a cross-departmental Ministerial Group on the Family was set up by the then new Labour Government, chaired by the Home Secretary. 1998 saw the publication of the Ministerial Group's Green Paper Supporting Families (Home Office 1998) and the announcement by the Treasury and the Department for Education and Employment of a major

£250-million programme – *Sure Start* – designed to deliver services to pre-school children and their families as part of an ambitious government strategy 'to end child poverty by the year 2020' (DfEE 2001). 1998 saw the establishment of a new unit within the Home Office, the Family Policy Unit (FmPU) who, among other things, were made responsible for administering the new Family Support Grant Programme, a multi-million pound grant programme over three years designed to fund services to families provided by the voluntary sector. At the Department of Health, the *Quality Protects* initiative was launched in April 1999, focusing on a framework of action to enable local authorities to deliver improvement to their services to children in care and at risk. Also around this time, the Crime Reduction Programme started to take a keen interest in family support as a means of preventing youth involvement in antisocial behaviour. To coincide with the introduction of a new disposal aimed at parents of young offenders – the Parenting Order – the new Youth Justice Board launched a national parenting programme that funded locally based Youth Offending Teams (YOTs) to provide parenting support and education services to parents of at-risk young people. Still on the theme of crime reduction, a new £30 million initiative, *On Track*, was launched at the end 1999 aimed at school-aged children in high-crime areas and those deemed to be at risk of developing conduct and behaviour difficulties. Last, in late 1999 the National Family and Parenting Institute was opened as an independent charity committed to 'providing a strong national focus on promoting families and parenting in the twenty-first century' across the social spectrum (NFPI 1999), and a few months later the Prime Minister established a cross-departmental Children and Young People's Unit to promote more coherent strategic planning for children and children's services.

Thus, the study took place during a time of unprecedented activity and development on the family support front. Developments continue apace and, at the time of writing, many of the new initiatives are in the process of being evaluated in respect of their impact on parents and children. Results are still awaited, but we hope that this book, which documents levels of need and use of support in poor neighbourhoods, will complement the evaluation evidence on the effectiveness of services for families. The extent to which there is overlap between what parents want, what services provide and 'what works' in supporting families remains to be seen, but a more thorough understanding of all three should help considerably in our efforts to improve the way in which we deliver services in this field.

Part One
Introduction and Background

CHAPTER ONE

Introduction

The changing policy context: parenting and family support

Although the last few years of the 1990s saw unprecedented growth in the number of players involved in the family support field, the study that is the subject of this book took place against a background not just of increased activity but of a more general shift of policy focus in children's services. The shift, broadly speaking, was away from a 'treatment' perspective, and towards primary prevention of child maltreatment and an increased interest in developing proactive rather than reactive services for parents and children. The backdrop to what became referred to as 'refocusing' included ongoing academic and practice debates about the definition of 'good enough', and indeed 'normal', parenting (Department of Health 1995) as well as a growing number of research studies that pointed to a lack of social consensus on what constituted 'abuse' or 'maltreatment' of children (Gelles 1975; Dingwall, Eekelaar and Murray 1983; Ghate and Spencer 1995). As a group, the influential Department of Health studies in the *Studies in Child Protection* series had highlighted widespread difficulties in establishing where the threshold for intervention should lie when there were concerns about a child's welfare. Moreover, research evidence was beginning to indicate that many children and families initially drawn into the child protection 'net' were subsequently allowed to slip back out, without receiving any further formal help or support (Gibbons, Conroy and Bell 1995). All of this seemed to indicate that there were likely to be families 'in need' in the wider community who for one reason or another were not getting into the system and who thus who might not be commanding the support they needed. Our study was therefore designed to address the issue of how such parents were being supported, and where the need for further support and help might lie.

Identifying the correlates of parenting problems: an ecological perspective

Risk factors

A key concept that has dominated research into parenting and family support has been that of risk, and the 'at-risk' family, usually defined as a family in which parents are experiencing frank difficulties with child care, or where there is considered to be a strong likelihood of difficulties without intervention.[1] 'Risk factors' are variables that research has shown to be associated with elevated levels of child maltreatment and which are assumed to act in an adverse way to undermine parenting skills or the ability to cope with the demands of child care. Today a relatively large body of research exists on the contexts for child maltreatment and the characteristics of 'at-risk' families, and much of the research endeavour has been directed at refining our understanding of the types of families who may be at risk for abuse, and hence at establishing models for both the prediction and prevention of child maltreatment.

Early studies focused on an 'individual pathology' or 'disease' model of abuse, locating its causes in the personality deficits and pathological interactions between certain types of parents and certain types of children (for example, Kempe and Kempe 1978; Steele and Pollock 1968). Another branch of the field laid the blame for parenting breakdown primarily at the door of social inequality and social deprivation (for example, Gil 1970, 1973). More recently, however, studies have shown that child maltreatment and parenting difficulties are associated with a complex web of interrelated factors in which social-structural and socio-cultural factors interact with and exacerbate psychological 'predispositions' to poor parenting in a 'diathesis-stress' process (Wolfner and Gelles 1993). This dynamic process is most clearly described within a model that has come to be known as the 'ecological model' of parenting (Bronfenbrenner 1977, 1979; Belsky 1980). As its name suggests, this model takes a systems perspective on family functioning, and it provides a framework for understanding how critical factors nest together within a hierarchy of four levels: the socio-cultural level (also called macro-system factors); the community (exo-system factors); the family (micro-system factors); and the level of the individual parent or child (ontogenic factors).

In empirical studies, three sets of risk factors have typically been found to be associated with parenting breakdown. First, at the community or exo-system level, living in an impoverished environment characterised by high concentrations of poor families and high levels of social and environmental problems has frequently been cited as a risk factor (Garbarino and Kostelny 1992; Coulton *et al.* 1995). Second, at the family and household level, high levels of poverty and social and material disadvantage characterised by lone parenting, low income, unemployment, living in poor housing, high mobility and so forth have consistently emerged as key correlates of parenting problems (Gil 1970; Pelton 1981; Straus, Gelles and Steinmetz 1980; Creighton 1988). Third, at the level of individual characteristics of family members, a diminished capacity to cope with stress in the parenting task, coupled with a tendency to show extreme responses to stress, seem also to enhance the risk of developing parenting difficulties. For example, studies have highlighted factors such as parental social isolation and depression, child ill health or challenging behaviour, parental psychological immaturity, and a host of other individual characteristics as potentially placing family functioning under stress (for example, Garbarino 1977; Helfer 1987; Gelles 1983; Belsky and Vondra 1989).

Protective factors

Yet, as previous authors have noted, the risk factors highlighted above are, of course, not unique to at-risk families. They also describe the situation of many thousands of families in the population who do not experience breakdown in parenting, although they may well be rearing their children under conditions of extreme difficulty – families that we refer to in this report as 'in need'.[2] Nevertheless, historically much of the research on parenting has focused on families at risk of child abuse and neglect, with relatively little attention paid to families in need more generally. Consequently, in recent years there has been a growing interest in the concept of resilience – that is, the ability of some individuals to maintain healthy functioning in spite of a background of disadvantage commonly associated with poor outcomes – and attention has turned to look for factors within the ecology of the family that might buffer families from stress and act as protective factors in terms of child and parent well-being. A supportive relationship with a spouse or partner, for example, help from friends and relatives; a close (but not oppressive) social network; and a temperamentally 'adaptable' child have all been shown to have a positive effect on parenting even where other conditions are not optimal (see Belsky and Vondra (1989) for a review). It has become clear that, to understand how better to support families in difficulty and implement primary prevention of abuse and neglect, it is important to learn not only from those families in which parents are struggling but also from those in which parents are still coping. It has also become increasingly clear that we know rather less about the factors that contribute to resilience in family functioning than we do about the factors that undermine it. In our study, therefore, we adopted an ecological perspective to conceptualise and explore parenting as a buffered system. We hoped to identify not only key risk factors that make parenting more difficult but also to shed light on what helps to make parenting easier.

Why study parenting in poor environments?

Since we wanted to explore not only risk factors but also protective factors in parenting, we took a general population, 'normative' approach to understanding parenting difficulties and successes. So, rather than sampling exclusively from an at-risk population (for example, from families known to child protection agencies or from families who defined themselves as experiencing problems in coping with parenting), we drew a community sample of parents but one which was at the same time representative of parents 'in need' – that is, living in the circumstances shown by the ecological model to present the greatest challenge to parenting. In practice, this involved identifying environments that were high in certain indicators of community and individual disadvantage and poverty (referred to in this report as 'poor environments'), and then drawing a random sample of parents from within these areas. Within such a sample we would expect to find many parents who were coping well with the demands of child rearing but others who were experiencing problems of varying kinds. That is, by definition, all families within the sample could be classified as 'in need' but only some will be 'at risk'. By holding certain factors in the parenting environment constant, we were able to make more meaningful comparisons between those parents who are 'in need but coping' as opposed to those who are 'in need and not coping'. We hoped we would thereby be able to identify more clearly the specific stressors and protective factors that are associated with a range of negative and positive outcomes for parents and children.

Social support for parenting

The study also focused strongly on the issue of social support to families in need.

Although we may as yet know relatively little about the precise correlates of coping with parenting, the literature provides a wealth of evidence to suggest that social support functions as one such correlate; that is, it acts as a protective factor (Garbarino 1977; Garbarino and Sherman 1980; Gaudin and Pollane 1983; Robertson et al. 1991; Belsky and Vondra 1989; Thompson 1995). Research suggests that social support can act as a stress-buffering factor by providing help or support at moments of particular need and as primary protective or preventive factor by bolstering parents' self-esteem and sense of efficacy, and generally enhancing healthy functioning. There is also a body of literature that suggests that poor environments may be deficient in social support for parents. In terms of informal social support (the kind of support that arises naturally from within parents' networks of family, friends, and neighbours) some research has suggested that poor environments suffer from social fragmentation and lack of community cohesion (for example, Vondra 1990), and that families in these areas may therefore be more isolated and less well supported than families living elsewhere. In terms of organised support, whether semi-formal (often provided by community groups) or formal (generally provided by statutory health or social welfare agencies), it is a matter of concern as to whether services are reaching those who need them most, with recent reports suggesting that poor areas may be particularly prone to deficits in support services, either because the services themselves do not exist or because they exist in a form that does not entirely meet the needs of local people (McCormick and Philo 1995; SEU 2000). Although our study was not able to audit the actual level of service provision to families in need in poor environments, in both survey and qualitative interviews we explored these questions in some detail, probing the extent to which parents were currently accessing social support of all kinds and their views on support deficits and how to overcome them.

Aims of the study

Above all, this was a study of parents' perspectives on life in a poor environment. The overall aims of the research were threefold. First, we aimed to explore the characteristics and life circumstances of a representative population of parents in need in Britain, using an ecological perspective to explore factors located at the community, family and individual level. We aimed to explore the contexts for stress and difficulty in parenting within poor environments and to identify some buffering factors that exist in parents' individual and social circumstances. In general, we wanted to seek parents' perspectives on how they cope with the challenges of child rearing. What makes life hard? What makes life easier, and why? Is living in a poor environment a risk factor in its own right and, if so, how? Second, we also aimed to explore in some detail the relationship between the social support received by families and coping with parenting. Do parents identify a need for more external support with parenting? What are the relative roles of informal, semi-formal and formal social support in the lives of parents in poor areas? What are the main sources of support, and what factors are associated with use or non-use of support? Are the poorest areas particularly deficient in social support and, if so, how? Lastly, we wanted to explore whether and how support could be better delivered to parents in need. If parents do perceive deficits in the current availability of support, how could these deficits be overcome? Who is most in need of extra support, and how can we identify such families?

Structure of the book

This book is divided in five parts, each of which contains several chapters. Introductory and background information is contained in Part I of the report. Chapter 1 sets the scene in terms of the policy background to the study and the key theoretical issues, and summarises the aims and objectives of the study. Chapter 2 details the methods used to draw the sample and collect and analyse the data, and outlines the key demographic characteristics of the sample. Part II takes up the theme of parents under stress, and is structured around the three key levels of the ecological approach to the study of family life. Chapter 3 explores stress and risk factors at the level of individual parents and children, Chapter 4 looks at stress factors at the household and family level and Chapter 5 takes up the story at the level of the community, exploring to what extent parenting in a poor environment is more difficult than parenting elsewhere. In Part III, we focus on social support to parents in poor environments. We begin with a short review of the literature and a discussion of the methodological approach we used to unpack the complex aspects of support, and in successive chapters explore parents' use of and attitudes to support at the informal level (Chapter 6), the semi-formal level (Chapter 7) and the formal level (Chapter 8). In Chapter 9, we pull together information on support deficits, asking whether some parents are less well supported than others and how we can understand deficits in different dimensions of social support. In Part IV of the report, we turn to the issue of coping with parenting in a poor environment. What do we mean by coping, and how can we measure it? In Chapter 10 we explore coping and not coping, focusing on identifying both risk factors (factors that seem to undermine coping) and protective factors that appear to enhance the odds of coping well. In Chapter 11 we investigate parents' coping strategies for dealing with key challenges and discuss how parents' coping strategies help us understand why certain risk factors appear more prejudicial to coping than others. In Chapter 12, returning to the issue of support, we ask to what extent social support is important in enhancing parents' ability to cope. Part V concludes the book with a summary of the key findings in relation to patterns of need and support within poor environments (Chapter 13), a discussion of what parents really want from support services and, last, the implications and messages for policy and practice that arose out of the study and some key recommendations for action (Chapter 14).

Notes

1. For example, cases where parents have become (or are deemed to have become) incapable of caring adequately for their children, or where there is child maltreatment or other seriously adverse conditions for a child.

2. Note that 'in need' also has a specific meaning under the Children Act (1989), and was spelled out in Quality Protects 1998 as connoting children who would be likely to suffer serious impairment if they did not receive services (Little and Mount 1999).

CHAPTER TWO

Methodology and Demographic Characteristics of the Sample

The study described in this book consisted of two components: a large-scale, nationally representative survey of 1754 parents in Great Britain and a qualitative follow-up study of 40 parents in particular circumstances. The fieldwork for the survey of parents was carried out in 1998, and qualitative interviews were carried out in the last half of 1998 and first half of 1999. In this chapter, we give brief details of the methodology used to conduct the study, including sampling and data collection procedures. The second half of the chapter describes the demographic characteristics of the families who took part in the interviews.

The survey of parents in poor environments

Sampling

The first stage of the survey was to develop a suitable sample frame consisting of areas corresponding to the concept of a 'poor parenting environment', where the word 'poor' is used not just to imply poverty but also in the sense of 'not optimal for parenting'. Such a sample frame would enable us to select parents living in areas of the country with high levels of social and material disadvantage where, according to the ecological model of parenting, community, family and individual circumstances would present particular challenges for parenting. Below we give a condensed account of the procedures used to select a sample for the study; fuller details are given in Appendix 2.

A number of indices and geo-demographic classification systems have been developed in recent years that enable the identification of areas of the country with particular socio-demographic characteristics (or constellations of characteristics) at varying levels of geography; for example, the Index of Local Deprivation or ILD (DETR 1998a, since superseded by the Indices of Deprivation 2000 (DETR 2000)). However, none of the existing systems was designed with parenting in mind. For example, although the data used for constructing the ILD are wide-ranging, including unemployment, income, health, education, land use, home insurance and housing, they are of varying levels of salience when considering the ecology of parenting.[1] Thus, although widely used for both research and planning purposes, our review of the existing instruments for classifying areas suggested that, while we could certainly identify poor areas using these methods, it was less clear how successful we would be at identifying 'poor parenting areas'. We therefore decided to create a new tool for generating a nationally representative sample frame of poor parenting areas specially designed for the proposed survey.

Our first step was therefore to develop a method of scoring areas of the country based on their relative levels of social deprivation, using indicators of particular salience to the ecological model of parenting. The scale we developed, which we refer to hereafter as the Poor Parenting Environments Index, or PPE-Index, was composed of a basket of indicators shown by previous research to be associated with parenting difficulties, about which information was available on the 1991 Census (thus allowing national application). Using Census data to construct such a scale had its drawbacks, not least that the data were rather old by the time work started on the study. However, on the plus side, Census data have the advantage of being robust and reasonably complete at small area level and in respect of national coverage, and are also readily available online.[2]

SELECTING THE VARIABLES FOR THE POOR PARENTING ENVIRONMENTS INDEX (PPE-INDEX)

We began the work of selecting the variables to go into the PPE-Index by reviewing recent literature on the correlates of child maltreatment.[3] A substantial number of studies (many from the United States) have explored these, mostly in relation to rates of child maltreatment reported to the authorities (for example, Garbarino and Kostelny 1992), although some studies (for example, Straus and colleagues 1980; Straus and Smith 1995) have also explored the relationship of demographic characteristics and self-reported child physical maltreatment. Allowing for cultural differences between the US and the UK, many of the variables identified in the North American literature are also consistently found to be associated with child maltreatment and at-risk status in British research,[4] and, taken as a whole, the studies we reviewed tended to give remarkably consistent findings. Isolating the variables of interest to go into our initial model of the index was therefore a relatively straightforward task. Essentially, the variables that are most consistently reported can be grouped into those connected with poverty (for example, low income/low affluence, unemployment, lone parenting, living in social housing, overcrowding); those connected with low social cohesion (for example, high mobility); and those connected with social class (socio-economic group, educational attainment).

Because not all of the variables found to be associated with poor parenting environments were directly available from the 1991 UK Census, some indicators were not able to be included in our model, and some proxy indicators had to be used.[5] For example, we used car ownership as a proxy for low income/low affluence. Thus the variables that were eventually chosen to go into the model are shown in Box 2.1.

Percentage of:

- unemployed adults aged 16 or more
- overcrowded households (defined as more than one person per room)
- lone parents
- households in social housing (owned by local authority or housing association)
- households of social class iii(n) or below (skilled non-manual occupations and below)
- households with no car
- households which had moved in the last year.

Box 2.1 Area-level variables included in the model of poor parenting environments

TESTING AND REFINING THE MODEL

To explore how well this model worked at identifying and ranking areas of the country, we carried out a series of tests using randomly selected pilot samples of Enumeration Districts (EDs) across the country.[6] We used factor analytical data reduction techniques to develop a weighted scale by which each ED in Britain could be scored; see Appendix 2 for details. Once a final scaling system was identified, it was run against a test group of 10,000 randomly selected Enumeration Districts and the distribution was examined. The point on the distribution of scores at which we defined 'poor environments' as beginning was, of course, essentially a subjective and arbitrary decision but one based on the shape of the overall distribution. We defined 'poor parenting environments' as those in the top 30 per cent of the national distribution. We then carried out a full pilot study of 40 addresses in six EDs across the country (see below) to verify that this system did indeed yield environments with high levels of social and economic disadvantage. Then, for the main survey, all EDs in the country whose score on the PPE-Index was within this top 30 per cent of the national distribution were used as the base for a further 135 randomly selected sampling points. The maps in Appendix 2 show the geographic distribution, first, of these 'top 30 per cent' Enumeration Districts ($n = 37,105$) across England, Wales and Scotland (Map A5), and, second, of the areas actually selected for the study (Map A6). It will be seen from the maps that, as we might expect, the high-scoring areas are clustered around the major conurbations (London, Birmingham, Merseyside, Newcastle upon Tyne, Glasgow, Cardiff, and so on), although there are also more sparsely scattered areas in rural locations.

Sampling of addresses and households for the survey then followed standard survey procedures, and full details are described in Appendix 2. The issued sample was formed by 10,500 selected addresses across the country. All selected addresses were visited by interviewers, who screened each household for the presence of a parent of a child aged 0–16 years, defined as a 'main carer' – that is, 'the person who is responsible for looking after or caring for the child for the greatest amount of time'. Where parents or parent-figures were located, they were invited to participate in the study. Where there was more than one parent in the household who considered themselves a main carer (for example, in households where mothers and fathers reported equal responsibility for child care), one carer was selected by random system and identified as the 'selected parent'. This yielded just over 2,800 households 'in scope' (that is, occupied households containing children under 17 years old, where interviewers could theoretically have completed an interview). Of those households which were identified as eligible for the survey, refusals from eligible parents (either direct or made by someone on their behalf) constituted 31 per cent of the in-scope sample, leaving a net response rate of 69 per cent of the eligible in-scope addresses, reducing to 62 per cent if households and parents who could not be contacted are included as potentially in-scope (that is, using a more stringent definition of eligibility). These response rates appear to be in the range that is typical for complex, large-scale surveys in the UK, and after considerable exploration of the distribution of the final sample (see Appendix 2 for information on sample outcomes, regional distribution, and reliability and validity issues) we were able to conclude that the final sample was, as far as can be determined, robustly representative of main carers of children in poor environments in Great Britain.

POOR PARENTING ENVIRONMENTS, POOR FAMILIES AND POVERTY

Since all areas selected for the sample were drawn from those in the upper 30 per cent of the national distribution in terms of their score on the PPE-Index, technically all the areas included in the survey can be thought of as above averagely 'poor parenting environments'. However, to what extent can we make statements about the impact of poverty, based on the data gathered in this survey? What is the relationship between poor *areas* (as measured by aggregated, area-level data) and poor *families* (as measured by individual level data)? As we know from work describing the 'ecological fallacy' (Robinson 1950; see also Davies, Joshi and Clarke 1997; Fieldhouse and Tye no date), not all materially poor families live in poor environments and, conversely, some poor areas are home to relatively affluent families. Nevertheless, research that has compared individual-level data on poverty against area-level data has shown that although the strengths of the relationships at individual level are not as powerful as aggregate data might suggest, comparable results are nevertheless obtained. Fieldhouse and Tye (no date), for example, conclude that 'multiple deprivation is heavily concentrated in particular social groups and particular geographical locations ...' and that 'the geography of deprivation is

... similar when using aggregate and individual level approaches'. Although the majority of deprived people may live outside deprived areas, deprived areas do contain large concentrations of deprived people. Our data bear this out: for example, data on household income in the sample (see Chapter 4) show that our poor parenting environments were indeed characterised by poor families; although income ranged substantially across the sample as whole, only a small minority enjoyed household incomes at or above the national average.

The strength of this design does, nevertheless, also entail some limitations. One is that it is difficult to disentangle the independent effects of individual- or household-level poverty as opposed to area-level poverty in our analyses. Although operationalised as a geographical indicator, like most other 'deprivation indices', the PPE-Index was constructed as a composite measure of poverty drawing on indicators largely located at the family and individual level. Although household income itself was not one the factors that formed part of the scoring system for the Index, there was a significant correlation between PPE-Index and household income ($r = -0.221$, $p<0.001$) because many of the factors that were used to construct the scale are themselves strongly associated with household income (for example, car ownership).

It is also important to note that the design of the study did not include a comparison group of parents living in average or affluent environments. We were able to make relatively firm statements about comparative levels of need between this sample and the wider population of families in Britain because there exist a number of large national data sets from which whole-population figures can be obtained. However, in many other areas touched on by the study (and particularly in the case of issues connected with social support), we have as yet no nationally representative data against which we can compare the figures obtained from the parents we interviewed. What we have done, however, wherever possible, is explore the impact of relative levels of poverty at both the community and the household level within the sample itself. One of the ways we achieved this was to further subdivide the sample of poor parenting areas into three equal bands or triciles, which we named 'poor', 'very poor' and 'extremely poor' areas,[7] and make comparisons on the basis of these groups. However, a limitation of this method is that in statistical terms we are dealing with a truncated distribution (that is, the highly skewed 'tail end' of a range of values). This means that when we find no associations between indicators of poverty (income, for example, or PPE-Index band) and any given dependent variable, we cannot always be sure whether this means that poverty is *not* a significant factor at all, or whether it has ceased to be a discriminating factor at some point earlier in the overall national distribution; that is, we have reached a point at which the effect of poverty no longer shows up not because it is unimportant, but because all the cases have crossed a threshold beyond which additional degrees of poverty make no difference. On the other hand, as a conservative test of the role of poverty *vis à vis* other variables, if we do find an association using this method, we can be fairly sure that poverty is indeed significantly associated with the dependent variable at issue.

The survey interview

All survey interviews (which took an average of 70 minutes) were conducted face-to-face by experienced field interviewers and, as far as possible, interviewers tried to ensure that they interviewed parents in private. The questionnaire for the survey was constructed with reference not only to the aims of the study but as far as possible by utilising questions already validated by previous use in other studies in order to maximise our ability to make comparisons with previous research. Most questions were administered directly by the interviewer, but for respondent privacy and confidentiality there was a self-completion supplement containing four short questionnaires that covered the most sensitive questions in the survey. Where there was more than one child in the household in the eligible age range, one was selected by random system to be the focus of detailed questioning and was designated as 'the index child'. The main topics covered by the survey interview are shown in Appendix 3. Further detail about the operationalisation of key constructs (social support, coping, current problems, etc.) is given in subsequent chapters.

Before the main survey, a pilot study was conducted replicating the sampling protocol to be used in the main survey and testing out the draft questionnaire. Interviewers piloted the household screening process and completed 27 full interviews. The results of these interviews were used to finalise the survey questionnaire and, in particular, to fine-tune response categories for questions of a fixed-response format. Last, to allow for the possibility that the interview could have raised issues that parents wanted to discuss further with an appropriate professional, at the end of the interview all respondents were given an information leaflet containing a list of contact addresses and telephone numbers of organisations that offer advice or counselling on various family, parenting and child care issues.

Survey data analysis

Full details of the procedures used for quantitative data analysis can be found in Appendix 4. We used a range of descriptive and inferential statistical techniques to explore the data, from simple frequency counts, cross-tabulations and comparisons of means to more complex multivariate techniques (that is, involving more than two variables), principally one-way analysis of variance and binary logistic regression. Percentages in tables are shown in whole numbers and therefore may not always add up due to rounding. Results below 0.5 per cent are indicated by an asterisk (*) in the body of the table. Bases (the number of cases on which the percentage is calculated) are given with within tables where results for subgroups are presented, or underneath tables for single groups. Where bases do not add to the full number of achieved interviews (1754), this usually reflects the fact that cases with missing data have been excluded. For the sake of brevity, where we compare two or more groups, only *p*-values (the level of significance), and not test statistics, are given in the text and tables. Unless otherwise stated in the text, where tests are for differences between two means the procedure used was a *t*-test for independent samples; where differences of means for three or more groups were being compared, analysis of variance (ANOVA) was used; and differences of proportion were tested using a chi-square. Tests of medians used the Mann-Whitney non-parametric test. All tests were two-tailed. The level of confidence used for all significance testing in the analysis was set at $p<01$; see Appendix 4 for further details.

The qualitative study of parents in especially difficult circumstances

Following the survey, 40 qualitative in-depth, unstructured interviews were conducted with parents in various parts of the country, in the following nine 'index situation' groups, shown in Box 2.2 (on facing page). Many of the parents, of course, could be classified as belonging to more than one group.

Parents sample:

- lone parents
- parents with very large families (five or more children under 16 in the household)
- very low income families (families with household income in lowest quintile of sample distribution)
- reconstituted families (step parent present in household)
- parents with serious health problems (a long-term health problem that affects functioning all or most of the time; or Malaise score 13+)
- parents with a seriously sick or disabled child (child in the household with a long-term health problem affecting functioning all or most of the time, who requires extra care)
- parents of very 'difficult' children (those with a very high SDQ score of 17+ or more)
- parents with serious accommodation problems (at least three separate problems reported).

Box 2.2 Groups of parents sampled for the qualitative stage of the study

The aim of the qualitative phase was not to study each of these circumstances in depth or to act as a stand-alone study, but to provide data from parents in a range of especially difficult circumstances to elaborate on and enhance our understanding of the survey findings. A topic guide was used to focus the interviews on the effect of the particular circumstances of the family on daily life, but allowed parents to raise the issues most pressing for them. Interviewers also referred back to survey questionnaire responses at some points, to clarify and explore particular responses in more detail. Qualitative interviews ranged in length from one to two hours, and all parents who participated in the qualitative stage of the study were given £15 as a thank-you for their time. All interviews were audio-taped (with respondents' permission) and transcribed verbatim and in full. Because the qualitative component of the study was intended to elaborate the survey findings, rather than to stand alone, we analysed the qualitative data according to themes we already knew we wanted to explore based on the preliminary results of the survey. Illustrative quotes were collated by themes, and are used throughout the text where appropriate to illustrate survey findings or provide explanatory context.

We found early on in the analysis process that, although we had sampled on the basis of the groupings described in Box 2.2, expecting that different groupings might generate different data, this was not generally the case. In many cases, what parents were most concerned to talk about did not reflect the 'index problem' as much as general difficulties faced by all parents, but perhaps exacerbated by additional problems in individual family circumstances. What stood out, therefore, were the similarities between parents rather than the differences. So, although we have provided attributions (labels) under the verbatim quotes in the report as an indication for the reader of the various areas of difficulties that parents faced, these should not be seen as necessarily having analytical significance.

Demographic characteristics of the sample

All 1754 parents we interviewed for the study were main or joint-equal carers of a child aged 16 years or less. Where there were two joint-equal main carers, interviewers selected one carer, using a systematic random method. For the sake of brevity, we tend to refer to main carers throughout the report as 'parents', although not all were biologically related to the children they cared for.[8]

Sex and age of parents

Reflecting the fact that it is still mainly women who care for children in our society, only about one in every 12 respondents was male ($n = 139$; 8% of the sample), with the great majority being female carers ($n = 1615$; 92% of the total sample). The relatively small number of men in the sample as a whole means that, in general, we do not in this book analyse the situation of fathers separately from that of mothers.

As well as being predominantly female, the sample of parents was a relatively mature one. The average age of respondents was 33 years, although ages ranged from 17 to 69 years. Only a small number (2%) of parents in poor environments were teenagers. Almost half (45%) of parents were in their thirties, about one-third were in their twenties (31%) and just less than one-quarter (22%) were 40 years old or more. Only three per cent of respondents were aged 50 years or more.

Marital and relationship status, and household composition

Figure 2.1 shows the marital status of respondents. Three in five respondents surveyed (61%) were living with partners, either married (48%) or living as married (13%). The remaining two in five were living with their children as lone carers (39%). This latter group of single carers was evenly divided between those respondents who had never married (19% of the sample) and those who were widowed (2%), divorced (12%) or separated (6%) from partners. Among male main carers the proportions of lone parents were lower, at 27 per cent of men interviewed ($n = 38$).

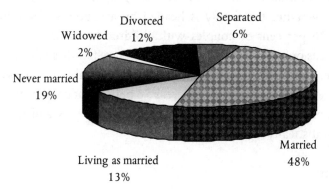

Base=1753

Figure 2.1 Marital status of respondents

The percentage of those who were married or living with a partner was substantially lower than figures reported for the general parenting population. In 1998, for example 79 per cent of dependent children were living in families with two parents and 21 per cent were living in households headed by lone parents (ONS 1999). One in ten (10%) respondents were living in step, or 'reconstituted', families.[9] This figure is higher than in the general population, where stepfamilies account for about one in 16 (6%) of all families with dependent children (ONS 2001).

The mean average size of household across the sample was 3.8 members, although the number of individuals in each household ranged widely from two to 11. Two-thirds of households were made up of three (30%) or four (33%) people, and a quarter contained five or more people (25%). The remainder contained just the parent and one child (13%). One in 20 respondents (5%) lived in 'extended' families containing parents, parents-in-law or other relatives.

Children in the household

The mean number of children in the families we interviewed was 1.98. Overall, the number of dependent children in the families ranged from one to eight, and one-quarter of the sample of parents (25%) had three or more dependent children aged under 17 living at home. In the wider population, approximately 22 per cent of families with dependent children have three or more children (ONS 2001), but the proportions vary widely depending on whether the family is headed by a couple or by a lone parent. Thus 26 per cent of couples with children have three or more children, whereas only 6 per cent of lone parents have families of this size. In our sample, there was much less difference in family size between couple and lone parent households. Whereas 26 per cent of couple families had three or more children, so did 22 per cent of lone parents, a difference that was not statistically significant.

THE INDEX CHILD

In households with more than one child aged under 17, one child was chosen randomly and systematically as the focus of more detailed questions about child characteristics. As would be expected, these 'index' children were equally divided between males (50%) and females (50%). The age of children ranged from under one year to 16 years old, more or less equally distributed between the year groups, and the mean age was 7 years and 5 months. Of the index children, 21 per cent were teenagers and one-third (34%) were under five.

In almost all families (97%) the main carer interviewed was the natural parent of the index child. Only 1 per cent of carers were the child's grandparents and 1 per cent were step-parents. Index children cared for by adoptive parents, foster parents, legal ward or other relations made up the remaining 1 per cent.

Ethnicity

Table 2.1 shows the ethnic group of parents. A large majority of the sample classified themselves as White British (89%). The next biggest ethnic group, Indian, represented only 2 per cent of the sample. Respondents classifying themselves as of 'mixed race' accounted for just 1 per cent of the sample. Overall, then, minority ethnic parents made up 11 per cent of the total sample ($n = 198$). These figures compare very closely with those drawn from other national studies. In 1998, of those families with dependent children responding to the Labour Force Survey, 90 per cent classified themselves as White.

Table 2.1 Parents' ethnic group	
Ethnic group	*% of parents*
White British	89
Indian	2
Black British	1
British Asian	1
Black Caribbean	1
Black African	1
Bangladeshi	1
Pakistani	1
White Other	1
Other	1
Mixed race	1

Base = 1753

Thus, it should be noted that in the sample as a whole we had a relatively small number of minority ethnic respondents, composed of a wide number of different cultural, religious and ethnic backgrounds. This means that, except in a very few places in this book, we are unable to comment on differences between White British and other parents because to do so would obscure important differences within the group broadly categor-ised as 'minority ethnic'.

Educational level

Respondents were also asked about their academic and vocational qualifi-cations. Academic or school qualifications were held by almost six in ten (57%) parents, meaning that more than two in five parents in the sample (43%) had no school qualifications at all. Qualifications attained by respondents ranged from GCSE/SCE Grades 4–5 to UK university degree. GCSE/SCE Grades 4–5 (or equivalents) were named by 7 per cent of parents as their highest level of examination passed. One in three (33%) respondents had attained an academic level of GCSE/SCE Grades 1–3 and 9 per cent had passed A-levels or Scottish Highers. Only one in every 25 (4%) of respondents were educated to higher education degree or diploma level.

The 13 per cent combined figure for parents achieving at least a level of A-levels or Highers is substantially lower than in the general popula-tion. The Labour Force Survey (1997–1998) indicated that 39 to 54 per cent of men and 25 to 36 per cent of women of working age, depending upon ethnic group, have obtained GCE A-level (or equivalent) or higher qualifications. In addition, the 43 per cent of parents in our sample not holding any academic qualifications is considerably higher than the figure for the general population of working age in the UK. The Labour Force Survey found that males with no academic qualifications ranged from 15 to 22 per cent of the population depending upon ethnic group, and females with no academic qualifications ranged from 15 to 33 per cent depending upon ethnic group (ONS 1999).

Two in five respondents (40%) had obtained professional or vocational qualifications. However, as Figure 2.2 shows, more than a third of parents (36%) did not have either academic or vocational qualifications.

Employment and activity status of parents

As we might expect in a survey of main carers for children, Table 2.2 shows that almost half (46%) of the parents surveyed in this study gave 'looking after the family or home' as their main occupation. This figure is margin-ally higher than the number of respondents presently in paid work (43%).

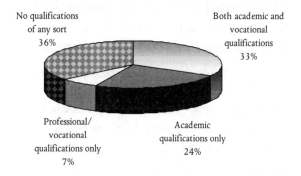

Base=1753

Figure 2.2 Respondents obtaining qualifications by vocational/academic type

The remaining 11 per cent consisted of respondents who classified themselves as unemployed; permanently sick or disabled; in full-time education; or otherwise occupied. A higher number of respondents worked part
time (25%) than full time (18%), but 8 per cent of those in work at present
(*n* = 60) occupied more than one job. The mean average number of hours
worked by those currently in paid employment for more than eight hours
per week was 27 hours a week, for part-time workers 18 hours a week and
for full-time workers 39 hours a week.

Table 2.2 Parents' main occupation	
Main occupation	*% of parents*
Looking after family or home	46
Part-time work (less than 30 hours a week)	25
Full-time work (more than 30 hours a week)	18
Unemployed and actively seeking work	4
Permanently sick or disabled	3
Full-time education	2
Unemployed and not seeking work	1
Other	1

Base = 1754

Most respondents who were out of the paid labour market ($n = 1008$) had been so for a substantial period of time; two in five (40%) respondents without paid employment at the time of the study had not had a paid job (for more than eight hours a week) in the past ten years.

Household activity status and social class

Half of all households in the survey had no adult in paid work (50%). In half of the families (50%) the respondent was also the chief income earner (that is, the person who contributes most to the household income). This figure fell to around one in five families (19%) where the main carer was living with a partner. Using the Registrar General's six-fold social class schema, based on the present or most recent occupation of chief income earner, the household social class of families in the sample is shown in Table 2.3. Just over one in ten households (12%) were classified as social class I or II (professional, managerial or technical occupations), about four in ten (42%) were in social class III (skilled occupations) and nearly half (45%) were in social classes IV and V or unclassified (partly skilled or unskilled occupations and long-term unemployed). Figures for the UK adult population as a whole are given for comparison (ONS 1999). As can be seen, our sample of households was skewed towards social classes III (m), IV and below.

Table 2.3 Household social class		
Registrar General's social class	*% of sample households (n = 1754)*	*% of UK population (n = 35.8m)*
I. Professional occupations	1	5
II. Managerial and technical occupations	11	25
III(N). Skilled occupations:non-manual	15	20
III(M). Skilled occupations: manual	27	18
IV. Partly skilled occupations	24	16
V. Unskilled occupations	7	5
(Unemployed 10 years or more)	14	12

Base = 1754

Household income

Respondents were asked to give their total disposable household income from all sources before housing costs but after other deductions. 1458[10] respondents (83% of the sample) provided a figure, with the remaining 296 unable to calculate the amount or declining to do so. The resulting figures were standardised using the McClements formula (ONS 1999, Appendix part 5) to give an 'equivalised' household income that takes into account the effects of household size and composition on the value of disposable income. This enables us to make meaningful comparisons of income between one household and the next. Equivalised average annual incomes across the sample as a whole were very low. The median annual reported household income was £7013 per year; that is, approximately half the median household income in the wider UK (ONS 2001).

Two alternative conventions for calculating the number of families living in poverty are in current use: one is to take a fixed 'poverty line' of half the mean national average household income, the other is to use 60 per cent of the median average income (Howard *et al.* 2001). Recent studies have reported that in 1996–97, approximately one-third of children in the UK lived in households with half or less of the national average household income using a measure of mean disposable income after housing costs (Gregg, Harkness and Machin 1999). In our sample, only around one in six households (16%) enjoyed an annual income at or above the national median average for 1998 (ONS 2001), and getting on for two-thirds of the index children (59%) were living in families with incomes at or below the poverty line when calculated as 60 per cent of the median before housing costs. The children in our sample were, therefore, considerably poorer than children across the UK as a whole. For lone parent households in the sample, the equivalised median annual income was even lower, at £5408, and the vast majority of index children of lone parents (83%) lived in households at or below the national poverty line.

Table 2.4 shows the income distribution (range and average) across the sample as a whole, by quintile groups. The low average income figures are reflections of the fact that only around half the sample reported that their main source of income for the household was earnings from paid employment. Almost all the remaining households (43%) relied on state benefits for the majority of their income – principally Income Support. The situation for lone parents was very different: only 19 per cent had earnings from paid work as their main source of income and 78 per cent were dependent on state benefits.

Table 2.4 Equivalised disposable household income, before housing costs, by quintile groups					
	Bottom fifth	Next fifth	Middle fifth	Next fifth	Top fifth
Income range £ per annum	1850–4824	4825–5994	5995–8476	8477–12,352	12,353–71,428[a]
Median average income £ per annum	3337	5409	7236	10,415	41,885[b]

Base = 1458

Notes: a top quintile is skewed by small number of high-income households. 80th percentile income range [a] £12,353–16,378; 90th percentile = 16,379–71,428. [b]80th percentile median income = 14,365; 90th percentile = 43,903.

Access to a car

Ownership (or the regular use) of a private car or van is commonly used as a proxy indicator of household affluence. Implications for easy access to child care facilities and services such as the doctor's surgery and shops make a car particularly relevant to parenting. As such, households in the general UK population are more likely to have access to a car if they contain children (79%) than if they do not (65%) (DSS 1998). However, parents in poor environments were less likely to have use of a car or van (56%) than either of these groups in the general population. In fact, respondents had a lower rate of access to a car than for households in the general population a generation ago (60% in 1981) (ONS 1999).

Tenure and length of time at current address

The pattern of tenure for households in our survey was markedly different from that of all UK households with children (Figure 2.3). The proportions of those renting and those who owned their property reversed the national picture. The two in three households in our sample (68%) who lived in rented accommodation were twice the national figure (35%). Conversely, the level of owner-occupancy in our sample of households (32%) was half that of the UK population of parents with dependent children (65%) (DSS 1998).

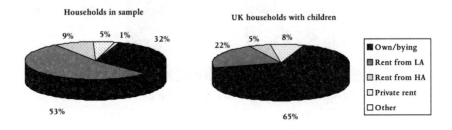

Base = 1754 households in sample; 8259 households in Family Resources Survey 1996-97

Figure 2.3 Household tenure: sample and UK population with children

Families in our sample were also considerably more mobile than those in the general UK population. Figure 2.4 shows that more than half of all families in our sample (55%) had moved at least once in the past four years, compared to just one-third of households nationally. This reflects the lower numbers of owner-occupiers in our sample relative to the population at large, as owner-occupiers tend to be less mobile than those in social or privately rented accommodation (ONS 1999). The higher degree of mobility for our sample may well reflect dissatisfaction with the quality of accommodation in poor environments as, nationally, the most common reason for moving across all types of tenure is 'wanting to move to larger or better accommodation'.

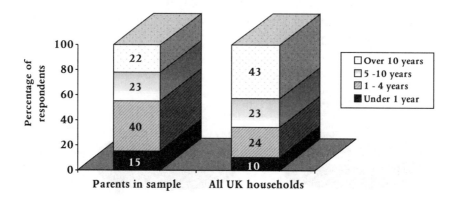

Base = 1752 households in our sample; 11,845 all UK households (General Household Survey 1996–97)

Figure 2.4 Length of time at current address: sample and UK households

Summary: the 'average' parent in a poor environment

Based on the foregoing, can we then draw a picture of what the 'average' parent in a poor environment might look like, demographically speaking? If we were to do this, we would highlight the characteristics shown in Box 2.3 on the facing page.

In the chapters that follow, we highlight other characteristics of the families in the sample.

Notes

1. For example, the ILD includes data on Standardised Mortality Rates for under 75s but not data on the proportion of households headed by lone parents.

2. We are grateful to the Manchester Computing MIDAS service at Manchester University for their assistance with access to the small area and local base statistics.

3. We include here only physical maltreatment and neglect, as child sexual abuse is thought to have different antecedents and to be far less strongly related to environmental variables.

4. An exception is ethnicity. The make-up of the UK population is very different to that in the US, and there is an absence of community data for the UK that speaks to a possible relationship between ethnicity and parenting breakdown. We did not, therefore, include ethnicity in our model.

5. For example, income data, data on educational attainment, and data on age of mother at birth of first child are not available on the 1991 Census.

6. See Appendix 1 for a definition of 'Enumeration District'.

7. See Appendix 1 for details.

8. Note that carers who were paid for caring (nannies, au pairs, etc.) were not counted as main carers in this survey, although grandparents or others with a main (unpaid) caring role were included.

9. We defined 'stepfamilies' as families where the respondent is partnered, and at least one child in the household is from a previous relationship of either the respondent or partner.

10. Two cases at extreme ends of the distribution were excluded as outliers.

Average parent:

- White

- married or living with a partner

- mature (median age 33 years old)

- around two children, and household size around four people

- an index child aged seven and a half

- living in social housing

- mobile: resident at current address for four years or less

- no or low academic qualifications

- household social class iii (n) or below (skilled non-manual occupation, or lower)

- low median equivalised household income (c. £7000 p.a.)

- more likely to be out of paid employment than to be working

- as likely to be reliant on benefits as to have income from paid work

- as likely not to have access to car as to have access to one.

Box 2.3 An 'average' parent in a poor environment

Part Two

Parents under Stress

We've seen the opposite end of the scale where we live. I will say to my dad, 'I'd love to put them in frilly little dresses and bring them up (protected from it)', but that's not the answer. We've seen alcohol abuse and drug abuse. We've seen the lower end of the scale.

(Mother, sick child, bad accommodation, low income)

It don't matter where (I could) go, there's drugs everywhere. Ideally I would like to live where there is no drugs, where there is no violence, no gangs, thugs – but that's living in my own fantasy world. There is nothing like that.

(Mother, low income)

As discussed in Part I, the study chose to focus on poor environments in part with a view to identifying the methods by which parents cope with difficulties – that is, in an attempt to establish what contributes to resilience in the face of challenges to parenting. However, before turning to an exploration of resilience and coping, in Part II we explore the risk factors present in the lives of the parents in the study. What are the correlates of parenting in poor environments? What kinds of disadvantage do parents face in these areas?

We use the term 'risk' to describe factors that have been shown by a substantial body of research to be associated with increased likelihood of difficulties with parenting and with poor child outcomes. We also use the term 'stressor' interchangeably with 'risk factor' to indicate that these factors place strains on individuals and families of varying kinds. In the chapters that follow, we discuss the extent to which stressors – both direct and indirect – were present in the daily lives of the families in this study. In Chapters 3 and 4 we explore some key stress factors at two levels of the ecological model – family and individual. In Chapter 5 we then explore the extent to which factors at a third level – the community and neighbourhood – may compound these problems. The question addressed in the final chapter of this part of the report is: does living in a poor environment make a difference? Does it create stresses over and above those already present in parents' lives by virtue of their household and individual circumstances?

CHAPTER THREE

Stress Factors at the Individual Level

Numerous studies have demonstrated a link between risk factors present in individual parents' and children's circumstances, and parenting problems (for example, Milner and Chilamkurti 1991; Belsky and Vondra 1989; Belsky 1980). Put simply, some parents are predisposed to have difficulties in meeting the challenges of parenting by virtue of their personal characteristics and circumstances, and some children are more difficult and less rewarding to parent than others (Pianta, Egeland and Erikson 1989). Moreover, each may influence the other, and as Belsky and Vondra (1989) have written: 'It is now widely recognised that what transpires in the parent–child relationship is determined not only by the parent, but by the child as well ... we speak, therefore, in terms of bi-directional influences' (p.170).

There are many factors that could be explored in this context, including individual attributes of parents and children that were beyond the scope of this study to explore, such as personality, temperament, genetic make-up, developmental history and early experiences. In this chapter, however, we focus on health – physical and mental, child's and parent's – since these factors appear repeatedly in the literature as playing a key role in the path to parenting difficulties. At the level of the parent, even for parents in good health, child care can be fatiguing and stressful, but for parents who are in poor physical health, or who are depressed, the parenting task can be especially challenging. Although parental physical health has perhaps received less attention, parental mental and emotional health has been extensively studied in relation to parenting difficulties, and it is now generally accepted that parents with poor mental or emotional health will be at elevated risk of experiencing a range of problems with child care (Belsky and Vondra 1989). At the level of the child, Belsky and Vondra (1989) comment: 'During the past 15–20 years an abundance of evidence has been amassed documenting the manner in which child characteristics influence caregiver behaviour' (p.170). As with the literature on parent characteristics, two child characteristics have been consistently associated in the research literature with parenting difficulties: long-term health problems or disabilities (for example, Kolko 1996; Roberts *et al.* 1995), and temperamental or behavioural characteristics such as irritability, fussiness, hyperactivity and other challenging behaviours (Bates 1980; Belsky and Vondra 1989; Parke and Collmer 1975).

In this chapter, therefore, we focus in on the extent to which parents and children in poor environments experience problems with health. At the parent level we explore physical health status and emotional and mental health problems, and at the level of the child we investigate the extent to which children in the survey were particularly challenging to care for, either because of physical illness or because of emotional or behavioural problems.

Parents' physical health

All parents were asked about their own physical health. The majority of the sample (84%) reported themselves generally in 'very' or 'fairly' good health. However, 7 per cent reported their health as middling ('neither good nor poor'), and one in 12 (8%) said their health was, for someone of their age, 'fairly' or 'very' poor.

However, despite parents' generally good perception of their health, when asked about sources of stress in their daily lives, nearly two in five parents (38%) reported that 'keeping themselves fit and healthy' caused them difficulties at one time or another, with 10 per cent of respondents finding this a source of stress 'all or most of the time'. Two in five parents (40%) also reported that they had a specific long-term physical health problem or disability, defined as a problem that they had or expected to have for at least six months. This figure is substantially higher than the national average for 16–44 year olds in Britain reporting long-standing health problems – 27 per cent of both men and women (ONS 1999, data from the General Household Survey (GHS) 1996–1997). Given the nature of this sample, the differences between the two figures undoubtedly reflect at least in part the well-established association between poor health and socio-economic status; for example, successive Health Surveys for England (for example, Department of Health 1998) have reported that in the population at large, both self-assessed general health and nurse-measured health indicators show a clear association with social class.

Of those who had a long-term physical health problem, the most commonly reported complaint was musculo-skeletal (over one-third of those with a health problem, or 15% of the sample as a whole). Other common complaints were respiratory conditions (one-quarter of those with a problem, or 10% of the sample as a whole), skin conditions and allergies (one in five of those with health problems, or 9% of the entire sample), and gynaecological problems (17% of those with long-term health problems, or 8% of the sample of women as a whole).

Table 3.1 on p.48 shows the distribution of health problems in the sample. Where known, national figures are also shown for comparison.[1] Although those with physical health problems were significantly more likely than those without to rate their health as poor ($p<0.001$), two-thirds (63%) of those who reported a long-term physical health problem also reported themselves as in 'very' or 'fairly' good health. Thus, in research, the real test of whether a health problem is significant or not is often taken to be the extent to which the condition affects or impairs daily functioning. In this sample, almost one-quarter of all respondents (23%) reported that their health problem 'sometimes' or 'always' had an effect on their daily activities, that is, over half – 56 per cent – of all those reporting a physical health condition (see Table 3.2). This compares with around 14 per cent of the wider population of men and women in this age group (Department of Health 1998). Furthermore, and particularly revealing for this study, over one in eight (12%) of all parents reported that a physical health problem 'always or sometimes' had an effect on caring for or doing things with their children, equivalent to nearly one in three – 29 per cent – of those reporting a long-term physical health problem (Table 3.3).

Table 3.1 Long-term physical health problems within the sample of parents, compared with British population			
	% of parents		% of British population aged 16–44 yrs[a]
Health problem	Parents with health problems (n = 695)	All parents (n = 1754)	
Musculo skeletal (including arthritis, rheumatism)	39	15	11
Respiratory	26	10	7
Skin conditions and allergies[b]	22	9	1
Gynaecological fertility	17	7	–
Heart/circulatory	13	5	1
Stomach/bowel/digestive	8	3	1
Vision (even with glasses)	8	3	1
Hearing (even with hearing aids)	3	1	1
Diabetes	4	1	1
Epilepsy/fits	3	1	1
Any long-term health problem	–	40	27

Note: respondents could report more than one health problem. [a] Base = 11,845 households; data from the General Household Survey 1996–97; (ONS 1999). [b] The elevated figure for 'skin conditions and allergies' in our data set relative to the GHS data may be due to differences of definition – for example, we included 'allergies' in with skin conditions whereas the ICD wording refers only to 'skin complaints'.

Table 3.2 Extent to which health problem affects daily activities		
	% of parents	
	Parents with physical health problems (n = 695)	All respondents (n = 1754)
All or most of the time	19	8
Some of the time	37	15
Never	44	(77)

Base = 1754

Table 3.3 Extent to which health problem affects caring for children		
	% of parents	
	Parents with physical health problems (n = 695)	All respondents (n = 1754)
All or most of the time	7	3
Some of the time	22	9
Never	71	(88)

Base = 1754

Qualitative interviews provided more details of the effects of health problems on caring for children. Parents described the frustration of not being able to take part in the same parent–child activities that they saw bringing other families closer together. They commented that many cheaper family leisure activities were precluded by ill health, leaving restricted options that were not affordable on a low income. For example, one mother with problems in walking explained:

> A lot of the children round here go with their parents on bike rides and they walk round the woods and things like that. Well I can't do that. The

activities that I can do with the children cost a lot of money, and on a budget it's very difficult (to afford them).

(Mother, lone parent, difficult child, poor health, sick child)

Parents also sometimes described more direct effects that their health problems could have on children. Apart from their acting as young carers, parents' ill-health could affect and constrain children's lives in a variety of other ways. For example, one mother with epilepsy described how her illness impacted emotionally on the children and affected day-to-day routines:

[The children] don't want to go out and play in case something happens [to me]. They don't want to go to school if I have a fit because they're worried that [when] they come home I might be in hospital or something and I won't be here.

(Mother, difficult child, low income, bad accommodation)

Parents' mental and emotional health

Parents were also asked to complete the Malaise Inventory developed by the Institute of Psychiatry from the Cornell Medical Index (Rutter, Tizard and Whitmore 1970). The Malaise Inventory is a checklist of 24 symptoms used to measure a tendency towards depression. A score of eight or more is known to be associated with elevated risk of depression. Backache, headaches, anxiety, extreme fatigue and difficulties in sleeping were widely reported by the parents in the sample and contributed substantially to the high Malaise scores shown in the Table 3.4.

Table 3.4 Mental and emotional health of parents in poor environments – scores on the Malaise Inventory			
	Women (n = *1604*)	*Men* (n = *137*)	*All respondents* (n = *1745*)
High scores (score = 8 or more) (%)	21	18	21
Mean score	4.7	4.0	4.6

Base = 1745

Overall, more than one-fifth of the sample (21%) had high scores on the Malaise Inventory. This is an extremely high proportion relative to that typically found in nationally representative samples of the population as a whole. For example, sweeps of the National Child Development Study (NCDS – a cohort of over 11,000 respondents born within a single week in 1958) show high Malaise score rates of only around 7.5 per cent at age 23 and around 7 per cent at age 33 for men and women combined (Cheung and Buchanan 1997). Thus, according to our data, parents in poor environments are approximately three times more likely to score highly on the Malaise Inventory than parents in a normal sample. Interestingly, our figures for both sexes are very similar to the scores for women who, while growing up, had experienced 'severe social disadvantage' within the terms of the NCDS study. For example, at 23 years, 19 per cent of disadvantaged women in that study had high Malaise scores, rising to 21 per cent by age 33.

Moreover, although Malaise scores are generally significantly greater for women than for men in national samples (Cheung and Buchanan 1997), in our sample, although women had somewhat higher scores on average, the difference between the mean score for the two sexes was not large enough to reach statistical significance. Over one in four women (21%) had high scores on this measure, and although the numbers of men with high scores were small ($n = 24$), the proportion of high scores among fathers (18%) was not greatly different from that found among mothers. This suggests, perhaps, that within poor environments, parenting may be a greater 'risk' factor for high Malaise scores than sex – where men are main carers for children they may be just as likely as women to suffer from symptoms related to depression.

Finally, showing how risk factors may be intertwined, like Rutter, Tizard and Whitmore (1970) we found that high Malaise scores were significantly associated with the presence of long-term physical health problems. Of those with a physical health problem, nearly one-third (32%) had a high Malaise score compared with only 13 per cent of those with no health problem ($p<0.001$.)

Children's physical health

Turning next to child characteristics that may present challenges to parenting, parents were asked first about the physical health of all children in their family, including that of the index child. Overall, two in five of the sample of parents (40%) were caring for a child in the family with a long-term health problem. Of the sample of parents, 17 per cent said that they were spending more time caring for a child in their family because that child had a long-term health problem. Notably, parents with a physical health problem were significantly more likely than others to have a sick or disabled child at home (50% compared to 33% of other parents; $p<0.0001$). A similar finding is reported in the 1995–97 Health Survey for England (HSE) on the health of young people (Department of Health 1999), in which children of a parent with longstanding illness were found to be two and half times more likely than those with 'well' parents to have a long-term health problem themselves.

As well as asking about the presence of children with health problems in the household, we asked in some detail about the physical health of the index children (that is, the child selected at random within each sample family to be the focus of more detailed questioning). Although most index children (93%) were reported by their parents to be in generally very good or fairly good health, over one-quarter (27%) were nevertheless reported to have long-term health problems or disabilities. This is only slightly more than the figure reported for the 1995–97 Health Survey for England (HSE), in which 26 per cent of boys aged 2–15 years and 22 per cent of girls were reported as having longstanding illnesses. The most common long-term health problem reported for index children was respiratory difficulties, including asthma (50% of those with health problems, 14% of all index children). Also commonly reported were skin complaints or allergies such as eczema (37% of children with problems, 11% of all). Other complaints included learning difficulties (10% of children with problems, 3% of all) and hearing problems, even when a hearing aid was used (6% of children with problems, 2% of all). Table 3.5 shows these figures, along with figures from the Health Survey for England for comparison.[2] Results below 0.5% are indicated by an asterisk (*) in the body of the table. Again, parents who themselves had a physical health problem were significantly more likely to report having an index child with long term health problems than other parents (53% compared to 34%; $p<0.0001$).

Table 3.5 Health problems of the index children, compared with children in England

Health problem	% of children		% of children in England [a]
	Index children with health problems (n = 507)	All index children (n = 1754)	
Respiratory (inc. asthma)	50	15	14
Skin conditions or allergies	37	11	4
Learning difficulties	10	3	–
Hearing (even with hearing aids)	6	2	3
Speech difficulties	5	1	–
Musculoskeletal	5	1	2
Stomach/bowel/digestive	4	1	1
Vision (even with glasses)	4	1	1
Heart/circulatory	3	1	1
Epilepsy/ fits	2	1	1 [b]
Diabetes	1	*	–
Mental illness	1	*	1
Gynaecological problems	1	*	–
Other problems	7	2	*
Any long-term health problem	–	27	24

Note that children could have more than one health problem.

[a] Base = 13,513
Data from the Health Survey for England 1995–97 (Department of Health 1999). Figures approximated from weighted data for males and females.

[b] Base 10,310
Data from Meltzer et al. (2000).

Somewhat under half of these children (45%, or 13% of the all index children) were described as being limited in terms of daily activities in some way 'all or some of the time'. This figure is very close to the 12 per cent figure (girls and boys combined) reported by the HSE. Taken together, with the possible exception of skin problems,[3] it seems that the children in our sample were not greatly dissimilar to children in the wider population in terms of the incidence in longstanding health problems. This is in contrast to the situation for parent health, which was markedly worse for parents in poor environments than in the population as a whole.

Although only one in every 14 (7%) of the index children with long-term health problems was officially registered as disabled, well over one-third of parents of children with problems (38%) said that they spent more time caring for this child than they would expect to do if the child were fully fit. Qualitative interviews revealed the real-life issues in coping with a sick child, and parents explained how this increased the stresses associated with parenting because of the additional effort entailed. A recurring complaint was that the ill health kept parents up at night, leaving them so tired that it created difficulties during the day:

> We have (always) got to see to them because they are ill … We are up and down to them all night. Because of our lack of sleep and being run down I just get bad tempered.
>
> *(Father, sick child, large family, poor health, bad accommodation)*

Balancing work and home commitments was also more difficult when caring for a sick child. Parents in this position gave accounts of how they found it impossible to maintain this balance, usually resulting in accepting the extra financial strain that came with having to give up work:

> She has a lot of physiotherapy and we're back and forth [to the hospital]. It's inconvenient to keep switching your [work] hours you see, because it's a monthly rota … you can't do it.
>
> *(Mother, lone parent, low income, sick child)*

Perhaps unsurprisingly, then, parents with sick or disabled children at home had significantly higher mean Malaise scores than other parents (5.51 compared with 4.07; $p<0.0001$).

Child behaviour

In addition to asking about children's physical health, we explored in some detail the index of children's emotional and behavioural characteristics. We used three well-known existing instruments to measure these, chosen to cover, as far as possible, the wide age range of children within the sample. All the instruments were self-completed by parents, after a short explanation by the survey interviewer. It is important, therefore, to stress that each of these instruments gives us only parent-perceived measures of child difficulty. We did not collect observational data, or data from other informants (e.g. teachers, or from children themselves) that would allow us to assess the relative difficulties presented by the sample children from alternative standpoints. Nevertheless, parents' perceptions of their child are known to be important factors in influencing parenting behaviours (for example, Rosenberg and Reppucci 1983) and it makes sense to measure these if we wish to assess the extent to which parents experience a sense of stress or challenge in their daily parenting role.

Full details of the instruments used and the modifications that were made can be found in Appendix 3, but, in brief, for babies and children under two years old ($n = 147$), we used a modified and shortened version (comprising two subscales) of the *Bates Infant Characteristics Questionnaire* (ICQ) (Bates, Freeland and Lounsbury 1979), an instrument developed to assess the concept of difficult temperament in infants. For children aged around three years ($n = 49$), we used the *Behaviour Checklist* (BCL) developed by Richman, Stevenson and Graham (1982). This 21-item scale has been widely used as a simple screening device to identify children whose behaviour might need further assessment. For older children (four years or more, $n = 1174$) we used Robert Goodman's *Strengths and Difficulties Questionnaire* (SDQ) (Goodman 1977). The SDQ is a 25-item checklist of child behaviours that is widely used and well validated. It includes questions on pro-social behaviour as well as problems, which is thought to make it especially acceptable to parents. There is a growing body of SDQ data based on normal community samples as well as clinic-based samples, and the SDQ has recently been used in a number of large-scale government-funded surveys including the Health Survey for England 1995–97. Through these instruments, our intention was to assess the extent to which children in the sample presented particular challenges to parents in terms of their emotional or behavioural characteristics. In total, 1413 children in the sample (81%) had valid scores on one of these instruments. Selected results for the SDQ, used with the largest group of children, are given below. Results for the ICQ and the BCL and further SDQ results can be found in Appendix 3.

The Strengths and Difficulties Questionnaire (SDQ)

The SDQ uses a cut-off score (the 'Total Difficulties' score) based on normed results (that is, results from using the scale with normal community populations). It consists of a 25-item symptom/attributes checklist, allowing children with scores above a certain point to be as rated as 'abnormal' relative to the wider population of children. The results are shown in Table 3.6 along with SDQ data from the Health Survey for England 1995–97 (Department of Health 1999) for comparison as a measure of scores in the wider population of children (shown in shaded columns). The children in our study had slightly higher scores than children in the HSE sample (13% were rated abnormal, compared to 10% in the HSE), although the differences are not substantial. Interestingly, recent surveys using other, more stringent, clinician-validated measures of childhood mental disorders have also found overall rates of mental disorder of 10 per cent for a slightly more restricted age group (Meltzer *et al.* 2000) from a survey of over 10,000 5–15 year olds in Britain conducted in 1999 by ONS.

As can be seen from the table, in our study boys were significantly more likely to have higher scores than girls ($p < 0.001$), a result also found in the Health Survey for England 1995–1997 (results shown in shaded columns), and in the ONS survey. Mean SDQ scores also varied significantly by age of child ($p < 0.01$), so that the older the child, the lower the mean score; see Table 3.7.

Table 3.6 Scores on the Strengths and Difficulties Questionnaire (children aged 4–16 years old), by sex of child, and compared with children in England

	% of children					
	Boys in sample (n = 599)	Boys HSE (n = 2843)	Girls in sample (n = 575)	Girls HSE (n = 2862)	All index children in sample (n = 1174)	All HSE children (n = 5705)
Normal (score 0–13)	74	78	81	84	77	81
Borderline (score 14–16)	11	10	8	8	10	9
Abnormal (score 17–34)	15	12	11	8	13	10
Mean score	10.4	–	9.0	–	9.7	–

Table 3.7 Mean SDQ scores by age of child

	4–5 years	6–8 years	9–11 years	12–14 years	15–16 years
Mean score	10.4	10.2	10.0	9.4	8.2

Base = 1217 children with valid scores

The direction of the relationship of age and SDQ scores bears comment. Although teenagers are often thought to be more difficult to manage, in this normative sample of parents and children in poor environments parents of pre-adolescent children in fact reported more difficulties, and our findings demonstrate that, in this sample at least, older children were not perceived by parents as more emotionally and behaviourally difficult to manage. This finding is consonant with other studies that have used the SDQ; for example, although the HSE reports 'no clear relationship between Total Deviance [Difficulties] Score and age' (Chapter 10, p.4), that survey did find a difference on the Conduct Problems and Hyperactivity subscales of the SDQ such that children aged 7–9 were more likely to score highly than older children; a finding that would seem to support our own findings with respect to age. However, other studies using more stringent and clinician-rated measures of mental disorders usually find the reverse pattern; that is, that older children show higher rates of disorder (see, for example, Meltzer *et al.* 2000). This suggests that the relationship of child age with emotional and behavioural problems may be affected by data collection method. Our findings may be an artefact of the component items of the SDQ, which may be more sensitive at picking up problems in younger children; or it may reflect a tendency for parents to over-report behaviour problems in younger children relative to professionals, perhaps as a result of relative inexperience. However, whatever the reason for the pattern we found, the implications are clear: parents themselves perceive younger children as more challenging – a finding repeated in other contexts later in this report.

'Difficult' children

In order to identify, in different age groups across the sample as a whole, children who were rated by their parents as 'difficult' or challenging, we created a composite category of 'difficult child'. This was achieved by grouping together children who had either a high score on *both* ICQ subscales, or a high score on the BCL, or an abnormal score on the SDQ. In total, 213 children met this definition: 15 per cent – one in seven – of the children for whom it was possible to calculate a valid child behaviour score. 'Difficult' children were more likely to be young (mean age in years = 7.50 compared to 8.82 for other children; $p<0.001$). They were also more likely to have some kind of long-standing physical health problem (45% compared with 28% of other children; $p<0.001$), a finding also reported in the HSE in respect of child emotional and behavioural measures (Department of Health 1999). Difficult children were also more likely to be the children of lone parents (47% compared with 38%; $p<0.01$) and to come from families in the lower income quintiles ($p<0.001$), as Figure 3.1 shows. For parents, there was also an extremely strong relationship between having a difficult child and having a high Malaise score (35% compared with 18%; $p<0.001$), although there was no relationship between having a difficult child and parental physical health problem.

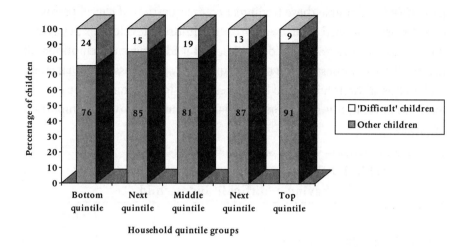

Base=1173

Figure 3.1 'Difficult' children by household income quintile groups

Clearly, then, having a 'difficult' child is strongly associated with a range of other risk indicators. What were the strongest predictors of having a 'difficult' child? A logistic regression model into which we entered the factors that were significantly associated with having a difficult child in cross-sectional analyses (child's sex, child's age, physical health of the child, parent's marital status, household income quintile, household social class and parent's Malaise score dichotomised as 'high' or 'low') showed that once other factors were taken into account, only the age of the child, whether a child had a health problem or not, the household income and the parent's Malaise score remained significant; Table 3.9. Note that once household income was accounted for, lone parenting *per se* ceased to be significant, suggesting that it is poverty, not single parenthood, that is most closely associated with having a behaviourally challenging child. Most noteworthy of all, however, the odds ratios obtained from the model indicated that a high parental Malaise score increased the chances of having a difficult child by a factor of three: in other words, those with high Malaise scores were almost three times as likely to have a 'difficult' child than those with normal or low scores. A similar association between parental emotional problems and child behaviour has been consistently found in other studies (for example, the HSE, Department of Health 1999; Meltzer *et al.* 2000). Of course these findings beg the question of causal pathway: does being depressed increase the risk of children developing behaviour difficulties, or does having a 'difficult' child lead to parental emotional ill health? This is a question we cannot answer from a cross-sectional study such as this, although it would be interesting to follow some of the parents who took part in this study longitudinally to shed light on this important question.

Table 3.9 Role of a range of factors in predicting having a 'difficult' index child	
	Odds ratio
Parental high Malaise score	2.96[a]
Child's age	0.92[a]
Household income (income quintile)	0.83[b]
Child's physical health problem(s)	1.70[b]

Base = 959; [a] *p< 0.01;* [b] *p<0.0001*

Note that the odds ratios for child's age and income quintile are negative (less than 1) because these two variables showed an inverse relationship with child difficulty ratings.

Conclusions

At the level of individual parents and children, we chose to focus on four key areas of risk that may make parenting more difficult and stressful: parents' physical health status, parents' mental and emotional health status, children's physical health, and child's behaviour.

Compared with general population samples of adults, parents in poor environments were in substantially worse physical and emotional health. While recent surveys of the general population (for example, ONS 1999) have found just over one-quarter of men and women aged 16–44 years to have long-term health problems (27%). In our sample of parents of broadly comparable age, the figure was closer to two in five (40%). Differences of survey method may of course account for some of this disparity. For example, although both studies used a similar definition of long-term health problems, the wording of questions about specific conditions varied in some respects and our wording – especially by including the term 'allergies', to which the Health Survey for England does not make reference – may have encouraged higher reporting of some conditions. However, even with this caveat in mind, it still appears that parents in poor environments do report more limiting long-term health problems across the board than adults in the general population. Thus, while only 14 per cent of adults in the HSE 1996 reported a health problem that impaired their daily functioning (Department of Health 1998), in our study, the figure was 23 per cent.

Similarly, general population surveys that have used the Malaise Inventory, as we did, to measure adult mental and emotional health have reported rates of high scores around 7 per cent for both men and women combined (Cheung and Buchanan 1997), whereas our rates were three times as high at 21 per cent. Moreover, although the small numbers of male main carers in our sample relative to female carers limits the generalisability of our results, there do appear to be indications that for male main carers, rates of depression may not be greatly below those for women, in spite of the fact that in samples of adults in the general population women typically show much higher rates than men. Given the substantial numbers of men who are now caring for children, either alone or as the main carer in a couple, this finding bears further exploration in a larger sample of fathers.

Interestingly, though, children in poor environments were more likely to have physical and behavioural problems than children in the wider population. The differentials were far less dramatic than those reported for adults. Among children in poor environments, the rate of long-term health problems was 27 per cent compared to 24 per cent in the general population as measured in the Health Survey for England. Based on the SDQ scores of children aged 4 year old or over, children in our sample were also only somewhat more likely to have abnormal scores indicating behavioural or emotional problems: 13 per cent compared to 10 per cent in the HSE (Department of Health 1999). In general, our results suggest that although children growing up in poor environments do appear to be a little more challenging to care for than other children in the wider population, the disparities at the child level are not nearly as stark as they are at the parent level.

Still, in terms of absolute numbers of children across the population as a whole, even small percentage differences have substantial implications.

Moreover, what our results also suggest rather strongly is that poor children may be 'storing up' physical and mental health problems for the future. Many of the children we surveyed will become the 'parents in poor environments' of the future. Although, as a group, the children included in our study may be in reasonably good physical and mental or emotional health, our data suggest that by the time they reach parenthood themselves they can expect to enjoy considerably worse health than parents in the population at large. There is, clearly, a need to address the living conditions and lifestyles of children in poor environments preventatively before the health problems of adulthood set in, as many other authors have urged (BMJ 1999; Roberts 1997).

Last, another key feature of our data is the remarkable overlap between problems, both within and between the generations. Thus, 'difficult' children were more likely than other children to have a physical health problem, and they were far more likely to be from the lowest income households and to have parents who themselves suffered from poor emotional and mental health. Parents with physical health problems tended to be more likely to have children with physical health problems than 'well' parents, and the parents of sick or disabled children had higher mean Malaise scores than others. Critically, the message is that parents who are least well equipped to manage the demands of challenging children are the most likely to face these problems.

Notes

1. It should be noted that both the GHS and the HSE provide a breakdown of long-standing illnesses based on conditions used in the International Classification of Diseases (ICD). Although broadly comparable to our list of common health problems, there are some differences in question wording that may in part account for differences between the two samples. Readers are referred to the HSE for further details.

2. It should be noted that the HSE provides a breakdown of children's longstanding illnesses based on conditions used in the International Classification of Diseases. Although broadly comparable to our list of common health problems, there are some differences that should be borne in mind when interpreting the table. Readers are referred to the HSE for further details.

3. As with our adult data, the elevated figure for skin problems in our data set relative to the HSE may be due to differences of definition – for example, we included 'allergies' in with skin conditions.

CHAPTER FOUR

Stress Factors at the Family Level

There has been a large body of work demonstrating that stress factors at the family and household level increase the risk of parenting difficulties and parenting breakdown. Two of the most important and frequently mentioned in the literature are poverty and family structure, and we discuss our findings in relation to these key risk factors in this chapter.

Poverty and its correlates – unemployment, low income, and poor housing – have long been known to be associated with higher rates of child maltreatment (Pelton 1978; Parton 1985; Jones and McCurdy 1992; Wolfner and Gelles 1993; Dietz 2000; Cawson *et al.* 2000), particularly those forms involving physical violence and physical neglect. In addition, numerous studies have demonstrated the deleterious effects of poverty and social disadvantage on parenting skills and parent–child relationships more generally (Madge 1983; Quinton and Rutter 1988; McLeod and Shanahan 1993; Conger *et al.* 1994). Poor parents are overrepresented in the case loads of agencies charged with responding to parenting problems (Dingwall, Eekelar and Murray 1983; Gelles 1987; Pelton 1981), as well as among those who self-report problems within the general population (Roberts *et al.* 1995). Hypotheses advanced to explain the consistent link between poverty and parenting problems have generally centred on identifying mediating variables that appear to be critical determinants of the pathway (Kaufman and Zigler 1989). Key among these are psychological stress that results from doing daily battle with tight budgets, debt, inadequate or overcrowded accommodation, long-term unemployment and so on (Pelton 1978). This is thought to affect adversely individuals' emotional and mental health, leading to impaired relationships between family members (Conger *et al.* 1994).

Linked to poverty, but also constituting a completely separate set of stressors, family structure and marital or relationship problems have also been consistently linked with parenting problems. Family breakdown and lone parenting have been shown by many studies to be strongly associated with parenting difficulties and adverse outcomes for children, substantially because of the impact on family resources that accompanies divorce, separation and lone parenthood (Buchanan and Ten-Brinke 1997) but also partly because of the psychological distress (of both parent and child) that may accompany these experiences. This may result in children who are harder to parent and parents who are less effectual at dealing with the challenges presented by distressed children (Burghes 1994; Simons *et al.* 1993; Rodgers and Pryor 1998). Moreover, family conflict (for example, fighting or hostility between adults) has also been shown to be associated with elevated rates of child maltreatment and hostility towards children in parents, and child behaviour problems and heightened aggression in children themselves (Belsky and Vondra 1989; Straus and Kantor 1987; Straus and Smith 1995; Conger *et al.* 1994; Grych and Fincham 1990). Conflict may of course precede family break-up; alternatively, it may be a chronic feature of family life in two-parent households. Last, family size (that is, the number of dependent children in a household) is also thought to be associated with parenting problems. Larger families are consistently overrepresented in child maltreatment statistics (Zigler and Hall 1989) and a recent study in the UK showed that large families (with four or more children) were twice as likely to report seeking help for a parenting problem than those with only a single child (Roberts *et al.* 1995). While the probability of encountering problems will obviously rise with each additional child in the family, it seems also that large families may be stressful in themselves, as parents have to manage a combination of increased demands, and limited material and personal resources to meet these demands.

By definition, the parents who took part in this study were living in areas that were selected for their unusually high concentrations of families in disadvantageous circumstances. It was not generally surprising therefore to find that stress factors at the level of the family were substantial for parents in the sample. In this chapter we explore the extent of key stress factors at the level of the family and household, focusing on material difficulties associated with low income and unemployment; practical problems such as difficulties with housing; and problems associated with family structure and relationships. We also present data from an instrument we called the Current Problems Questionnaire, a composite measure of stressors at the family and household level.

Financial stressors

Low income

Financial strains loomed large in this sample. Indeed, it is difficult to overstate the importance of financial difficulties as a source of stress in the daily lives of families in poor environments. As already noted in Part I, half of the households in the sample had no one in paid employment, and the median average income for the sample families (equivalised to reflect household size) was just over £7000 per annum – approximately one-half of the average annual household income for the UK general population. Only one in six families in this sample reached the national average household income, and a similar proportion (16%) lived on one-third or less of what most families in the UK have to live on.

Consequently, parents reported severe limitations in their spending power. For example, we gave parents a short list of eight items that most families in Britain would take for granted as basic aspects of family expenditure (that is, not 'luxury' items). The list was constructed with reference to previous, more detailed studies of poverty and social exclusion (for example, Kempson 1996) and was designed to assess whether both adults and children in the household had adequate food, clothing and warmth at home, as well as exploring whether they were able to participate in basic social activities that are considered a normal part of life in modern Britain. Detailed and careful studies that have been conducted since the fieldwork for this study took place confirm that these areas of expenditure are considered by most of the population to be a necessary part of a decent standard of living (for example, Gordon *et al.* 2000).

We asked parents to tell us whether there was anything on the list they could not afford. Strikingly, only two in five parents (38%) said they could afford *all* the things on the list (that is, they lacked none of them) and this figure went down to less than one in five for lone parents (17%). Although we cannot compare these figures directly with other studies, due to differences in methodology, a recent national study reported, by contrast, that 58 per cent of the general population lacked none of the items on a (longer) list of basic necessities (Gordon *et al.* 2000). As Table 4.1 shows, the most likely area of expenditure to be cut when family resources are scarce is the family holiday. Indeed, in poor environments, family holidays are enjoyed by only a minority of households. A majority of households in the sample – nearly two-thirds, rising to more than three-quarters among lone parent households – missed out on an annual family holiday away from home. By contrast, Gordon and colleagues report that only 18 per cent of the wider population say they cannot afford a holiday away from home (other than with relatives) on an annual basis. Moreover, one in seven children lived in households in which even a day trip or an outing once a year was not affordable. Among lone parent households, almost a quarter of families did not take day trips. These findings strongly echo those reported by Kempson (1996) in her detailed study *Life on low income.*

Table 4.1 Basic items of expenditure that cannot be afforded by parents	
Item of expenditure	*% of parents*
Family holiday away from home once a year	60
Family day trip or outing once a year	15
Heating whenever it is needed	8
Basic toys and sports gear for children	8
Warm winter clothes for each adult	6
Warm winter clothes for each child	5
Cooked main meal every day for each adult	3
Cooked main meal every day for each child	1
(None – we have or can afford all of these things)	(38)

Base = 1754

Note: Respondents could cite more than one item that could not be afforded.

Nearly 1 in 12 families (8%) lived in homes in which heating was not always available when needed (as compared with only 1 per cent in the wider population according to Gordon *et al.* 2000), and the same proportion could not afford basic toys and sports gear for children. One family in 20 (5%) said they could not afford warm winter clothes for all children in the household. Like Middleton, Ashworth and Walker (1994), Middleton, Ashworth and Braithwaite (1998) and Gordon *et al.* (2000) we found that parents in poverty usually manage to ensure that their children do at least get a decent meal once a day but, even so, a small minority of parents (3%) reported having to skimp themselves on hot meals in order to provide this.

Discussions with parents highlighted the importance of these findings in terms of their impact on quality of life. For example, both the value of holidays and the frustration of not being able to afford them were strong themes in the qualitative interviews. Parents emphasised how holidays helped to 'bond' the family and provide brief respite from stressors at home, but simply weren't an option financially. One mother described how much her family had enjoyed a recent week's caravan break paid for by a relative – her first holiday for 22 years.

> It was nice because we were together all the time. We sat down and had our meals together. There was an indoor swimming pool so we were all together ... I think you get closer (on holiday) ... and I wish I could go away every year, but I can't.
>
> *(Mother, lone parent, large family, low income)*

Financial strain

It is important and useful to measure actual levels of material deprivation, using indicators such as annual income and perceptions of purchasing power. Lists of things which families cannot afford, as in Table 4.1, give a vivid picture of the lives of some parents and their children, living in homes which lack basic creature comforts that most would take for granted these days, and where escape – even for a day a year – is often not possible. However, in terms of appreciating the extent to which life on a low income impacts upon family life and on parenting more generally, it is perhaps equally useful to consider the concept of 'financial strain'. By this, we mean the way in which the constant effort of managing money and making ends meet creates a sense of stress and strain for parents that permeates family life and can come to characterise the atmosphere at home. To what extent is low income a source of ongoing stress for families with children? As we show in Part IV, many families had creative and effective ways of managing to make ends meet; nevertheless, a sense of financial strain was pervasive within the sample as a whole.

In total, although a majority of parents (43%) said that they were 'getting by all right' and over one-third (35%) felt they were managing 'very' or 'fairly' well, one-fifth of parents (22%) reported that they were not generally managing financially (see Figure 4.1). Comparable figures from a national survey carried out in 1992 (Berthoud and Kempson 1992) show that in the wider population, by contrast, only around 6 per cent of households were in financial difficulties; 51 per cent were 'just getting by' and 43 per cent were managing well. Moreover, confirming that, in matters of household finance, subjective perceptions on the whole reflected objective fact, parents' perceptions of whether they were managing financially were strongly related to their actual household income. The median equivalised household income for those who were managing very or fairly well or getting by all right was £7672 as compared to £5465 for those who were not managing well or not managing at all $(p<0.0001)$.[1]

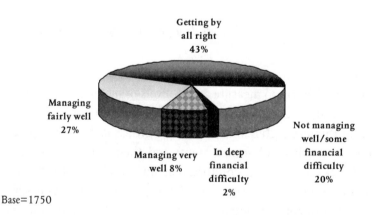

Base=1750

Figure 4.1 Perceptions of how well the family is managing financially

Although the majority of the sample said they were managing their family financial matters to a greater or lesser degree, anxiety about finances was common, indicating that in poor environments, even those who were managing financially did so at some personal cost. Nearly two-thirds of parents (60%) reported frequent worries about money, and over one-third (37%) said they worried about money 'almost all the time' (rising to 50% for lone parents). One quarter (24%) worried 'only sometimes', and only one in seven parents (15%) reported living a life more or less free from financial anxieties. Moreover, further evidence that financial strain can impact negatively on emotional health is contained in the finding that there was a strong relationship between household income levels and parental Malaise score. Malaise scores were strongly inversely associated with household income: the median household income for those with a high Malaise score was £6103 compared to £7432 for those with a low or average score; $p<0.0001$.

What were the reasons for this sense of anxiety? For most, the reasons were described in straightforward terms: household income was 'too low to cover our commitments'. Of those who were not managing, 75 per cent of respondents cited this as the reason. In addition, one in five (19%) of those who were not managing said they had had 'unexpected or unusual' expenses in the recent past, as Table 4.2 shows. In addition, one-fifth of parents (21%) reported chronic, long-term debts (apart from a mortgage) of two or more years' standing, and a similar number admitted to 'problems with owing money' – for example, getting behind with repayments, or being regularly hassled by credit card companies and other lenders. Many poor families rely on credit (usually catalogues and store cards) to manage on a day-to-day basis (Berthoud and Kemspon 1992) and, for some of the parents in our sample, one of the main reasons for financial difficulties was credit/debt repayments. In total, out of those who identified that they were not managing well financially, nearly one-third (29%) cited credit and debt repayments as part of the problem.

To what extent is financial mismanagement on the part of parents a source of financial strain? Kempson (1996, p.28) states: 'while some people manage to balance their budgets more successfully than others, the evidence for fecklessness is scant'. Our findings support this, and in our sample a relatively small number attributed their difficulties to mismanagement of money. Only one in ten (9%) said they thought they themselves were 'not very good at managing money', very few of those who weren't managing admitted they 'spent money on the wrong things' (6%), and a tiny proportion (3%) blamed their partner as not good at money management.

Table 4.2 Reasons for not managing financially	
Reason not managing financially	**% of parents**
Income not enough to cover commitments	75
A lot of credit or debt repayments to make	29
Unexpected/unusual expenses recently	19
Respondent not good at managing money	9
Family spends money on the wrong things	6
Partner not good at managing money	3
Some other reason	9

Base = all those not managing financially (*n* = 392). Respondents could cite more than one reason

The necessity of having to juggle finances while living in a constant state of debt was a dominant theme in qualitative interviews. Parents explained that on a low income it was impossible to cope with periods of high expenditure such as Christmas and school holidays without incurring debts. Even for those parents who did manage to keep on top of repayments, the regular cycle of these high cost periods meant that they were continuously faced with the pressure of catching up with 'never-never' payments.

> Well you've just got to get yourself into debt … to try and get the kids their things for Christmas. And then by the time I pay that off, it starts up again. In between that I've got four [children's] birthdays.
>
> *(Mother, lone parent, poor health)*

Parents who weren't managing repayments described how having to handle creditors added to the stress of trying to bring up a family. Apart from the problems of securing future credit after being 'blacklisted', some parents recounted how they had suffered harassment from debt collectors.

> Yes they harass you on the phone, knocking on your door. They're not really nice, they're nasty. Mind you, it's their money, so they're bound to be nasty.
>
> *(Mother, low income, reconstituted family)*

Moreover, illustrating how financial strain may interlock with family conflict, parents also reported other forms of 'harassment' or stress because of low income, this time from within the family. For example, a prominent theme in qualitative interviews concerned the pressure parents felt to buy children and young people expensive, 'designer' fashion goods for school or leisure. While expensive, branded clothes for children and teenagers may not seem like a vital necessity to some, it is clear that, in poor environments, failure to supply these for children has very real implications both for the children's social relationships and for family harmony. Many respondents described the strain of knowing that children were being bullied by peers because they 'didn't wear the right clothes', and felt frustration at not being able to do anything to change this. In short, they described a situation of 'social exclusion' for children because of these visible signs of poverty.

> Well, they've got to be in the fashion. They've got to be the same as their friends. If not, they're called 'tramps' or they get picked on at school. They make your life hell, because the kids are calling them [names] at school and [daughter] has ended up on the phone to me crying (from school), wanting these Adidas [trainers]. But, I can't get them, where am I supposed to get [the money] from?
>
> *(Mother, lone parent, poor health)*

Accommodation problems

Strongly related to low income, another major material stressor that emerged from the study was the poor quality of housing of families in poor environments. Many houses were cramped, uncomfortable and dilapidated, but respondents could not afford to move. Overall, two in five respondents (41%) reported serious problems with the quality of their accommodation. Although methodological differences make it difficult to compare our data precisely with national data (for example, those from the English House Conditions Survey (EHCS), Department of Environment, Transport and the Regions 1998b), our measures probably come closest to the EHCS definition of 'poor housing' (housing which is either unfit, in substantial disrepair or requires essential modernisation) which in 1996 stood at a much lower figure of just over 14 per cent of households. Consonant with national housing study data, those in the lowest income quintile were twice as likely to report accommodation problems as those in the highest quintile (49% compared with 26%; $p<0.0001$), and those in rented accommodation were twice as likely to have accommodation problems than owner-occupiers (49% compared with 24%; $p<0.0001$). Privately rented properties marginally beat local authority housing as the worst accommodation in this respect, as Figure 4.2 below shows. Specific problems reported included problems with damp or wet or dry rot (16%), insufficient heating in bedrooms or living rooms in winter (15%), excessive condensation (14%), infestation by insects or rodents (9%) and water leaking through roofs, windows and doors (6%) – all of which constitute a risk to the health of children and their parents. Lack of space was also problematic for some, and one in six (17%) of households were officially 'overcrowded' in terms of the ratio of people to rooms.[2] This figure is three times higher than the national rate of overcrowded homes (6% in 1995) (ONS 1999). Furthermore, 17 per cent of parents also said they felt they did not have enough privacy at home, and one in ten (9%) reported that they were 'having trouble finding a place to live that is suitable and that we can afford'.

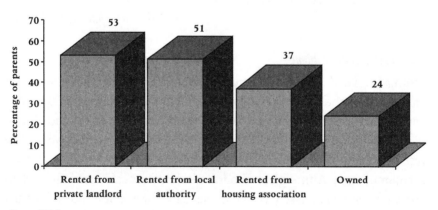

Base=1713

Figure 4.2 Parents reporting serious accomodation problems, by tenure

In terms of basic amenities at home, however, most families reported having essential items, in line with recent national findings that the number of dwellings that lack basic amenities has fallen away to a very small number over the last decade (DETR 1998b). It was nevertheless noteworthy that one in ten households (10%) did not have a private telephone in the home and 13 per cent did not have even partial central heating, although this figure is only marginally higher than the national average of 12 per cent (DETR 1998b).

Qualitative interviews suggested that problems with accommodation were a major stress factor for families trying to cope in poor environments. Parents emphasised the anxiety they felt at having to struggle with problems in a place where they just wanted to feel 'at home'. Parents rarely presented a wish-list of luxury, but just referred to the need for basic amenities to keep their children healthy.

> Let me live in a house, a decent house (where) my kids are going to feel they're at home and not like living in a squat, because that's what they all feel like. And just something with central heating like everybody else has got. I don't want a car or anything fancy, I just want a house. Somewhere nice to live that I can walk in and say, 'Thank God I'm home', not 'Oh God, here we go (facing problems)'.
> *(Father, lone parent, bad accommodation, low income, sick child, poor health)*

Parents described a variety of different problems with their accommodation, commonly having to deal with multiple difficulties in old or dilapidated properties. Damp and wet was a recurring complaint. One mother described the far-reaching ways that this affected her family.

> There's loads of things I can't have in the house. I can't have curtains because they mould, so everywhere is blinds. My kids beds, their quilts go mouldy. If anything touches the walls, any sort of quilt – a cuddly toy for instance – that will go mouldy and so will the wall where they're touching. Well that's terrible.
> *(Mother, bad accommodation)*

A second housing problem that caused parents considerable anxiety was infestation. This mother winced when she recalled how, in her last council flat, her family had been forced to live with an infestation of cockroaches.

> [Cockroaches were] running along the ceilings you know ... Sitting watching the telly and they'd drop on to them ... It was horrible. I just hated it. It just really made me feel dirty. And you say to the council, 'It

makes you feel disgusting' and they said 'There's nothing you could do, it's the whole block that's affected.'

(Mother, bad accommodation, large family)

Family structure

The other major group of stressors that we explored at the level of family was the extent to which family structure and/or family relationships created difficulties for parents in the sample.

Lone parenting

As we noted in Part I, although the majority of index children in the sample were living in two-parent families (61%), this is a much lower percentage than recent figures reported for the general population of parents. Thus, parents in poor environments are far more likely to be bringing up children on their own than parents in the wider population. Furthermore, for those in poor environments, living as a lone parent tends not to be a short-term, temporary situation but more of a chronic stressor. In addition to the one in four (23%) of lone parents who reported that they had never lived with a partner, only 19 per cent of lone parents had lived with a partner in the previous 12 months. Over a quarter (26%) had been living apart from a partner for at least five years. For parents with older children (children aged 12 years or more), this figure rose to 57 per cent, meaning that in poor environments over half of all adolescents are growing up in families in which they have had only one resident parent for at least five years.

Being a lone parent can be considered a risk factor for parents in many senses, in particular because lone parenting tends to be associated with lower household income, greater financial strain, and all that goes with it (for example, Bradshaw and Millar 1991). In this study, as in others, lone parents were indeed more likely than parents with a partner to experience various forms of material disadvantage. For example, the median equivalised household income for lone parents was £5408 compared with £9750 for parents with partners ($p<0.0001$), and two-parent households were 11 times more likely to have an adult in paid work (77% compared to 7%; $p<0.001$). Lone parents were also more likely to be living in rented accommodation (81% compared to 52%; $p<0.001$), and to have serious problems with their accommodation (47% compared to 38%; $p<0.001$).

However, material disadvantage was not the only source of stress for lone parents in our study, and many lone parents experienced higher rates of other difficulties at the individual level, such as emotional and mental health problems, or difficulties in managing their children. For example, whereas the mean Malaise score for parents with partners was 4.1, for lone parents it was 5.4 ($p<0.001$). Lone parents were also somewhat more likely to have an index child rated as 'difficult' on our composite measure (18% of index children of lone parents were 'difficult' as opposed to 13% of children of in two-parent families; $p<0.01$). However, it should be noted that, to some extent, the higher level of problems at the individual level that lone parents experienced were attributable to the strong underlying association between marital status and household income. For example, in logistic regression analysis, marital status in fact ceased to be significant as a predictor of having a 'difficult' child once income was taken into account. By contrast, although, marital status *remained* a significant predictor of high Malaise scores even after income was controlled for, suggesting that the lack of support that lone parents experience may have real and independent implications for their emotional health (see Table 4.3 below).

Table 4.3 Role of marital status and household income in predicting having a 'difficult' child and having a high Malaise score			
Outcome variable: 'difficult' child (n = 1458)		*Outcome variable: high Malaise score* (n = 1453)	
	Odds ratio		**Odds ratio**
Household income (income quintile)	0.99**	Household income (income quintile)	0.99**
Marital status	1.21 (n/s)	Marital status	1.50*

$p<0.01$; **$p<0.001$; n/s = not significant

In discussions, lone parents' comments about the emotional strain of raising children without a partner illustrated why this may be.

You haven't got a partner to discuss things with, or to lean on, or just to talk to … There's nobody there, you're on your own and you've got a child or two children or three children or whatever …

(Lone mother, low income)

It is hard on your own, mind. I've got to be honest, it is hard. You're trying to work, trying to correct them, trying to give them a good home life, make the house nice for them and everything. And then, sometimes you sit there and think, 'What is the point? What is the point?'

(Lone mother)

Family relationships and conflict

However, while not having a partner could be stressful, many of those with partners reported that their relationship was a source of problems; indeed, one-quarter of respondents who were married or living as married said that 'lack support from their partner' caused them stress to some extent. A number of questions in the survey measured specific difficulties in relationships with partners that were considered to be 'currently a problem' for respondents. Of those with partners, one in six parents (17%) were currently in relationships with partners who had verbally abused them (defined as 'your partner has said things to you on purpose to make you feel really bad or worthless'), 8 per cent (just under one in 12) of respondents said they were having 'regular fights or arguments' with their current partner, and one in 20 (5%) had been physically assaulted by their current partner. These figures are very close to the most recent British Crime Survey annual incidence figures on physical assaults by partners, in which 4 per cent of men and women questioned said they had been hit by a current partner in the year preceding the survey (Mirlees-Black 1999)

In qualitative interviews, some of these parents described how their partners shirked parental responsibilities, leaving them to struggle alone. Indeed, some felt that in many ways struggling when one had a difficult partner was worse than being a lone mother or father – a theme to which we return in Part IV when we explore coping with parenting in more detail. For example, parents described how uncooperative partners could make parenting harder.

> I'd have to go to my parents to ask them for money for food and things like that. His money was his, you know? If the kids wanted feeding that was my job to arrange somehow to find money.
>
> *(Mother, reconstituted family, large family)*

In addition, the particular problems for parenting faced by those in an abusive relationship was a recurring theme in qualitative interviews. Again, parents argued that trying to cope with parenting while in a violent relationship was in many ways more stressful than having no partner at all.

> It's better as a single parent, you have not got that pressure … Well, he was a wife beater and he made your life hell, day to day. How could you be a decent mum?
>
> *(Mother, lone parent)*

> You wasn't allowed to talk to no one. You wasn't allowed to talk to family about any problems. So you were stuck indoors 24 hours a day, seven days a week … I used to have my Mum saying something, 'well talk to me, tell me what's going on'… if you do, when you come home you'll pay for it. So it was a choice between not talking to my Mum or go home and get a good hiding. So I kept my mouth shut.
>
> *(Mother, reconstituted family, large family)*

Family size

The mean number of dependent children per family in our sample was 1.98, a figure not greatly dissimilar to the national average family size. One quarter (25%) of all the families we interviewed had three or more children under 16. There were no significant differences between parents with partners and lone parents in terms of numbers of children, nor by ethnic group.

Large families (those with three or more children) were disproportionately likely to be in the lower ranges of the sample household income distribution ($p<0.0001$), even although for the purposes of analysis income figures were already adjusted ('equivalised') for household size and composition, as Figure 4.3 below shows. This means that large families were not enjoying the same standard of living as smaller ones, and not surprisingly parents with large families were also much more likely than others to say that they felt they were not generally managing financially (27% compared to 21%; $p<0.01$).

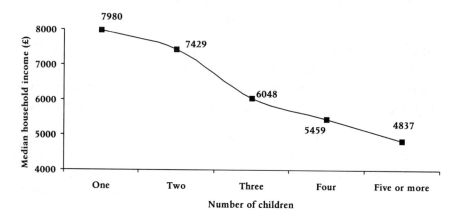

Base = 1458 respondents who disclosed income

Figure 4.3 Average equivalised household income by number of dependent children

The effect of family size on other risk factors revealed some other interesting findings. Mean Malaise scores, for example, were relatively stable with increasing family size up until the fourth child, after which they increased rather dramatically ($p<0.0001$), see Figure 4.4.

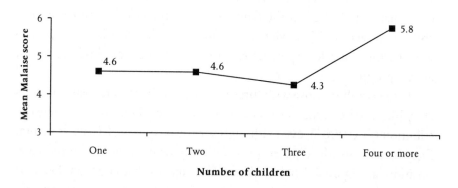

Base=1745

Figure 4.4 Mean Malaise Inventory score by number of dependent children

A composite measure of problems at the family level: the Current Problems Questionnaire

One of the most important measures of stress factors at the family level that we used in the survey was the Current Problems Questionnaire, or CPQ. Adapted by us from an American instrument known as the 'Difficult Life Circumstances Questionnaire' (DLC) (Mitchell *et al.* 1998), see Appendix 3 for further details, the CPQ consisted of a simple self-completed binary checklist of 23 questions that were not covered elsewhere in the survey, which asked respondents to indicate which of the family-level problems on the list 'are currently a problem for you'. The items covered relationships with current and former partners, financial problems, problems with work and accommodation, problems with substance misuse, and difficulties with children including problems at school and involvement with social agencies such as the police or social services. Critically, the CPQ does not so much measure whether a particular risk factor is present as whether it is present *and* is perceived to be a problematic. By adding up the number of affirmative answers, an overall CPQ score for each respondent can be computed. The scale therefore provides a snapshot of the extent to which respondents are exposed to multiple difficulties at the family level in simple numeric terms.

Results for individual items on the CPQ are referred to throughout this report and are also given in Table 4.5. The most common areas of difficulty for parents were debt, followed by various forms of abuse experienced by respondents, problems with accommodation and problems with children. Overall scores ranged from zero to 20 problems, and the mean score for the sample as a whole was 1.85. Those with high Malaise scores and those with a 'difficult' child had significantly higher mean CPQ scores than other parents. Those with a high Malaise score had a mean CPQ score of 2.84 compared with 1.61 ($p<0.0001$); and those with a difficult child had a mean score of 2.61 compared with 1.75 for other parents (p<0.01). Parents with large families also had higher mean CPQ scores: 2.19 compared with 1.74 for those with two or less children; $p<0.0001$). CPQ scores did *not* vary significantly with household income or by marital status within the sample as a whole.

Table 4.4 Problems on the Current Problems Questionnaire (CPQ): parents reporting item as 'currently a problem'

Current problem	*% of parents*
Money problems	
Long-term debts (2 years or more) other than a house mortgage	21
Problems with owing money and getting behind on repayments	19
Relationship problems	
Respondent abused physically, sexually or emotionally by someone other than present partner	17
Current partner said things on purpose to make respondent feel bad or worthless	15
Partner away from home more than half the time for job or other reason	11
Problems with former partner	8
Current partner has hit or injured respondent	5
Regular arguments/fights with current partner	6
Partner in prison	1
Problems with accommodation	
Not enough privacy at home	17
Trouble finding place to live that is both suitable and affordable	9
People living in home who respondent wishes were not there	2
Trouble with landlord	2

Current problem (cont.)	% of parents (cont.)
Work-related problems	
Respondent's work interferes with family life	12
Partner's work interferes with family life	11
Problems with children	
Problems at school with a child that mean has to visit teacher or other staff	14
Child in family abused by someone physically, sexually or emotionally	6
Currently in contact with social services for child-related issues	4
Child in family in trouble with police or courts	2
Child in family on Child Protection Register	1
Problems with substances	
Personal problem with alcohol or drugs (prescribed and other)	1
Partner has problem with alcohol or drugs	2
Someone else in household has problem with alcohol or drugs	1
Mean number of problems	1.85

Bases vary by item: $N = 1693-1726$. Note that respondents could report more than one problem.

Note that 'current/present partner' could mean resident or non-resident partner.

Figure 4.5 shows the distribution of total scores on the CPQ, and in later analyses we refer to 'high' scores on the CPQ, taken to be scores of 3 or more problems (30% of the sample overall).

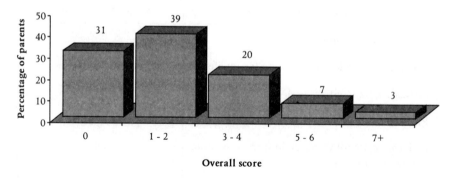

Base=1745

Figure 4.5 Overall scores on the Current Problems Questionnaire

Conclusions

At the level of the family, we focused on stressors relating to material poverty and disadvantage, family structure and relationships, as well as a composite measure that assessed the number of risk factors that were considered by respondents to be currently problematic.

As with stressors at the individual level, parents in poor environments were extremely disadvantaged relative to families in the wider population. They were dramatically poorer, with very low incomes. Only one in six households reported an equivalised household income at the level of the national average. Only 38 per cent lacked none of the items on a list of essential expenditure headings, compared to 58 per cent in the wider population. Moreover, this disparity is almost certainly underestimated due to methodological differences between our survey and other more detailed studies of family finances. Levels of anxiety about money were high, and one in five parents reported being in financial difficulties. Still, overall parents were perhaps remarkably positive about their financial situation, with the majority claiming to be managing financially, and there was little indication that financial difficulties were attributable to poor budgeting skills – a theme to which we return in Part IV of the report where we explore coping with parenting in a poor environment.

Accommodation problems loomed large, however, in this study, with 40 per cent of parents reporting 'serious' deficiencies with their housing. Chief among these were damp, wet, and inadequate heating, and in qualitative interviews many parents told horror stories of housing conditions that many would consider unfit for child rearing. The present Government's housing policy aspiration, 'To offer everyone the opportunity of a decent home, and so promote social cohesion, well being and self-dependence' (DETR 2000) will require some further substantial effort if it is to be achieved in poor environments, according to our study.

In terms of family structure, the number of children in the family was related to lower equivalised household incomes – a 'double whammy' for larger families, who not only had greater demands placed on them but fewer resources to meet them. Unsurprisingly, larger families with three or more children were disproportionately likely to say they were having difficulties managing, financially speaking, and parents with four or more children were also more likely to report higher Malaise Inventory scores. Families in poor environments were also disproportionately likely to be headed by lone parents, and a key finding of the study was the chronic nature of this situation. Three-quarters of lone parents had been alone for at least three years, and one-quarter had never lived with a partner at all. There was, moreover, a strong and independent association between lone parenting and poor parental mental health as measured by the Malaise Inventory, and qualitative interviews clearly indicated that, for many, raising children alone can be a very lonely and depressing experience.

Our findings may, however, debunk some common myths about lone parents. Although lone parents were indeed more likely to have problems such as those we discussed in Chapter 3 – for example, problems with 'difficult' children – our analysis suggested that this was not necessarily a function of lone parenting *per se*; that is, not necessarily a result of ineffective parenting, for example, or inadequate discipline and supervision of children by single parents. In the case of child behaviour, for example, poverty rather than marital status appeared to be the significant factor, and in logistic regression analyses lone parenting was not an independent predictor of child behaviour problems once household income was controlled for. Moreover, life with a partner was not necessarily any more rosy than life without, and we uncovered a number of dispiriting findings about the state of many parents' relationships with their partners. Over one-quarter of those with partners reported stress arising from lack of help and support from partners, almost one in six rated verbal abuse from a partner as a current problem, and one in 25 had been hit or injured by their present partner. We return to these issues later in the report, in Part IV, where we explore how support and coping with parenting relate to one another.

Last, we used a composite measure – the Current Problems Questionnaire or CPQ – to assess the extent to which parents were subject to multiple stressors at the family and household level. Although the mean number of co-occurring current problems for the sample as a whole was less than two, nearly one in three (30%) of respondents reported three or more problems and one in ten reported five or more. CPQ scores were not related to income with in the sample overall, although they were strongly associated with mental health problems and problems with child behaviour as well as with larger family size.

Overall, however, the picture painted by these results is one of rather remarkable optimism against a background of substantial disadvantage. That so many parents reported managing family finances well despite very low incomes is, in itself, noteworthy. It is a testament to the coping skills of parents in poor environments; a theme to which we return in Part IV. Nevertheless, some of the problems reported in this chapter, such as the very poor condition of much of the housing of families in poor environments and the inability of so many parents to afford even basic necessities for themselves and their children, indicates that there is clearly plenty of room for improving the lives of families in poor neighbourhoods. Moreover, while the situation of lone parents is undoubtedly extremely disadvantageous in terms of standard of living and emotional health, the strained nature of many marriages and co-habitations is also cause for concern, given what we know about the relationship between conflict between adults and poor outcomes for children.

Notes

1. Comparisons of median household incomes were carried out using the Mann Whitney Test.
2. That is, the household contained more people than rooms, following the ONS formula derived by dividing the total number of people in the household by the number of non-utility rooms (i.e. excluding kitchens and bathrooms).

CHAPTER FIVE

Stress Factors at the Community and Neighbourhood Level

So far we have explored some of the stressors and risk factors reported by parents in poor environments at the level of the individual parent or child, and at the family and household level. In this chapter we investigate parents' reports of stressors and difficulties within the local community and neighbourhood – that is, the difficulties for those raising children within poor environments, irrespective of, or additional to, other adverse circumstances they may face.

There is a large, mainly American, literature on the relationship between parenting difficulties – and especially child maltreatment – and poor environments. So numerous and consistent are the studies that have linked high rates of child maltreatment to community indicators that some have gone as far as to suggest that 'child maltreatment is but one manifestation of community social organisation … its occurrence is related to some of the same underlying macro-social conditions that foster other urban problems' (Coulton *et al.* 1995). As with other urban problems such as crime and delinquency, the indicators most frequently found to predict child maltreatment at the community level can be conceptualised at both the infrastructural and the social level. Each level can be seen as strongly interconnected to the other so that physical impoverishment and disintegration of the environment at the infrastructure level undermines community and neighbourhood cohesion at the social level and so fosters what has been termed 'a vicious cycle of decline' (Skogan 1990). Evidence for this can be drawn from a number of sources. For example, several studies by Garbarino and colleagues (Garbarino and Crouter 1978; Garbarino and Sherman 1980; Garbarino and Kostelny 1992) found that in addition to high concentrations of residents exposed to multiple risk factors at the household and individual levels, high-risk areas for child maltreatment (that is, those areas in which reporting rates were especially high) were physically degraded and run down, had less positive neighbouring and more stressful day-to-day interactions for families. Zuravin (1989) found that, together with low income (a household level risk factor), the level of vacant housing in the local area – that is, a community level risk factor – was the strongest predictor of child abuse and neglect. Lack of basic services in these areas (public transport, child care, recreation facilities – what Vondra (1990) calls 'community "quality of life" markers') – are seen as further contributing to the problem. For example, lack of services may drive out more affluent families, leading to a high residential turnover rate and leaving only the poorest households, who may be limited in their ability to participate in 'neighbourly exchanges of services and goods' (see also Page (2000) on impoverished housing estates in the UK). Ultimately, it is argued, the sense of community that promotes the involvement of local people in community endeavours is weakened in a way that fosters a range of social problems.

In this sense, then, child maltreatment can be viewed as just one of a number of social problems that characterise poor areas. Thus, in the same way that students of child abuse have found strong links between environmental indicators and child maltreatment, there is a wealth of evidence demonstrating that the same factors are implicated in high rates of neighbourhood criminality, delinquency and antisocial behaviour by young people, substance misuse and other local problems (Simcha-Fagan and Schwartz 1986; Sampson 1992; Furstenburg 1993; Rutter, Giller and Hagell 1998). In this chapter, we explore how some of these issues relate to the situation in our sample of poor parenting environments. We first document parents' reports of the physical characteristics of their neighbourhoods and their perceptions of the level of social problems in their local areas. We then turn to explore some of the evidence for 'social disorganisation' and lack of community cohesion that the literature discussed above leads us to expect in poor environments,[1] and question the extent to which living in a poor neighbourhood compounds or exacerbates the problems families already face on account of their personal or family circumstances.

The extent and impact of environmental and social problems in the local area

We asked parents in the sample to report on problems in the neighbour-hood in which they lived by showing them a list of common problems highlighted in other studies and by the pilot study for the survey, and asked them to assess which were a 'serious problem', 'a bit of a problem' or 'not a problem' in their local area. By definition, of course, all areas selected for the study were areas with high levels of social disadvantage, and so we expected most parents to report generally high levels of environmental and social problems; see Table 5.1. The picture presented in the table certainly confirms what we already know about poor areas – they are considered physically dirty and degraded, crime-ridden, dangerous and generally unpleasant by those who live in them. Overall, only one in 25 respondents said there were no problems of any kind in their neighbourhood and half of the sample (51%) cited six or more different problems. What is perhaps most interesting, although, is the order in which problems were nominated: simple environmental hazards (streets and other public spaces made unpleasant by dog fouling and by uncleared rubbish) were mentioned more frequently than property crime, for example.

The frequency with which specific issues were identified as 'problems' within the neighbourhood, however, was an imperfect guide to what was reported to have the greatest impact on families in a direct way. For example, although over one-quarter of the sample (26%) reported that there was 'serious' problem in their area with drugs, when we asked parents to indicate whether the problems they identified had affected them or their family personally, less than one in five parents considered that they or other members of their family had been directly affected by this problem. Although the phrase 'personally affected' could be interpreted in a number of different ways, from 'has happened to my family' (in the case of crime) to 'impacts on the way we live our lives' (in the case of environmental hazards), piloting established that the underlying meaning of the question was generally interpreted as implying that the problem had identifiable adverse effects on the quality of respondents' family life.

Table 5.1 Respondents' reports of problems in their local area

	% of parents		
	Bit of a problem	Serious problem	Any problem
Dog fouling	29	40	69
Litter/rubbish on streets	35	28	63
Property crime	34	22	56
Drugs	19	26	45
Vandalism/graffiti	28	20	48
Danger from traffic	28	19	47
Stray or loose dogs	24	19	43
Drunken disorderly behaviour by young people	25	14	39
Drunken/disorderly behaviour by adults	22	10	32
Joy riding	20	11	31
Violent crime	17	8	25
Poor state of buildings	15	10	25
Noisy neighbours	14	9	23
Pollution	14	8	22
Poor street lighting	12	7	19
Racial/other abuse or harassment	7	5	12
(None)	–	–	(4)

Bases vary according to item from 1752 to 1743. Respondents could cite more than one problem.

Parents reported being personally affected most by environmental hazards. For example, over half of parents felt personally affected by the problem of dog fouling (54%). Other key environmental problems that directly impacted on families in the study were litter and rubbish in the streets (42%), danger from traffic (36%), stray or loose dogs (29%), and pollution from traffic or factories (17%) (see Figure 5.1).

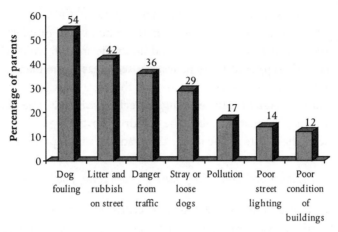

Base=1752

Figure 5.1 Environmental problems in poor neighbourhoods – perceptions of personal impact on family

Qualitative interviews revealed that the impact on families of environmental hazards was often to make parents anxious about children's health and safety. This tended to mean that children's freedom of movement was restricted, and that parents had to take special measures to circumvent these problems. For example, dirty streets and parks curtailed use of (already limited) grass and play areas, and traffic danger prevented children from playing out safely near their houses.

> Bob would love to play on the grass and pick up things, but there's always dog thing on there.
>
> *(Mother, minority ethnic, poor accommodation)*

> On Sunday afternoon (on this road) it's like a rally – they just zoom up and down ... and my kids have got no road sense. And then we're waiting for a bigger fence to be put round the garden ... [to stop] the dogs jumping over and messing. I don't think it's safe – my brother is blind in his one eye through messing in dog mess when he was little. Sometimes I leave the back door open, and one time I heard something in the kitchen and I went in and it was one of [my neighbour's] dogs weeing in the kitchen ...

(Mother, poor accommodation, low income)

There is nowhere safe for the children to play ... I'm not particularly happy if they want to play outside. There is a number of problems. There is the traffic which is quite severe, and limits the areas in which they can play. There is supposed to be pedestrianised areas at the back and they have put bollards across to stop cars, but there are boys on mopeds that ride around the estate in the evenings especially, which can be quite dangerous. There's a park ... but the children have to go accompanied because of the nature of the road ... and anyway, it's a pretty unsavoury place.

(Father, sick child, large family, poor health, poor accommodation)

On the whole, problems connected with crime and antisocial behaviour were less keenly felt in terms of actual impact on the family. Just over one in four parents reported that they felt, or had in the past felt, personally affected by property crime in their area (29%). Just under one in five said they felt personally affected by drugs in their area (18%), and a similar proportion were affected by noisy neighbours, vandalism and graffiti in the

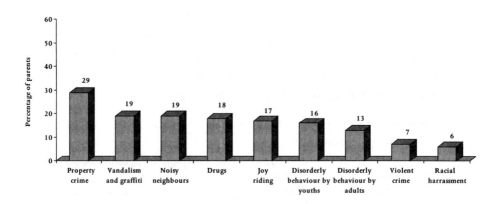

Base=1752

Figure 5.2 Crime and anti-social behaviour problems in poor neighbourhoods – perceptions of personal impact on family

local area, joy riding and by unruly or drunken behaviour by young people; (see Figure 5.2).

Qualitative interviews demonstrated the sometimes far-reaching effects of these problems. Showing once again how freedom of movement is curtailed for families by area-level problems in poor neighbourhoods, fears about drugs and violence on the streets were cited as reasons why children could not be allowed to play outside in the evenings.

> There would be prostitutes on the corner, and there would be people fighting after dark, and they were employing children on BMXs to run crack from the dealers to the buyers and back again. So we were worried about children getting caught up in people fighting over drugs [if they played outside]. It just meant, stay indoors. Most of my friends don't let their children out to play at all.
>
> *(Mother, lone parent, low income, bad accommodation)*

> One of the main reasons [wife, with psychiatric problems] got psychologically poor was due to harassment and things in the area. She was threatened – someone threw a brick at her and it barely missed the pram ... There's been quite a lot of crime, and it does affect you as a parent because you feel unsafe in your property. John [son with learning difficulties] doesn't play out with the other kids ... I wouldn't want him mixing with these (kids round here) because he's going to pick up bad practices...and there's the safety element.
>
> *(Father, sick child)*

> In the summer it's not a pleasant place to be – it can be very noisy with my neighbours playing their music very loud and sitting on their front porch with their friends and their beers, and they have the windows open so they can listen to their stereo ... Then if you want to get away from it there is the worry that you are going to come back and find that you have been burgled. I haven't been, but I must be one of the few that hasn't.
>
> *(Mother, lone parent, low income, bad accommodation)*

Social fragmentation as a stressor?

How do these problems impact upon the social fabric or community cohesion of an area? As we noted above, one of the central hypotheses of the ecological approach to understanding parenting and family functioning is that, in materially disadvantaged neighbourhoods, parenting is made more difficult not just by the correlates of poverty themselves (high crime rates, dirty streets, etc.), but by the socially fractured nature of these communities (Vondra 1990). A degraded physical environment, high crime risk and high mobility of the population, it is argued, tend to militate against community cohesion, so that residents are less likely to organise together to lobby for badly needed services or resources and less likely to feel a sense of civic pride that encourages proactive efforts to maintain homes and neighbourhoods in good order. One consequence of this, it is hypothesised, is that the sense of community which fosters social support networks may be impaired, leaving the poorest families living in neighbourhoods lacking in 'a sense of community involvement, mutual caring and social cohesion' (Vondra 1990, p.22). Some writers (for example, Sampson 1992) have characterised this social disorganisation as overlapping with a lack of 'social capital' in poor environments, defined by Coleman (1988) as the social relationships that serve as resources upon which individuals with the community can draw, including interpersonal ties and reciprocity, opportunities to share information, and other resources that facilitate social action. In areas that lack social capital, there may be 'a shift from collective to individualistic strategies of family management ... and ... a disengagement of the family from the community' (Furstenburg 1993, quoted in Thompson 1995; see also Brooks-Gunn, Duncan and Aber 1997; Furstenburg et al. 1999).

Most of the research on social disorganisation and social capital has been conducted in the United States, but to what extent does this picture of socially impoverished, fractured communities hold for parents in poor environments in Britain? Our findings suggested that, for a minority of parents, this was indeed their experience of living in a poor environment. For example, relatively high levels of mobility are to be expected among families with children, whose housing needs change as children grow up. However, it has been noted that the families in this sample were particularly mobile, with the majority having moved at least once in the past four years (see Part I) and more than one in seven families (15%) having moved within the past year. High mobility in some neighbourhoods certainly limited the extent to which people could get to know one another, let alone build a sense of community.

People are coming and going, moving every day. You can't really keep up with who's [here]. You see somebody [in a house] and a couple of weeks later you just see somebody else. It's never the same.

(Mother, ethnic minority, poor health)

People don't mix with each other now … If anything was wrong with the kids, you [used to] help. But they don't do that now … I don't think that it's a close community anymore … They just mind their own business. Once they come in through their door [at home], they don't bother coming out. They just keep to themselves.

(Mother, low income, bad accommodation, poor health)

There were, however, signs that even despite these problems, the majority of the parents in the sample did not, in fact, perceive their neighbourhood as characterised by a sense of isolation and lack of community. For example, the majority of parents (78% – over three-quarters of the sample) described the people in their neighbourhood as 'generally friendly', and over half of respondents claimed to know 'a lot' of their neighbours personally (defined as 'knowing their name and stopping to talk to them at least every once in a while'). Less than one in ten thought their local community generally unfriendly, or said that they did not know any of their neighbours to talk to. Despite high levels of mobility, nearly three-quarters of the sample (70%) felt that their community was relatively stable and one in which people tended to settle and live for a long time (see Figure 5.3). Indeed, most parents were coping well with the stresses of living in a poor neighbourhood, and it was striking that the majority of parents were generally rather positive about their area as a place to live, when asked in broad terms. Although just under half of the sample (46%) thought that, given the choice, they would move to another area (as compared with a national figure of about one in three households in the general population) (DETR 1998), when asked how they would rate their area as a place to bring up a family, the majority of parents (66%) said their area was 'very' or 'fairly' good (18% and 48% respectively), one in seven (15%) were ambivalent (rated it as neither good nor poor), and less than one in five (18%) rated their area as 'fairly' or 'very' poor (10% and 8% respectively).

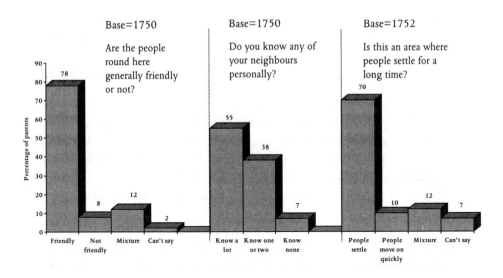

Figure 5.3 Perceptions of neighbourhood friendliness and stability

The relationship between stressors at the community, family and individual level

To what extent is being a parent in a poor environment more difficult than being a parent elsewhere? We have already identified a host of family and individual level stressors that were disproportionately found within the sample relative to general population rates, but to what extent is it possible to say that being disadvantaged in a poor area is worse than being disadvantaged elsewhere?

In fact, we can only partially answer this question, because we did not directly compare parenting in poor as opposed to affluent areas, and so we cannot know how families with similar individual and household level characteristics would fare in more favourable environments. However, two aspects of the study design enable us to draw some conclusions in response to this question. First, we were able to compare and contrast our data with data from other, national, sources to assess the particular hardships that parents in poor areas might face. Second, as discussed in Part I, within our sample of areas drawn from the 30 per cent most disadvantaged enumeration districts in the country, we had a fairly wide distribution of PPE-Index scores. This enabled us to group areas into three equal bands – 'poor', 'very poor' and 'extremely poor' – according to ascending scores on the Index. When we compare the incidence of risk factors relative to scores on the PPE-Index, it becomes clear that in some respects, even within what are already classified as poor parenting areas, there is what we might term a 'hierarchy of risk'. The poorer the environment on the PPE-Index scale, the greater the likelihood of facing a number of risk or stress factors that potentially make parenting a more difficult task.

Poor environments, and family and individual level risk factors

The preceding chapters indicate that at both the family and household level, and at the level of the individual, parents in poor environments could be distinguished from parents in the wider population on a number of counts. However, families in the study did not differ only in relation to the broader population in terms of the prevalence of risk indicators. They also differed from one another within the sample itself, and the level of risk in terms of the distribution of stress factors varied with the objectively-rated quality of the area according to the PPE-Index. For example, taking stressors at the family and household level first, median income decreased with increasing PPE-Index score, so that the average household income in extremely poor areas was substantially lower than in poor or very poor areas (£9224 in poor areas, £7359 in very poor areas, and £5824 in the extremely poor areas; $p<0.0001$).[2] In the extremely poor areas, nearly half of all households in the sample were headed by lone parents, as compared with less than one in three in the least poor areas. Similarly, in extremely poor areas almost two-thirds of households had no adult in paid work compared to just under two in five in the least poor areas. In respect of accommodation problems, the proportion of households in the extremely poor areas was also significantly higher than the proportion in the least-poor areas; see Table 5.2.

		% of households	
	Poor areas (lowest PPE-Index band)	Very poor areas (middle PPE-Index band)	Extremely poor areas (highest PPE-Index band)
No adult in paid work (n = 858)	38	47	65***
Accommodation problems (n = 705)	38	37	49***
Lone parent (n = 668)	30	37	49***

Table 5.2 Problems at the family and household level, by type of area

*** = $p<0.0001$

At an individual level, although the actual correlation co-efficient was low due to the large sample size, parents' Malaise scores were extremely significantly correlated with PPE-Index scores ($r = 0.1$; $p<0.001$). As Figure 5.4 shows, parents were very much more likely to have higher mean Malaise scores if they lived in poorer areas ($p<0.001$). Whereas in the extremely poor areas nearly one-quarter (24%) of parents reported 'high' Malaise scores, the corresponding percentages in the middle-ranking and least poor areas were 21 per cent and 17 per cent respectively. However, it is important to note that a number of risk factors were not significantly associated with scores on the PPE-Index. Whether parents said they were managing financially, for example, was not strongly associated with the area of residence but rather with household income levels. Mean Current Problems Questionnaire score was also not significantly associated with area of residence and nor was physical health (for either parents or children, and irrespective of whether we looked at index children or other children in the household). Neither family size nor child behaviour (in terms of whether the child was classified as 'difficult' on our composite indicator) were significantly associated with the area of residence, and within poor environments children were no more likely to be difficult in the very poorest areas than they were in the least poor.

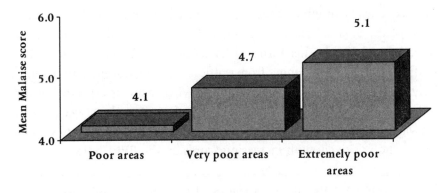

Figure 5.4 Mean Malaise Inventory score, by type of area

Poor environments and community level risk factors

Another way of looking at the relationship between area of residence and challenges to parenting is to examine parents' subjective ratings of the specific problems in their neighbourhood and of the overall quality of their area, relative to PPE-Index scores. That is, to explore the extent to which community level risk factors (as opposed to family or individual level factors) vary by area, *within* the context of poor environments. This gives us an insight into the special 'environmental' characteristics of poor neighbourhoods that may make parenting particularly challenging. In general, our findings showed that the poorer the environment, the less positive parents were about the area and the more likely they were to rate it as problematic. They were more likely to report local environmental and social problems, less likely to rate the area as a good place to bring up a family, and less likely to want to stay in the area in the long term. Taken together, there appears to be fairly strong evidence for an 'added effect' of residence in a poor area in terms of the challenges presented to parents. Below we discuss this in more detail.

PROBLEMS IN THE AREA

In terms of specific issues within local communities, of the 16 indicators used in our checklist of local problems, ten were significantly more likely to be reported as problems in the poorest areas, as Table 5.3 shows. By chi-square tests, only six did not reach statistical significance in terms of the frequency with which they were reported relative to the PPE-Index band of the area. These were property crime, dog fouling, poor street lighting, racial and other forms of harassment or abuse, pollution from traffic or factories and danger from traffic, all of which seemed to be similarly problematic in our sample of poor environments irrespective of the difference in objective levels of poverty that existed between areas. However, the incidence of the ten problems listed below did vary significantly and positively with increasing scores on the PPE-Index.

Table 5.3 Problems in the local area, by type of area			
Problem	*% of households*		
	Poor areas (lowest PPE-Index band)	Very poor areas (middle PPE-Index band)	Extremely poor areas (highest PPE-Index band)
Litter/rubbish on streets	58	63	70**
Drugs	42	45	60**
Vandalism/graffiti	40	50	55**
Stray or loose dogs	33	43	56**
Drunken/disorderly behaviour by young people	35	37	46**
Drunken/disorderly behaviour by adults	28	31	41**
Joy riding	28	33	37*
Violent crime	21	25	34**
Poor state of buildings	17	22	37**
Noisy neighbours	19	22	30**

Bases vary by item from 1609 to 1710; * = $p<0.01$; ** = $p<0.001$

OVERALL PERCEPTIONS OF THE AREA

At the same time, there was a clear relationship between the PPE-Index band and residents' perceptions of the overall quality of the neighbourhood. As Figure 5.5 shows, the poorer the area in terms of PPE-Index score, the less satisfied parents felt. The study found that the higher the neighbourhood score, the less likely parents were to classify the area as a good place to bring up a family ($p<0.001$). The poorer the area, the significantly more likely were parents to want to move and to say that the people in their area tended to move away fairly quickly rather than settle (both $p<0.001$), as Figure 5.6 shows. Nevertheless, respondents did not uniformly give poorer areas negative ratings in all respects. For example, we saw earlier that most parents thought their local community 'generally friendly' and knew their neighbours by name. Neither of these indicators varied significantly by index banding. These findings perhaps help explain why, as can be seen from Figure 5.5, even in the 'extremely poor', highest scoring areas (that is, those that would be in top 10% of national scores), respondents were still almost twice as likely to rate the area as 'good' as they were to rate it as 'poor'.

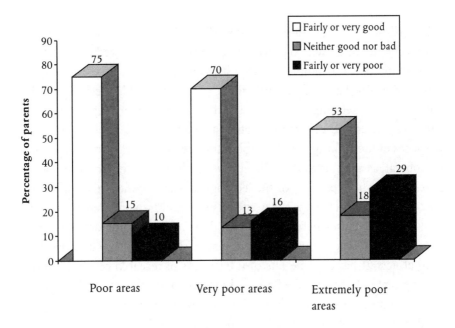

Base = 1716

Figure 5.5 Ratings of the local area as a place to bring up a family, by type of area

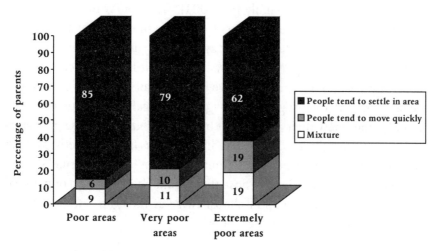

Base= 1671 excl. Don't knows

Figure 5.6 Perception of neighbourhood stability, by type of area

Implications: risk and parenting in a poor environment

In this chapter and the two preceding ones we have explored the extent to which parents in the sample reported stressors at three levels of the ecological model: the level of the individual parent or child; the level of the family and household; and the level of the community or neighbourhood. Although these levels were treated as conceptually distinct for the purposes of identifying and describing the specific risk factors that parents in poor areas may face, in reality these levels are of course interrelated: indeed, the whole premise of the 'ecological' framework – in terms of the way people experience everyday life – is that children and parents inhabit ecological systems where these levels flow into, and interact with, one another to produce complex, nested relationships and layered or overlapping effects. It has become one of the truisms of research on family functioning that risk factors, like London buses, tend to come in batches. Those who face problems in one dimension of functioning are often at heightened risk of problems in other dimensions, and our research largely confirms this.

Is parenting likely to be more difficult when living in a poor area? The findings of the study suggest that the answer to the question is 'yes' on a number of counts. There is clearly an interrelationship between living in a poor environment and a range of risk factors at the household and individual levels. Although we cannot make direct comparisons between 'poor' and 'not poor' neighbourhoods in this study because the sample design did not include a control group of parents in average or above averagely affluent areas, we can compare many of our data with published figures taken from large-scale general population surveys that include both poor and affluent areas. When we do this, the parents in our sample are revealed as disadvantaged across a range of indicators compared to the wider population of parents. Moreover, even within our sample of poor areas, the poorer the area, the more disadvantage across a range of indicators at all three levels of the ecological model. To this extent, parenting in poor environments is a more 'risky' business than parenting elsewhere, and it gets riskier the poorer the area.

Some caveats are important to note, however. As we noted in Part I, statistically speaking it is sometimes difficult to disentangle the independent effects of area-level and individual-level poverty. Thus, when we conducted further multivariate analyses of the relationship between area and risk factors, we found that often, where we have uncovered what appears to be a relationship between area of residence and certain stressors, what we are picking up is in fact an underlying association between family poverty (as measured by low income) and those stress factors. For example, a series of separate logistic regression analyses showed that the significance of PPE-Index banding as a predictor of a range of family and individual level stress factors disappeared once household income was taken into account, as Table 5.4 demonstrates. However, at the community and neighbourhood level, we obtained a different (reversed) pattern of relationships between risk, family-level poverty and area. For example, when both area of residence and household income were entered into logistic regression models predicting rating of the area as a good place to bring up a family, or predicting desire to move away, environment was clearly the stronger predictor of negative perceptions, as Table 5.5 shows:

Table 5.4 Role of household income and area of residence in predicting a range of risk factors at the household and individual level

	Odds ratios				
	Lone parenting (*n* =1427)	Accommodation problems (*n* = 1427)	High parent Malaise score (*n* = 1422)	Child with health problems in home (*n* = 1427)	'Difficult' index child (*n* = 1145)
Household income (Income quintile)	0.50***	1.24*	78***	0.83***	0.79***
Area of residence (PPE-Index Band)	1.18 (n/s)	0.88(n/s)	1.12(n/s)	0.98(n/s)	1.18(n/s)

* *p*<0.01 ***; *p*<0.0001; n/s = non significant

Table 5.5 Role of household income and area of residence in predicting perceptions of the neighbourhood

	Odds ratios	
	Area is a not a good place to bring up a family (*n* = 1420)	Desire to move out of the area (*n* = 1392)
Household income (Income quintile)	0.92 (n/s)	0.96 (n/s)
Area of residence (PPE-Index band)	1.50***	0.75***

*** *p*<0.0001; n/s = non significant

What these results tell us is that within the contexts of environments already classified as poor, all of the household and individual level risk factors or stressors that we measured (with the exception of parental physical health problems, which were predicted by neither factor) were more strongly predicted by household income than by the area in which respondents live. In this sense, it is not living in a poor environment that heightens parenting risk so much as being poor. At the community or neighbourhood level, however, exposure to risk factors *is* predicted by area and, in this respect, living in a poor area clearly does contribute independently of other factors to parenting stress. These quantitative findings bear out the qualitative data presented earlier: that many families living in poor areas feel oppressed by their fear of crime; that parents perceive environmental hazards in their local area as a threat to the health and safety of their families; and that some parents feel isolated in communities in which neighbours do not know one another due to high turnover of residents. All of these things constrain both parents and children in terms of freedom of movement, and can make living in a poor environment a limiting and stressful experience.

Despite these fairly negative findings, however, regarding the impact of area on parenting, it is worth concluding this part of the report by reiterating that it was not generally the case that poor neighbourhoods were experienced by parents as terminally unsatisfactory places to bring up families. Indeed, the study suggested that many parents hold a substantial reservoir of pride in, and affection for their local neighbourhood, even if the neighbourhood is objectively classified as 'poor' by national standards. Despite complaints about poor infrastructure, many parents described their community in warm terms.

> I love the area. I love the house, and you know it's a nice area to live in… It's quite quiet…and I like this area because it's a mixture. There's children, there's young couples without children, there's elderly couples…it's just a mixture.
>
> *(Mother, large family, health problems)*

Thus, although parenting in poor environments is clearly a more difficult task than parenting elsewhere in a number of ways, many parents expressed remarkably high levels of general satisfaction about their local neighbourhoods, and had positive things to say about the area in which they lived. Although, overall, reports of the prevalence of social and environmental problems and the numbers of families who were dissatisfied with their area rose steadily with increasing scores on the PPE-Index, we did not in general find widespread evidence of 'social disintegration', as evidenced by lack of a sense of community, in the areas included in the study. According to our respondents, people do still talk to each other, associate with one another and 'feel at home' in poor environments. Although there may be pockets where local conditions are particularly bad, or particular groups that are disproportionately affected by problems that our analysis does not reveal, overall our findings give some cause for optimism. As we show later in Part V, there are many ways in which poor environments can be improved for parents and children, and from our study it does not look as if these areas are disintegrated beyond saving.

Of course, a critical factor in determining how parents experience the neighbourhood in which they live may of course be the quality of their social relationships and interactions, as the quote above hints. In the rest of this book, we explore further the extent and quality of social support of all kinds with in poor parenting environments, and return to the concept of social capital to explore whether our conclusions here are borne out in relation to the prevalence and quality of social support within poor environments.

Notes

1. A discussion of services (awareness and use) is included in Part III in the context of more general findings on support to parents in poor environments, and so is not included in this chapter.

2. Kruskal-Wallis test.

Part Three

Social Support to Parents
in Poor Environments

When you grow up in the same area, you know each other and trust each other. But when you move in, they don't know you … And sometimes if you're in trouble, you don't think anyone could help you here. You have to do it on your own.

(Mother, ethnic minority, bad accommodation)

Everybody is about, and they're interested in my well-being – they're just there for you; if you need anything, they're there. They're supportive, not just financially, I mean – my mam has nothing really but if they've got it, they'll give it. If you need emotional support, they're just there. It's the same with a lot of families up here. There's quite a lot of extended families on this estate.

(Mother, sick child)

One of the main aims of the study was to explore the extent and quality of social support available to parents in poor neighbourhoods. There is a complex and extensive literature on social support. It provides a wealth of evidence to suggest that support functions as a protective factor in parenting and that its absence (that is, a deficit of support, often called 'social isolation' in the practice literature) is a definite risk factor for parenting difficulties of all sorts, including child maltreatment (Garbarino 1977; Garbarino and Sherman 1980; Gaudin and Pollane 1983; Robertson *et al.* 1991; Belsky and Vondra 1989). In particular, the research suggests that social support can act as a directly protective factor by actively providing help or support at moments of particular need and as an indirect factor by bolstering parents' self-esteem and sense of efficacy (Vaux 1988). Another way of describing these multiple effects has been to talk of support as being both stress buffering, by providing instrumental and emotional assistance at times of need, and stress preventive, by enhancing the overall healthy functioning of the individual so that problems with stress do not arise so easily (Thompson 1995; Barrera 1986; Cohen and Wills 1985; Lazarus and Folkman 1984).

In this study, we explored the role of social support in parenting in its broadest sense, following an operational definition offered by Thompson (1995):

Social support consists of *social relationships* that provide (or potentially provide) material and interpersonal resources that are of value to the recipient, such as counselling, access to information and services, sharing of tasks and responsibilities, and skill acquisition. [our emphasis]

Thompson's definition emphasises that social support has two dimensions (practical or instrumental, and emotional), and also reminds us that, whatever the type, relationships between individuals lie at the heart of support.[1] This is an important issue that has sometimes been overlooked by researchers when developing ways of operationalising and measuring social support in empirical studies. Moreover, meaningful analyses of support must focus not only on the structural properties of support (that is, what is provided, or the shape that the support takes) but also at the affiliative properties (that is, what the support 'feels' like to the recipient). Many analyses have focused only on the structural, more quantitative aspects of support, measuring, for example, the extensivity of support networks (for example, size of network or the frequency of use of support services) but have ignored the affiliative, more qualitative properties such as how useful the help was perceived to be, or whether accepting the support carried with it negative implications. When the affiliative, relationship aspects of social support are ignored, research runs the risk of obtaining only half the picture in terms of how support relates to outcomes for parents and children. How the support feels may be as important as, if not more important than, what it actually consists of (Vondra 1990), and several authors have cautioned against simplistic concepts and measures of social support in research (for example, Barrera 1986).

Therefore, in conceptualising 'social support' and in operationalising the concept (that is, translating the concept into ways of measuring or exploring its component elements), we attempted to separate out the structural from the affiliative properties, as shown in Box III.1. We hoped that this multi-dimensional approach would give us a well-rounded picture of the role of social support in parenting as well as making it easier to identify deficits not only in the quantity of support available but also in the quality of what is on offer to parents in poor environments.

To measure social support, we used a three-fold model that included informal, semi-formal and formal sources of support. Informal social support can be thought of as the kind of support that arises naturally from within parents' networks of family, friends and neighbours; semi-formal and formal support, on the other hand, tends to be organised to a greater or lesser degree and to be provided by community groups and formal helping agencies.

Structural properties:

- size (how many important people in network)
- embeddedness (how frequent is contact)
- dispersion/proximity (how accessible – e.g. distance away)
- stability (how long known/how stable/consistent is relationship)
- intimacy (is contact one-to-one or in group)
- form/type (what forms does enacted and received support take – e.g., instrumental, emotional, both).

Affiliative properties:

- valence (positive, negative, or mixed)
- reciprocity (is support reciprocal; does it incur obligation)
- homogeneity (are supporters similar to self/on same 'wavelength')
- density/complexity (supporters similar to one another/does advice complement, conflict, etc.)
- multi-functionality (supporters fulfil different functions)
- situation specificity (what kind of support in which contexts)
- perceptions/expectations (how 'supported' does recipient feel; how much can supporters be relied on; how useful is support).

Box III.1 Structural and affiliative properties of social support

Box III.2 shows how we defined these three different types of social support for the purposes of the study.

In the chapters that follow, we explore in turn informal support (Chapter 6), semi-formal support services (Chapter 7) and formal support services (Chapter 8). These chapters focus on identifying the structural and affiliative aspects of support that parents receive. In the last chapter of Part III (Chapter 9), we switch perspectives to address the concept of support deficits to try to understand more about why support fails for some parents.

Notes

1. Note that Thompson's definition, with its stress on relational aspects, overlaps considerably with Coleman's conception of social capital, discussed earlier.

Informal support (support which arises from pre-existing personal social networks):

- often provided by single individuals
- arises from pre-existing social networks
- may not have direct relationship to perceptions of 'need'
- operates at all preventive levels.

SOURCE

- within household (e.g. partner, older children)
- within family (e.g. grandparents and relatives)
- within peer group (e.g. friends)
- within community (e.g. neighbours, community groups).

Semi-formal support (community based, organised activities for parents, children or whole families):

- provided by small groups and organised networks
- frequently provided in response to a generalised need or perceived 'good'

- fluid or no referral system
- mainly targeted at primary preventive level.

SOURCE

- Organised voluntary sector open-access activities and services.

Formal support (services provided by statutory sector alone or in partnership with voluntary sector):

- provided by large organisations
- usually in response to a specific and identifiable need
- often filtered by referral system
- targeted mainly at secondary and tertiary preventive levels.

SOURCE

- Often statutory sector, or voluntary sector in partnership with statutory sector.

Box III.2 Three-fold model of social support

CHAPTER SIX

Informal Support

In this chapter we explore the extent and quality of informal support – that is, support arising out of a person's own network of family and friends. There is an abundance of literature demonstrating that lack of support at this level in particular is associated with parenting difficulties and parenting breakdown. Drawing on the conceptualization of social support detailed earlier, we explored both the shape of the support and the form that it takes, as well as the quality or 'valence' of that support.

Structural aspects: the extent and composition of informal support networks in poor environments

In an earlier chapter we showed how, in terms of parents' own perceptions of the area in which they lived, the stereotype of the 'socially fragmented' poor environment did not necessarily hold true for the majority of parents in the sample. Most rated their area as a reasonable environment in which to bring up their family and claimed to know at least some of their neighbours personally and to find people in their local area generally friendly. At least half had no desire to move out of the area. We suggested that this went against the view that poor environments are necessarily lacking in social cohesion. To what extent did data on perceptions of the availability of informal social support back up or modify this conclusion?

Network size and frequency of contact

A largely positive picture emerged in relation to structural properties of the informal support networks of parents in the sample, at least in terms of extensivity and composition. When we showed parents a list of potential sources of informal support[1] only 3 per cent of the sample said they had no one in their personal network to call upon for support or help, while over nine in ten cited at least one person (97%). The mean number of supporters cited was six, and one in eight respondents had large support networks consisting of over ten different individuals. The most common size of informal support network was three people (see Figure 6.1).

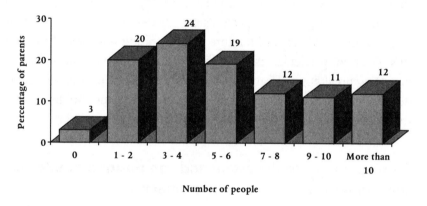

Base = 1744

Figure 6.1 Number of individuals in parents' support network

These findings seem to argue against a view of poor environments as socially fragmented but, as we noted earlier, simply counting the number and type of supporters may give a relatively crude idea of the quality of support networks. For example, it is possible that people could name a large number of individuals as being in their network but have relationships with these people that were, in fact, geographically and practically distant. We therefore asked in some detail about the 'three most important' people in each respondent's network to get a picture of how often supporters were physically present and available to talk to.[2] For example, if not a member of the household, were there nevertheless regular meetings or conversations? As Table 6.1 illustrates, the picture that emerged was in fact one of close-knit support relationships characterised by regular contact, both in person or by phone, and close physical proximity. Even among second and third most important supporters, a majority were in frequent contact with the respondent.

	Table 6.1 Frequency of contact in support networks: attributes of the three most important supporters		
	% of supporters		
	First most important person (*n* = 1701)	**Second most important person** (*n* = 1561)	**Third most important person** (*n* = 1350)
Member of household, or lives less than 10 minutes away	74	55	52
Sees daily or most days	81	61	54
Speak on phone daily or most days	67	59	47

Figures exclude cases where respondents did not speak on telephone because supporter was member of household.

Composition of support networks: who are the supporters?

Figure 6.2 shows the top ten and bottom ten sources of informal support for the sample as a whole. Apart from the wide range of supporters nominated, what is immediately apparent is the predominance of family, and of females, in the 'top ten' list. Family members feature strongly, but it is interesting to note that in this representative sample of parents in poor environments, mothers were more frequently cited than partners as providers of support. Indeed, when the figures are based on the sample as a whole, partners came lower on the list than female friends and were closely followed by sisters. In poor environments, then, it is women who are largely supporting parenting at the informal level.

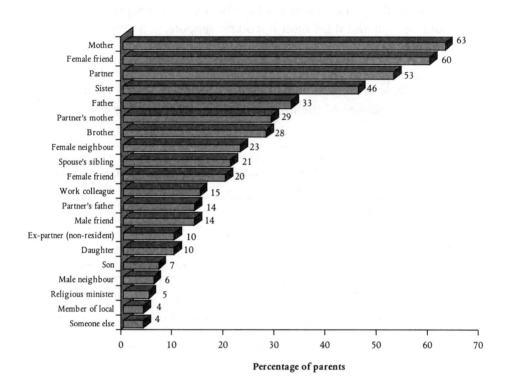

Base = 1698

Figure 6.2 Sources of informal support for parents in poor environments

Factors affecting the extent and composition of networks

A number of factors at all levels of the ecological model were associated with the size of support networks reported by parents in the sample, and composition of networks also showed some variability.

At the level of the individual, parents with high Malaise scores reported a mean of 4.70 supporters compared to 6.39 for others ($p<0.001$). Although these data cannot tell us anything about the causal direction of the link, parents who tend towards depression are – at least in terms of numbers – less well supported than those in better mental and emotional health. Confounding some of the cultural stereotypes of minority ethnic families as being more likely to have large extended networks of family and friends, ethnic minority parents also reported fewer average supporters than white parents (mean = 4.98 compared to 7.17; $p<0.01$).

At the level of the household and family, family structure appeared to be important. Lone parents, for example, cited significantly fewer supporters in their network (mean number of supporters = 5.02, compared to 6.69 in couple households; $p<0.001$), and there was evidence that family structure influenced not only the extensivity but also the composition of informal support networks. Figure 6.3 illustrates how sources of support varied depending on type of family, and the results are revealing. Whereas spouses and partners were the most frequently named sources of help and support among parents with a resident partner (86%), for lone parents, their own mother was the most frequent source of help (65%). Strikingly, less than one-quarter (23%) of lone parents named an ex-partner as a source of support or help (meaning that over three-quarters got no help from former partners). Moreover, lone parents lost out on the support of a wider extended family. For example, whereas partners' relatives – especially mothers-in-law or the equivalent – were prominent supporters for parents with a partner, it appeared that lone parents had lost the support of their partner's wider family along with that of their partner. So, for example, while 41 per cent of parents with partners cited a mother-in-law as a source of support and 20 per cent cited a father-in-law, the corresponding figures for lone parents were 10 per cent and 4 per cent. Whereas 30 per cent of parents with a partner named that partner's sibling as a source of support, only 7 per cent of lone parents enjoyed support from this source. Although lone parents filled these support deficits to some extent by turning more to siblings, neighbours and friends, overall they still had more restricted support networks than parents with partners.

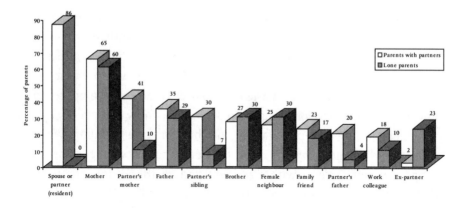

Base = 1046 parents with partners; 646 lone parents. Note: Only differences between groups of five percentage points or more are shown.

Figure 6.3 Sources of informal support for parents in poor environments, by marital status

Family stage as well as structure proved to be associated with network composition. In the sample as whole, there was strong evidence that the network of informal supporters – particularly in respect of family members – shifts over time, so that the people who are prominent in a parent's support network vary according to stage in the family life cycle. For example, the profile of support for parents with a teenager in the household looked somewhat different from that for families with only pre-school children. Parents with younger children were much more likely to report turning to their own mother and father, and also their partner's parents, for support than parents with teenagers, while parents of older children called far less on the grandparental generation. Conversely, as children themselves grow up, they begin to be named as important parts of their parents' support network. One-fifth of parents with teenagers named a daughter, and one in seven named a son as someone from whom they received informal help and support. Thus, support networks are not static over time; as families mature, and parents themselves accrue experience, they begin to rely far more on the resources available within the immediate

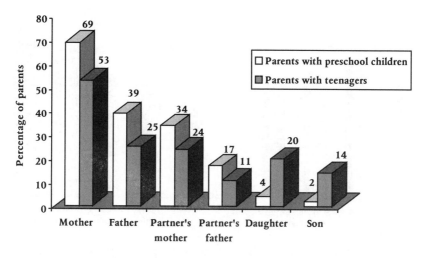

Base = 598 parents with teenagers; 812 parents with preschool children

Figure 6.4 Sources of informal support within the family, by family lifestage

nuclear family (including their own children) and less on those that could be provided by the extended network of parents and parents-in-law.

Also at the level of the family, poverty at the household level made a difference to network size: for parents in the poorest household income quintile the average number of supporters was 4.26 whereas, by contrast, parents in the wealthiest quintile group in our sample reported an average network size of 7.93 supporters ($p<0.001$) (Figure 6.5). Similarly, those with high scores on the Current Problems Questionnaire reported an average of 5.48 supporters in their network, compared to 6.28 for those with lower levels of problems by this measure ($p <0.01$). Last, at the community level, area of residence was highly significantly associated with smaller network size. Figure 6.5 shows the mean number of supporters by area of residence. Parents living in the poorest areas according to the PPE-Index reported an average network size of 5.11, compared to 6.83 for those living in the least poor areas ($p<0.001$).

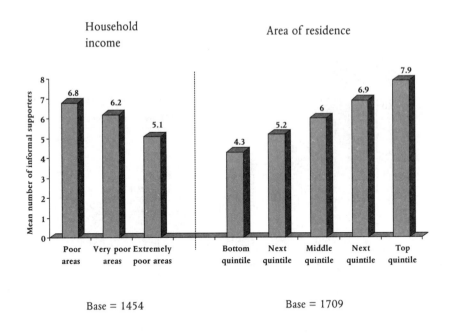

Figure 6.5 Mean informal support network size, by area of residence and household income

To summarise, taken together, the various factors associated with network size indicated, overall, that most parents reported reasonable numbers of supporters. However, it was also the case that the higher the level of need (whether measured at the individual, family or community level) the smaller the networks, and some groups of parents reported substantially fewer people they could call on did than others.

Affiliative aspects: the quality of informal social support in poor environments

As we indicated earlier, although structural aspects of support networks are important, the affiliative quality (or 'valence') of support relationships is also thought to be a critical component in understanding how they operate in parents' lives. Regular contact, for example, although seemingly beneficial, could in fact be experienced as undermining rather than being supportive if the parties did not have positive regard for one another, disagreed about significant areas of family life or did not feel they could rely on the other for help at times of greatest need. To explore these aspects, we asked parents to tell us about the affective quality or valence of their support relationships, with reference to their three 'most important supporters'. As Table 6.2 shows, parents were on the whole extremely positive about the valence of their support relationships. Respondents reported extremely positive affect; high (although not total) levels of agreement about parenting issues; and a strong sense of the general reliability of the support at times of need.

Table 6.2 Valence of informal support networks: attributes of the three most important supporters			
	% of supporters		
	First most important person (n = 1701)	Second most important person (n = 1561)	Third most important person (n = 1350)
Usually get on well together	93	93	94
Usually agree about families and children	65	62	64
Can always count on person to give support when needed	76	71	67

This general perception of the high quality of informal support networks was a strong theme in our in-depth discussions with parents. Showing how physical proximity and emotional connectedness interacted to provide a strong sense of reliable support, some described the way that several members of their extended family might live near one another on a local estate, seeing each other regularly and helping each other in a variety of ways.

> Everybody is about, and they're interested in my well being – they're just there for you; if you need anything, they're there. They're supportive, not just financially, I mean – my mam has nothing really but if they've got it, they'll give it. If you need emotional support, they're just there. They're willing to have [child] every week, they would have her every weekend

> for me ... It's the same with a lot of families up here. There's quite a lot of
> extended families on this estate.
>
> *(Mother, sick child)*

Showing how the sense of being supported could seem just as important as
the actual practical benefit derived, one mother commented:

> Sometimes my brother comes and he says, 'Come on sister, we are going
> out'. I say, 'Where to?' 'You have got to get some food.' I say, 'I have got
> no money' (and he says) 'Come on, we work as a family.' And you know,
> it's really nice to know you have got friends.
>
> *(Mother, large family, sick child, difficult child)*

Friends were also important as informal supporters as well as family.

> You know when you've got a friend yourself, you just ... you don't talk to
> your friends like you do to your husband do you? You complain more! I
> can *talk* to my friends.
>
> *(Mother, bad accommodation, large family)*

Limits to informal support in poor environments

Despite this generally rather positive picture of informal social support in
poor environments, we also picked up many hints that there may also be
limits to the capacity of informal networks to support parents in need. In
particular, despite the overall picture of reasonably extensive networks of
supporters, limits to informal support from friends, family and neighbours
were strongly apparent when we asked about parents' perceptions of the
reliability of support in relation to specific, rather than general, situations.

Perceptions of the accessibility of informal support

We showed earlier that a majority of parents expressed a sense of being
able to 'count on' key individuals for help and support should the need
arise. However, this optimism in relation to hypothetical situations was not
so apparent when we asked parents to assess the chances of finding reliable
help with reference to specific dimensions of need. For example, Figure
6.6 shows the results of asking parents how confident they were that if
they needed help across a range of specific situations that might commonly
arise in the course of day-to-day child rearing, they could find it.[3]

Although in every area of support on the list a majority of parents were sure they could find help at least sometimes, two findings were striking here. The first was that a small but not insignificant minority of parents said that they would never ask for various types of help, suggesting that there are barriers to the uptake of support connected with negative perceptions of asking for help. We return to this issue, and its wider significance in Chapter 9. The second was that substantial numbers of parents thought they would never be able to find certain types of support, even if they wanted it. In short, when questioned about the specifics (as opposed to the generalities) of the reliability of informal support in poor environments, the picture looked rather less rosy.

Actual support received

As well as asking parents about their confidence in finding support at times of need, we also asked about 'enacted' support – that is, *actual* support received within the recent past (defined as 'the last four weeks').[4] The

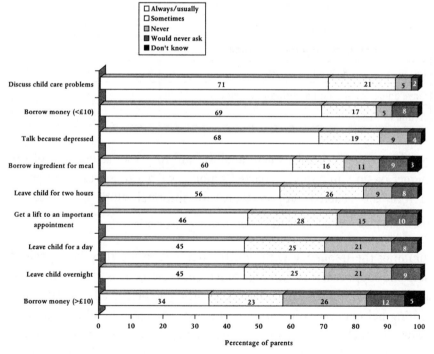

Base = 1745

Figure 6.6 Parents' perceptions of how often they could find someone to help out

results again showed substantial limits to support in poor environments. Across a range of ten specific types of support or help listed in Table 6.3 – both practical and emotional, and both directly and indirectly related to the parenting role – relatively few parents reported having received help. One in five parents (21%) said they had received none of the types of help on the list in the past four weeks.

Table 6.3 Types of support received in past four weeks	
Practical help/support: Someone ...	*% of parents*
Minded a child during day	42
Gave you a lift somewhere	28
Helped with chores, shopping or errands	23
Minded a child overnight	19
Took a child somewhere for you	18
Lent you a small sum of money (<£10)	17
Looked after you because you were ill or tired	11
Lent you a sum of money over £10	8
Emotional support: Someone ...	
Listened or was a shoulder to cry on	39
Gave advice or shared parenting experiences	25
(None of these)	(21)

For the purposes of subsequent analysis and to get an assessment of the 'bigger picture' in terms of enacted support, we put these results together to form an 'enacted support score' for informal support, derived by

Base = 1744. Respondents could report more than one type of help

summing the frequency with which parents reported they had received help and support across the range of ten dimensions. This gave each parent a score in the range 0–10, with 0 representing no help at all, and 10 representing help in every dimension on the list. The mean number of dimensions on which support had been received in the four weeks prior to the survey was 2.30. One in five (21%) of parents had received *no* help in the past four weeks, 20 per cent had had help in one area only, which we termed a 'low' score, and 35 per cent – just over one-third – had a 'medium' score (that is, had help in two or three areas). One-quarter (24%) scored 'high' relative to the rest of the sample (that is, had received help in at last four of the areas of the list).

FACTORS ASSOCIATED WITH ENACTED SUPPORT

What factors were associated with the overall amount of enacted support that parents reported? The results revealed a relatively complicated relationship between the different dimensions of support. For the sample as a whole, network size and the total score on the enacted support scale were strongly and positively related; analysis of variance comparing mean enacted support score with the number of people in the support network showed that while those with fewer than three supporters had a mean score of 1.43, the mean score for those with more than ten supporters was 3.19 ($p<0.0001$). (See Figure 6.7.) Thus, overall, the larger the network, the higher the levels of enacted support in the recent past.

Despite this clear relationship between network size and enacted support score across the sample taken as a whole, however network size was an imperfect guide to enacted levels of informal support when particular subgroups of the overall sample were investigated. For example, although

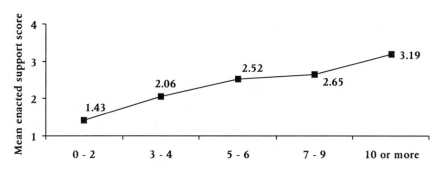

Base = 1744

Figure 6.7 Mean score on the enacted support scale, by network size

parents with high Current Problems Questionnaire scores reported smaller networks, they in fact received *more* enacted help than those with average or low scores on the CPQ. Thus, parents with high CPQ scores reported a mean score on the enacted support scale of 2.61, compared to 2.17 for other parents ($p<0.001$). Following a similar pattern, although parents with high Malaise scores reported fewer people in their personal networks, they also reported higher enacted support scores, although the differences did not quite reach significance at the 99 per cent confidence level (mean enacted support score for high-scoring parents = 2.50 compared to 2.26 for others; $p = 0.044$). These results suggest, to a limited extent, that those with higher levels of need are receiving more informal social support – that is, that support is reaching at least some of those who may need it most. On the other hand, parents with large families (three or more dependent children) did not report more enacted support than others, and furthermore, lone parents, who reported smaller networks overall, also did not differ significantly in terms of enacted support scores compared to parents with partners.[5] By contrast again, ethnic minority parents not only had less extensive networks, they also received less enacted support. While white parents reported a mean enacted support score of 2.37, minority ethnic parents reported a mean of only 1.77 ($p<0.001$).

Similarly, although household income showed a strongly negative linear relationship to network size, it showed a less clear-cut relationship to enacted support. Those in the highest income quintile were significantly more likely to report higher levels of enacted support than those on the lowest quintile (mean = 1.99 compared to 2.55; $p<0.0001$), but the relationship between income and enacted support was in fact more bell-shaped than linear, with those in the middle-income quintile reporting the most enacted support of any group (mean = 2.60). Last, community-level poverty as measured by the PPE-Index score, although strongly associated with network size as we reported earlier, was not associated in any clear way with enacted support scores. Those in the poorest areas reported only slightly less enacted support than those in the least poor.[6]

Conclusions

The findings of the study in relation to informal support show that in terms of extensivity of support (numbers of supporters available within the network and frequency of contact) most parents in the sample appeared relatively well supported. Overall, only a small minority of parents (3%) had no one they could turn to, and most had supporters within the immediate local area with whom they had frequent face-to-face or telephone contact. Moreover, most reported close-knit and warm relationships with their most important supporters, in which family members and women played the key roles. These findings chime well with a large body of research on natural social support networks that has also found kin relationships to be dominant, followed by friends (Cochran et al. 1990; Gunnarsson and Cochran 1990), and to be generally strong in terms of size, frequency of contact and overall feeling of 'closeness', even in high-risk samples (Tracy 1990). These findings seem to argue against a view of poor environments as socially fragmented. The study also found evidence that the composition of support networks may change over time, perhaps in relation to changing needs as families move through different life stages. This finding is borne out by other studies that reveal natural networks have a high level of turnover and that different components of networks may show differing degrees of stability over time (Larner 1990).

Nevertheless, there were limits to informal support in poor environments. First, some groups did report more restricted networks than others; for example, ethnic minority parents, those with high levels of problems as measured by the Current Problems Questionnaire, those with emotional health problems, those living on the lowest incomes and those in the poorest areas. In general, there seemed to be an inverse relationship between need, as measured at various levels of the ecological model, and network size. Although, as we have shown, small networks did not necessarily mean less actual support, it is nevertheless of interest that higher-need parents often reported more restricted networks.

Second, and arguably more important, there were widespread limits in terms of actual, enacted informal support. Even in the sample as a whole where most parents described generally strong networks of potential supporters, when asked about concrete examples of enacted support, many reported receiving relatively little help. Although in relation to named individuals the majority of respondents said they felt they could count on help from these people if they needed it, when questioned in more detail about help in relation to specific dimensions of parenting, many were unconfident about their ability to locate assistance in times of need. In short, although parents reported extensive support networks, they did not necessarily seem able or willing to draw on them in relation to 'real-life' parenting situations. We concluded therefore that first, much parenting in poor environments is conducted without a great deal of instrumental or emotional support and, second, that some groups who reported both fewer supporters, *and* less enacted support (in particular minority ethnic parents, and low income households) seem to be even less well supported than others.

Were overall levels of enacted support low because they reflected a lack of need among parents, or did they reflect a lack of access to support? It could be, for example, that parents reported low levels of enacted help or support because they had not needed support – at least in the areas about which we asked or within the time frame we specified in our survey question (that is, the last four weeks). We explore this further in Chapter 9, and conclude that, in part, lack of need or desire for help on the part of some parents may to some extent explain the low levels of actual support we uncovered. Some parents simply do not perceive themselves as requiring help with parenting. On the other hand, our data on parents' relatively low confidence in finding specific types of help suggest that at least part of the explanation may lie with the availability or accessibility of support at times of need. These data suggest that there is, perhaps, a difference between feeling that one can turn to others for support in a general sense and actually doing so when the need arises. Some parents may be unwilling to ask for help in some areas, perhaps because they feel it is inappropriate, or they may simply find that in the context of life's daily hassles help is not always at hand at the time it is actually needed. Again, we will return to these questions in Chapter 9.

Taken together, the results of the study underline the importance of distinguishing between different aspects of informal social support in trying to understand how support networks operate in everyday life. For example, the extensivity of networks, although interesting, is a very imperfect guide to the actual practical significance of support. Overall, despite generally extensive networks, many parents reported receiving remarkably little enacted support in key dimensions of the parenting task. Moreover, parents in some groups (for example, those with high CPQ scores, those with high Malaise scores, those in the poorest neighbourhoods or those who are parenting alone) received the same or more enacted support than others, despite having more restricted networks. Our data seem to argue that some parents may in fact get better 'value' out of the supporters that they have – that, despite having fewer people to turn to, they still manage to garner as much, and sometimes more, support than others with wider networks. Similar findings have been noted by previous studies. As Cohen and Wills (1985) observed long ago, a large personal network is not necessary to social support, although network size is certainly an important dimension. Based on a review of the literature Thompson (1995, p.31) cautions that 'network size is a rather insensitive measure of the supportive features of social networks' and, supporting our own findings in respect of lone parents, notes that in the case of single mothers, for example, research has shown that they have smaller personal networks but can nevertheless rely on those supporters they do have for more in the way of tangible aid and emotional support.

Clearly, in order to understand how informal social support networks operate to bolster parenting, it is necessary to take into account a complex web of factors. In particular, how parents feel (that is, whether they perceive themselves as supported) may be just as, or more, important than any objective assessment of how that support manifests itself. We return to this question in Part IV, where we explore the correlates of 'coping' with parenting. However, before we do that, we first assess the evidence on the extent of awareness and use of other dimensions of the support matrix: semi-formal, and formal, support services.

Notes

1. We showed them a list of 20 different types of people both inside and outside the household and family, and asked them: 'Do you have any people like this to whom you can talk, get practical help or favours, information, advice or any other form of help or support connected with parenting or family issues?'

2. We asked: 'Including the people you live with as well as those outside your household, which of the people you have mentioned are the three most important in terms of help and support with parenting?'

3. We asked: 'If you needed any of the following things, could you always/usually, only sometimes, or never find someone to help you out?' The specific aspects of help we asked about included: borrowing small and large sums of money; obtaining

emergency child care in the day time and at night; getting emotional support at a time of anxiety or depression; getting emotional support or advice with a child care issue; getting help with transport to an important appointment; and borrowing an ingredient for a meal.

4. We showed parents a list of types of help and asked them to tell us whether they had received: 'any of these types of help and support in the past four weeks. Please include help from people inside and outside your family or household, but do not include help you have paid for.'

5. The mean enacted support score for lone parents was 2.36 versus 2.26 for parents with partners; $p = 0.296$.

6. Mean enacted support scores were as follows: Poor areas 2.40; Very poor areas 2.29; Extremely poor areas 2.21; $p = 0.289$.

CHAPTER SEVEN

Semi-formal Support

We turn next to parents' use and experiences of semi-formal support, which we defined in this study as organised forms of help and support for families and children that parents might receive from community groups or from neighbourhood-based services. These support services are frequently (although not always) provided by the voluntary sector, and are sometimes staffed by volunteers as well as, or of instead, of paid staff. Semi-formal support services may be thought of as complementary to informal support. These services potentially give parents (and children) access to a wider social network, to resources and facilities not available at the individual family level, and to specialist advice or assistance that may be beyond the capacity of friends and family to supply. Examples of semi-formal support services that we focused on included services for families with pre-school children as well as older children, but were weighted towards younger children as this is the age group more generally catered to by services in this sector. The services we asked about are shown in Box 7.1.

> *Services (semi-formal sector):*
>
> - parent and baby/toddler groups
> - playgroups
> - toy libraries and play facilities
> - after-school clubs and holiday playschemes for school-age children
> - day care
> - parent support and befriending groups or schemes
> - parenting education
> - in-home parent support (e.g. Home Start)
> - services for families of children and with special needs
> - lone parents' services (e.g. Gingerbread groups).

Box 7.1 Services in the semi-formal sector

To determine the extent of use of semi-formal services, we asked parents first, what services they were aware of in their local area, second, whether they had ever made use of these services themselves and, finally, whether they had used the services in the recent past (defined as the last three years). For parents who had used a service recently, we then went on to explore in more detail the reasons for starting and ceasing to use that service, and perceptions of the quality of the service received.

Extent of awareness and use of semi-formal support services

Awareness and overall levels of use

Semi-formal support services, being generally located within local communities and often run by volunteers or staff from the local neighbourhood, are often thought of as more accessible to parents than formal support services. However, with the exception of toddler groups and playgroups, a picture emerged from this study of relatively low awareness and use of these kinds of services. In total, over one in ten parents (11%) said they were not aware of any of the services on the list being present in their area,[1] two in five (40%) of all parents had never used any of the services at any point, and nearly two-thirds (60%) had not had contact with any services in the past three years.

As Figure 7.1 shows, by a large margin, the most frequently used types of semi-formal services, whether recently or in the past, were services offering some kind of direct child care or activity for children. Among this group of services, the most frequently used were parent and baby/toddler groups or playgroups, with two in five parents in the sample as whole (42%) having used such a service at some point. For the sample as a whole, just under one-quarter (23%) had used a service of this type in the past three years, and among parents with a child in the household currently aged seven years or less,[2] the figure for use in the past three years rose to 35 per cent.

Holiday playschemes or afterschool clubs were the next most frequently used type of service, with over one in six parents (18%) having made use of these at some point and one in eight (12%) having used them recently. Among parents with a child in the family currently aged 8 years or older, the figure for use in the past three years rose slightly to 15 per cent. Next came day nurseries and creches, which had been used by 17 per cent of the sample at some point. Ten per cent of families in the sample overall had used a service like this in the recent past, but this figure rose to 18 per cent when only parents with a child in the appropriate age range were included (that is, parents with a child in the household currently aged four years or less).

By contrast, the other types of services on the list, which mainly offered services directed at parent support rather than child care *per se*, were very infrequently used. However, although overall levels of use were low, once parents made contact with a service they tended to make fairly extensive use of it. Thus, among parents who had used one or more of the services in the semi-formal support category in the past three years, frequency of use had been generally high. Out of 980 cases of service use, two-thirds of services had been used by parents more than ten times (66%), with only a relatively small proportion (just over one in six, or 15%) of services used only once or twice and then not visited again. Overall, in well over half of the cases (59%), parents were currently still in touch with the service at the time the survey interview took place.

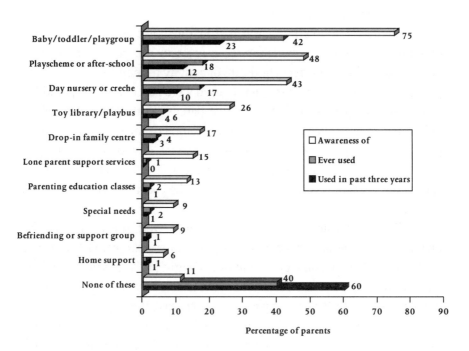

Base=1754

Figure 7.1 Use of semi formal support

Reasons for use

Consonant with the types of semi-formal support services most frequently used, parents' reasons for using services reflected a strong concern with children's needs. However, responses to the question 'why did you start using that service?' illustrate how services which are ostensibly aimed at providing child care and developing children's play or education are also seen as meeting parents' own personal needs. As Figure 7.2 shows, the reasons that parents gave for using any of the semi-formal services in the recent past can be summed up as a combination of socialisation (for children), access to material resources (to make use of toys etc. that might otherwise not be available to the family), social interaction (for parents) and, to a lesser extent, respite (a break for parents from child care). Thus the predominant reasons parents gave for using these services were: to give their child 'an opportunity to mix with other children of the same age' (66% of users); 'to use the facilities – e.g. toys, equipment' (more than one-third – 36% – of users); 'to meet or make contact with other parents in the local area' (one-quarter – 25% – of users); and 'to get child care in order to have a break or do something else' (one in five, or 21% of users).

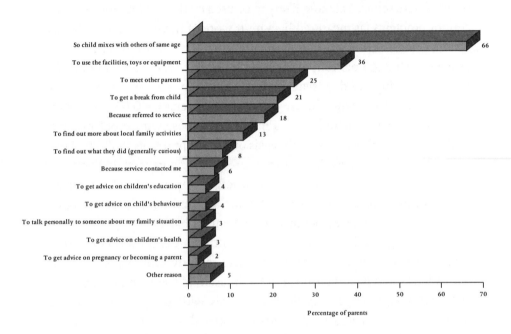

Base = 980 instances of service use in past three years. Respondents could use more than one service

Figure 7.2 Reasons for using or contacting semi-formal support services

Who uses semi-formal support services?

Reflecting the types of services on our list, age of children in the household was a major determinant of service use. Parents with a pre-school child in the household and those with a child under eight in the household were much more likely than other parents to have used semi-formal services in the past three years. Of parents of pre-school children 56 per cent compared to 26 per cent of parents without, and 52 per cent of those with under eights compared to 17 per cent of parents without a child in this age range had used one or more of these services (both $p<0.0001$). Conversely, households with older children (aged 12 or older) were very unlikely to report having used a semi-formal service in the recent past, and only 22 per cent reported doing so ($p<0.0001$).

To a limited extent, 'need' at the individual or family level also appeared to be associated with semi-formal service use. Semi-formal services were somewhat more likely to be used by those with high levels of current problems (as measured by a high score of three or more problems on the Current Problems Questionnaire) than those with lower levels of problems. Thus, 45 per cent of those with a high level of current problems reported having used a semi-formal service in the past three years compared to 38 per cent of those with fewer problems ($p<0.01$). However, services were still reaching only a minority of those with problems, and well over half of those with high levels of current problems (55%) had not used a service in the past three years. Furthermore, in general there was no significant increase in the level of use of services by parents who had particular kinds of problems at the individual or family level; for example, whether parents reported being a lone parent, or having a physical health problem, a high Malaise score, or a 'difficult' index child was not associated with having used semi-formal services recently. Only having a child with a long-term health problem in the household was significantly associated with recent use of semi-formal services, with 46 per cent of parents of such children having used services compared to 37 per cent of other parents ($p<0.0001$); but again, the figures still indicate that less than half of these parents reported using a service.

However, need as measured by household or community level poverty was not statistically associated with use of semi-formal services. Those in the poorest areas as measured by the PPE-Index were no more likely to have used a service than those in the least poor areas, and in the case of household income, the trend for use of services ran in the opposite direction to other indicators of need. Thus, those who had used a service recently had, on average, higher household incomes compared to those who had not used a service (median average income £7482 compared to £6783; $p<0.01$).3

Finally, minority ethnic parents were significantly less likely to have used semi-formal services in the recent past (29% compared to 42% of white British parents; ($p<0.01$) (see Table 7.1).

Table 7.1 Use of semi-formal support services in the past three years, by current problems, presence of a sick child and minority ethnic status

	% of parents
High levels of current problems ($n = 524$)	45
Household with sick child ($n = 709$)	46
Minority ethnic parent ($n = 198$)	29
All ($n = 1753$)	40

Relationship between semi-formal and informal social support

Are those using semi-formal support services doing so because of support deficits at the informal social support level? We did not find evidence that this was generally the case. In fact, lower numbers of informal supporters were associated with *lower* levels of use of semi-formal services. Thus, the mean network size for those not using semi-formal support services in the past three years was 5.79, compared to 6.41 for those using a service – a result that just missed statistical significance at the 0.01 level ($p = 0.010$). Similarly, the mean enacted support score of those who had not used services in the past three years was lower, at 2.00, than for those who had used services, who had a mean score of 2.74 ($p<0.0001$). Thus, those who were drawing more extensively on informal support networks were also making greater use of semi-formal services and, conversely, those who reported lower levels of informal support were also the least likely to be using services in this sector.

Quality and value of semi-formal support services

Quality of services

Among those who had experience of using services in this sector, perceptions of the quality of semi-formal services were largely positive, as we might perhaps expect given the heavy frequency of use by those who had actually tried services in this sector. In over two-thirds of the instances of service use (65%), parents rated the service they had used as 'very helpful', and a further quarter (27%) of the services were rated as 'fairly helpful'. In only 7 per cent of cases of service use ($n = 68$) were parents ambivalent or negative about the usefulness of the service.

Value of services

When we explored parents' reasons for feeling positive about the services they had used, once again, child-centred issues topped the list (Figure 7.3). The fact that the service was of value to the child was most frequently cited as a positive factor. The vast majority of parents who had found a service helpful said that one of the 'helpful or good' things about the service was that their child had enjoyed it (85% of cases). The next most frequently cited positive factor, in well over half the cases (59%), was that the service had helped the child's learning or development. Service professionalism came next on the list of positive perceptions: parents cited the service being 'well organised' as a positive factor (47%), and having staff who were 'well trained and good at their job' (43%). After these, the next most popular factors cited as helpful were a group of factors related to the value to the parent. Over one-third of parents cited having a break from child care, and convenience or accessibility as positive aspects of the service (both 37%), and over one-quarter mentioned having a break from the house as helpful (26%). One-quarter also said they personally enjoyed visiting the service (25%). In total, in an impressive 96 per cent of cases, parents said they would recommend the service they had used to other parents in a similar situation.

In terms of the value to the child, in-depth interviews highlighted the opportunity for children to mix with others through these services, providing the important double benefit of being fun for children and helping their social and educational development.

> It's just a bit of freedom for the children and it's something different for them to do, get them out of the house, mixing with children, experience other children.
>
> *(Mother, lone parent)*

At the same time, the services provided value to the parent by also giving them the chance to mix with other adults. Parents gave enthusiastic

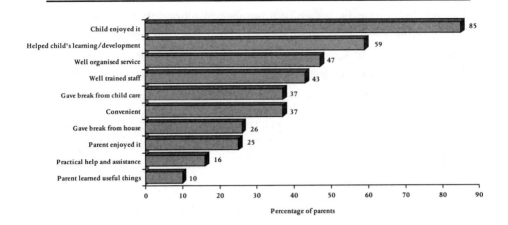

Base = 901 instances of 'helpful' service use in past three years. Respondents could use more than one service

Figure 7.3 Parents' experiences of what was helpful about semi-formal support services

accounts of their time at local groups and centres, stressing their appreciation of the opportunity to socialise with other adults.

> You talk to parents, don't you? You swap stories and you just talk. And it gets you out of the house and while the kids are playing you're sat talking to other people. And it's time for yourself you see...you meet new friends and you meet people all the time you see. That's a good thing, it's good for you to get out and have a chat.
>
> *(Mother, sick child)*

An indirect benefit mentioned by some parents was that mixing with other adults at services provided an opportunity to increase their informal social support network. One respondent described how joining a local church group had provided him with a new set of friends who had subsequently helped him out in times of difficulty:

> I suppose if you really got into any real bother there are people there that can help you and back you up ... I think you know people that would just be there for you if you have got any sort of ... problems ... you would have someone to talk to, someone to turn to.
>
> *(Father, sick child, difficult child)*

One mother with a large family, a number of whom attended the Boys' Brigade, illustrated this combination of benefits that parents got from semi-formal support services. Discussing the merits of their involvement, she initially stressed the experiences and opportunities the service gave for her children.

> (My son aged 12), he's been on a submarine. He wouldn't have been on one if it wasn't with the Boys' Brigade. So all them things, that's why I find it is good.
>
> *(Mother, large family)*

However, later in the discussion she revealed that she was also positive about her children's involvement because it provided an important indirect benefit for her – an increasingly rare opportunity to get a break from child care.

> I used to be able to get (someone to babysit) the kids, but not now they're getting older… That's why I want to keep them in the Boys' Brigade because they can go away for weekends.

Reasons for ceasing to use semi-formal support services

Finally, where parents had ceased to use a service in the past three years ($n = 324$), we asked their reason(s), to ascertain the extent to which dissatisfaction with the service had been influential in the decision to leave. Consonant with the generally positive user perceptions outlined above, the major reason that parents gave to explain having left a service was that either the child had outgrown the service, or that the service had been time limited (for example, a holiday playscheme) and had simply come to an end (75%; in a further 7% of the cases, the service had actually closed down completely, however). In only 5 per cent of the cases ($n = 16$) did the parent say that the reason for leaving was that the service was unhelpful, and other reasons (lack of time, inconvenience, cost, unfriendly staff, etc.) together accounted for only 13 per cent of reasons.

Conclusions

The study indicated that in general, awareness and use of semi-formal services was relatively low among parents in poor environments. The low levels of awareness revealed by the study are in themselves interesting, although we cannot tell to what extent this reflects an actual lack of services in poor environments, (that is, a failure in provision), or a failure in marketing services to local families. However, for those parents who do use them, these services fulfil an important role: not only do they relieve the social isolation of both children *and* parents but they allow families on low incomes access to toys and equipment that they might otherwise not be able to afford. To an extent, use was associated with higher levels of need, at least in terms of levels of current problems as measured on our composite scale, and with having a child with a health problem.

However, it was also clear that substantial numbers of parents with problems who might benefit from these services were not using them. Moreover, semi-formal services did not appear to 'compensate' for lower levels of informal support, since those who reported lower levels of support from within their personal networks were also less likely to have used a service. Although we cannot draw conclusions about the direction of causality here, our data do suggest that rather than forming two discrete domains of social support, informal and semi-formal social support may instead overlap and 'feed' one another. For example, some of our qualitative data clearly indicate that the benefits of semi-formal services include meeting and making contact with other local parents. It therefore seems likely that semi-formal support services may provide a way for parents to enhance their social networks which may in time come to function as a source of informal support.

Equally, having wider informal social support networks may be a way for parents to increase their awareness of organised services, and may perhaps act to encourage them into services in the first place. Last, the significantly lower levels of use by ethnic minority parents raise some questions about the inclusiveness of family support services, especially given that these parents also appear to be more isolated in terms of informal support networks than white British parents.

We explore in more detail some of the reasons for non-use of services in Chapter 9. The next chapter focuses on the third dimension in the support network of parents in poor environments – examining the awareness, use and perceptions of formal support services.

Notes

1. Lack of awareness does not, of course, necessarily mean that there were no services in the area; services could have existed without parents knowing of them.

2. That is, the group most likely to have used a service of this type in the recent past.

3. Mann Whitney test.

CHAPTER EIGHT

Formal Support

We defined formal support services as services provided by the statutory sector alone or in partnership with the voluntary sector, often provided by large organisations, and in general accessed by a referral system.[1] Using a list of services which included both 'universal' services (for example, health services such as health visiting and ante-natal classes) and 'targeted' services for families in need or at risk (for example, social services, referral-based family centres, child psychology services, speech therapy), we generated questions for paretns.

Services (formal):

UNIVERSAL

- health visiting
- antenatal classes.

TARGETED

- social services
- referral-based family centre or family service unit
- speech therapy
- educational psychology, child psychology and psychiatry, child guidance
- educational social work.

Box 8.1 Services in the formal sector

We asked parents to tell us whether they were aware of such service as being available in their area; whether they had ever had contact with any of these services; and whether they had had recent contact (that is, in the past three years). The services we asked about are shown in Box 8.1.

Extent of awareness and use of formal support services

Awareness and overall levels of use

Awareness and use of formal services was somewhat higher than the corresponding figures for semi-formal support services (Figure 8.1). Overall, only 6 per cent of the sample were unaware of at least some formal support services within their local area, and only 19 per cent of respondents reported never having used a formal service at some point. Just over half (54%) of parents had been in touch with a formal service in the past three years.

Awareness and use of services in the formal family support sector varied, as would be expected, by whether the service was of the 'universal' or 'targeted' type. Taking universal services first (that is, health visiting and ante-natal services), there were some surprising findings. Although awareness was generally high, it was noteworthy that, given the widespread availability of these services, substantial proportions of the sample were unaware that such services existed in their area, and claimed *never* to have used the services. For example, in the case of health visiting services, nearly one in eight (13%) was unaware that such a service was available to parents in their area, and nearly one-third of all parents, or 32 per cent, said they had never been in contact with a health visitor. Sex of parent and age of children in the family played some role in these findings, however: when the results were examined only for women with a child in the household aged under five years (that is, the group mainly targeted by health visitors for whom recall of the visit(s) should not have been a problem), the figure for those who said they had never had a health visitor dropped by half, to 17 per cent. However, this means that one in six mothers of pre-school children did not recall having ever had a visit from a health visitor, suggesting that a sizeable proportion of parents in poor environments are not being reached by the health visiting service.

Moreover, ante-natal classes followed a similar pattern – in theory, these are available to all pregnant women, but were unknown to over one-third of the sample (38%) and unused by two-thirds (67%). In this case, the recency of having a baby appeared to make very little difference to these figures. Of those women who had given birth in the last five years, 36 per cent thought ante-natal classes were not available in their local area, and only two in five (40%) had actually attended such a class.

Turning to targeted family and child support services (services which, although often widely available on a statutory basis, would generally be reserved for those in particular need), levels of awareness still showed some gaps, although actual usage was perhaps relatively high (and, in general, high relative to use of semi-formal services). For example, although nearly two in five of the sample did not think social services were available in their area (39%), nearly one in eight families had contacted a social services department at some point in connection with parenting, and nearly one in 12 had done this within the past three years (8%). Furthermore, one in 25 (4%) of parents also told us that they were 'currently in contact with social services because of a problem with one of the children'.

Relatively extensive use was also being made of speech therapy and child psychology or psychiatry services. One in eight parents had been in touch with speech therapy services at some point (13%), and nearly one in ten (9%) had used child psychology, child psychiatry or child guidance services in the past.

As with semi-formal services, once parents were in contact with a service, they tended to make relatively extensive use of it, and among parents who had used one or more of the services in the formal support category in the past three years, frequency of usage had been generally high. Of 1433 instances of service use, three-quarters (75%) had been used at least three times, and over one-third (36%) had been used on more than ten different occasions. Overall, in half of the cases (53%), parents were currently in touch with a service at the time the survey interview took place.

Reasons for use

We asked parents who had been in contact with a formal service in the past three years about their reasons for using the service. Whereas the main reasons given for using semi-formal services revolved around social contact for children and parents, and to some extent access to resources that were not available at home (for example, toys and play facilities),

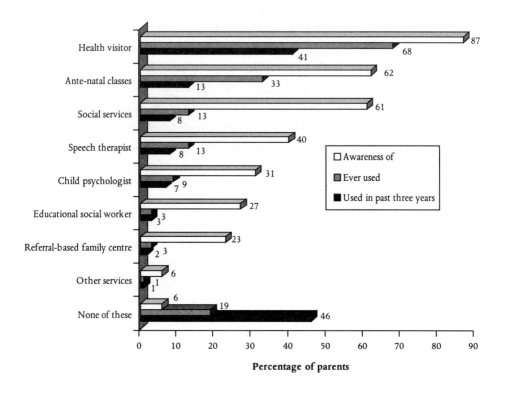

Base = 1754

Figure 8.1 Use of formal support

reasons for using formal services were rather different, and appeared to be more parent centred than child centred. For many parents, of course, the main reason for using a service was that they had been referred to it (50% of users) or had been contacted directly by the service itself (33%). However, when more self-directed reasons were given, they tended to be more instrumental than social in character, as Figure 8.2 shows. Thus, parents had contacted formal support services mainly to get advice on a range of parenting issues or to talk to someone about their personal family situation, rather than to meet other parents or to give their child wider social experience.

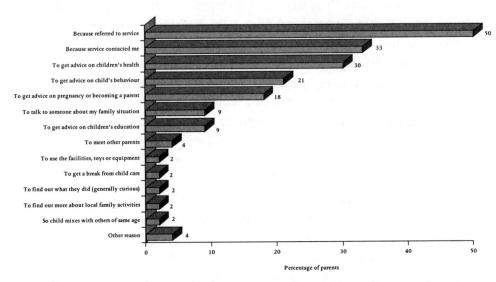

Base = 1416 instances of service use in the past three years. Respondents could give more than one reason

Figure 8.2 Reasons for using or contacting formal support services

Who uses formal support services?

As with semi-formal types of support, parents with a pre-school child, or a child under eight years old in the household were most likely to report having used formal support services in the recent past. Of parents of pre-schoolers' 83 per cent had used a service, compared to 28 per cent of those without pre-school children in the household and 71 per cent of those with under eights had used a service compared to 22 per cent of others (both $p<0.0001$).

Households with teenagers, however, had made somewhat more use of formal services than semi-formal services, reflecting the inclusion in our list (and the general availability within this sector) of more services aimed at older children as well as younger ones. Nevertheless, it was still the case that services in this sector were far more likely to be reaching 'younger' families than older ones: only 32 per cent of parents of teenagers compared to 66 per cent of those without older children reported having used a service in this sector in the past three years ($p<0.0001$).

In some respects, there were stronger signs for formal support services than for semi-formal ones that services were reaching parents with higher needs. At the level of the individual, relative to semi-formal services, parents with a wider range of particular problems were more likely to have accessed formal services in the last three years: having a high Malaise score, having a child in the household with health problems, and having a 'difficult' index child were all significantly associated with making greater use of formal services, as Table 8.1 illustrates ($p<0.01$, $p<0.0001$ and $p<0.0001$ respectively). At the level of the family or household, as with semi-formal services, those with higher levels of problems as measured by a score of three or more on the Current Problems Questionnaire were more likely to report having used formal services (68% of those with high levels of current problems compared to 48% of other parents; $p<0.0001$). However, unlike semi-formal services, formal services had been accessed by a *majority* of this group, with only one-third (32%) of those with high levels of current problems having not been in touch with a service. Parents with larger number of children were also more likely to have used a formal service recently, with 62 per cent of parents with three or more children having used a service compared to 51 per cent of those with one or two children ($p<0.0001$). However, as with semi-formal services, use of formal services did not appear to be directly related to poverty, whether measured in terms of household income or in terms of the respondent's area of residence. Those on low incomes and those in the poorest areas of our sample were not more likely to report using a formal service recently. Lone parents were also no more likely to have used these services than parents with partners.

Table 8.1 Use of formal support services in the past three years, by high level of current and other problems	
	% of parents
High level of current problems ($n = 524$)	68
Parent with high Malaise score ($n = 360$)	60
Child with health problems in household ($n = 709$)	62
'Difficult' index child ($n = 213$)	64
All respondents ($n = 1753$)	54

Last, as with semi-formal services, ethnic minority parents were significantly *less* likely to report having used a formal service in the recent past (43% compared to 55% of white British parents; $p<0.01$).

Relationship between formal and informal social support

We showed in the previous chapter that semi-formal services were not necessarily providing an alternative source of support to those with low levels of informal support. Were formal support services, then, acting as a safety net by reaching those who were less well supported at an informal level? In general, it seemed not. Those with low numbers of informal supporters were no more likely than those with average or high numbers to be using formal services in general.[2] Moreover, as with services in the semi-formal sector, those with greater levels of enacted support at the informal level were also more likely to be drawing on formal services for assistance. Thus, those who were not using formal services had a mean enacted support score of 1.92 compared to a mean of 2.63 for those using services ($p<0.0001$). Again, as with semi-formal support, the more support at the informal level the greater the likelihood of using organised services.

Quality and value of formal support services

Among users, perceptions of the quality of formal services were largely positive, although somewhat less so than perceptions of semi-formal services. In half of the instances of service use (52%), parents rated the service they had used as 'very helpful', and a further third (31%) of the services were rated as 'fairly helpful'. Twice as many respondents who had used formal services were either ambivalent or negative about the usefulness of the service compared to users of semi-formal services (16% compared to 7%).

When we explored parents' reasons for feeling positive about the formal services they had used,[3] reflecting the main reasons for using these services, 'parent-centred' responses tended to predominate. (See Figure 8.3.) Whereas with semi-formal services the main reasons for finding services helpful were given as the value to the child, for formal services, factors relating to practical value to parents topped the list. Given that by far the most frequently used service in the past three years was the health visitor service (and so most parents were answering with this service in mind), this suggests that in terms of parents' perceptions, this service is seen as being of particular value to parents rather than to children. So, for example, the most appreciated attribute of formal services was that 'practical help and assistance' had been received (55% of cases), and two in five formal services (43%) were praised because 'they came to see me in my own home'. In over one-third of the cases (35%), parents appreciated the fact that they 'had learned useful things'. Note however that 'value' to parents is not synonymous with 'enjoyment': only one in ten parents (10%) praised formal services for being enjoyable (in contrast to one-quarter – 25% – of semi-formal services).

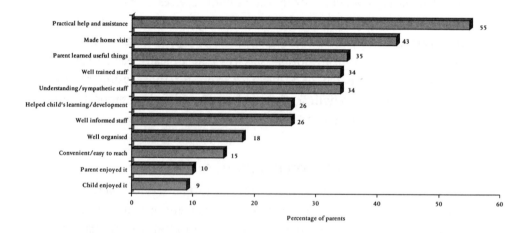

Base = 1058 cases of 'helpful' service use in the past three years

Figure 8.3 Parents' perceptions of what was helpful about formal support services

As with semi-formal services, although, the professionalism of the service was cited as helpful, with parents praising the 'well trained' and 'understanding or sympathetic' staff (both 34% of cases). By contrast with reasons for finding semi-formal services helpful, only a small proportion cited the child's enjoyment of the service (9%), and whereas with semi-formal services 59 per cent of services were praised because they 'helped the child's learning or development', the proportion for formal services was less than half this figure (26%).

In total, in 88 per cent of cases, parents said they would recommend the formal support service they had used to other parents in a similar situation, and in only one in ten instances of service use would parents definitely not recommend the service to others (9%). Although a somewhat lower proportion of parents were satisfied with formal as opposed to semi-formal services, this is still a high figure and suggests that, in general, parents found these services satisfactory.

In qualitative interviews, we explored in more detail the aspects of formal services that were most valued. Discussions tended to concentrate on the extent to which service providers had successfully addressed parents' own self-defined needs. A consistent and important message (and one that we return to in Chapter 9) was that parents' satisfaction with services depended substantially upon whether the professionals involved had made them feel respected as adults and had treated their concerns as legitimate.

> He [doctor] treats you as an individual. You know – he doesn't talk down to you or anything like that, he treats you as a normal person, where you can get others that don't.
>
> *(Mother, reconstituted, large family)*

Parents clearly felt that an important part of showing respect was listening carefully to what they had to say. They particularly valued all types of professionals who would take time to hear about their problems and who were able to offer guidance or advice without judging or criticising their parenting skills or style.

> She [health visitor] was nice. I could sit down and talk to her in confidence, and she wouldn't knock anything I had to say.
>
> *(Mother, lone parent, poor health)*

Reasons for ceasing to use formal support services

Last, when asked about their reason(s) for ceasing to use a service ($n = 580$), the overwhelming reason cited by parents (as with semi-formal services) were 'natural' ones: 'the course ended' or 'my child outgrew the service' (almost one in nine of those who had left a service in the past three years – 88%). In only a small proportion of cases (10%; $n = 58$), did parents say they left because 'the service wasn't helpful'.

Conclusions

The findings in this chapter have shown that there is a relatively high level of awareness and use of both universal and targeted formal support services. However, levels of use – although higher than for semi-formal services – were not especially high, given the 'high need' nature of the sample for this study. Only around half the parents interviewed had used a service in the past three years, and although the majority (four in five) had accessed a formal service at some point in their parenting career, the proportion claiming never to have received so-called 'universal' services such as health visiting will no doubt surprise some. Although this result may in part reflect problems with recall (perhaps parents did not remember being visited, or misconstrued the health visitor's identity), we found no evidence of confusion or recollection problems concerning health visitors in the qualitative interviews. We therefore suspect that this figure does tend to reflect gaps in service coverage rather than in respondents' understanding or memory.

The most common routes to formal service use were being referred to, or contacted by, the services directly, and reasons for use tended to be described in terms of parent-centred, instrumental needs rather than the child-centred or social reasons given for using semi-formal support services. Overall, parents were largely positive about the quality of services, although slightly less so than for semi-formal support. Parents valued practical assistance from understanding staff who respected them as adults by listening to their concerns and who addressed their self-defined needs directly. However, although there were signs that services are reaching those in the greatest need, some groups appear particularly badly served: ethnic minority parents and families with older children in particular are unlikely to have used formal services recently. Like semi-formal services, formal services do not necessarily appear to be an alternative source of support for families with low levels of informal social support. In terms of measuring actual received support, parents are ranged along a distribution in which informal enacted support and use of services are positively related to each other. Thus, while some parents have low levels of enacted support at both the informal *and* the organised level, other have high levels across both dimensions, while still others report 'medium' consumption rates of both forms. In other words, those who were low on informal enacted support also tended to be low on service use, and conversely those who were high on service use also consumed greater levels of enacted informal support. This is very clearly illustrated when we look at use of organised support services in both semi-formal and formal sectors against levels of enacted informal support. As Figure 8.4 shows, enacted informal support scores were strongly and positively associated with increasing levels of use of organised support, so that those parents who had used neither semi-formal nor formal services in the past three years had a mean enacted informal support score of 1.74, those who had used *one* of the two types of organised services had a score of 2.37 and those who had used both types of organised service had the highest score of all, 2.87 (*p*<0.0001). Put another way, some parents appear to have relatively high 'consumption' levels across all dimensions of social support while others have low consumption levels.

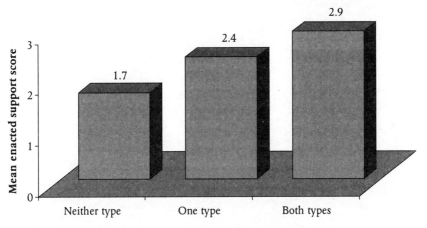

Base = 1754

Figure 8.4 Mean informal support score, by extent of organised service use

Completing our analysis of social support to parents in poor environments, the next chapter reviews the evidence on support deficits. It explores parents' perceptions of the extent and quality of social support across the board to unpack the relationship between subjective and objective assessments of 'supportedness', and asks to what extent consumption of support indicates need. For example, do low consumers of social support need more support, or are high consumers the more needy group? How can we identify and make sense of support deficits, and what do these tell us about the prospects for meeting them more effectively through policy and practice?

Notes

1. We asked parents to tell us about contact 'specifically in connection with being a parent' with 'services for children and families which may be provided by your local authority, council or health authority'.

2. Mean network size for those using a service = 5.92 compared with 6.18 for those not using a service; $p = 0.283$).

3. We asked parents who had found the service helpful, 'What was helpful or good about this service?'

CHAPTER NINE

Support Deficits in Poor Environments

To recap on the complex pattern of results in the previous three chapters, our picture of support for parents in poor environments so far is a mixed one. At the level of informal social support – that is, support arising naturally out of individuals' own social networks of family and friends – we picked up a pattern of reasonably extensive and close-knit networks. Relatively few respondents reported themselves as entirely without an informal support network, and in qualitative interviews many described themselves as enjoying substantial, high-quality levels of help and assistance from friends, family and neighbours. Nevertheless, when we tried to ascertain in concrete (and quantitative) terms what actual help and support parents were receiving in their day-to-day lives by asking about help in specific domains of family life over the recent past, we formed a rather different picture. In terms of informal support, parents on the whole did not feel very confident in their ability to recruit help if the need arose. Moreover, reports of enacted informal support were low. It may be that a different, more 'micro' approach to collecting data (such as a daily diary keeping exercise) might have revealed higher levels of 'hidden' or unacknowledged support within parents' daily lives, and more detailed research in this area might shed light here. Nevertheless, on our 'macro' measures, the results were clear: most parents in poor environments currently do not receive a great deal in the way of help and assistance through their informal networks.

At the level of semi-formal and formal support, such as services provided either by local community or statutory organisations, the picture was also mixed. Those parents that had used services tended to have had relatively extensive contact with them, and were on the whole satisfied with the quality of provision. Most said they would recommend the service to other parents. Levels of awareness of services showed some gaps, however, and overall actual use of services was low, despite the fact that the sample for the study was drawn from a high need population. Use of formal services was somewhat higher than use of semi-formal services. Even so, a substantial minority claimed never to have used a formal service, despite the fact that universal services such as health visiting were included in our list.

Bearing in mind that parents were asked to consider all kinds of help, both informal and agency-based, instrumental and emotional, from all sources including resident partners and other close family members as well as local community and statutory services, an unavoidable conclusion is implied: there are clearly substantial gaps in support across all dimensions within poor environments. Although some parents do make use of a range of different types of support, others reported low levels of support across all sectors.

To what extent should these gaps in support for parenting in poor environments give cause for concern? For example, do parents themselves perceive a need for more support? The answer is that many do not. When we asked parents whether they desired more help with parenting,[1] half (52%) said no and, of these, two-thirds – 66 per cent, or 35 per cent of the sample in total – said they had never at any point felt this way since they first became a parent. We return to these parents later in Part IV of the report to explore in more detail what strengths and strategies these 'copers' have, and what we might learn from them about successful parenting in poor environments.

However, not all parents were content with the levels of support and assistance they were currently receiving. Although half of the sample was satisfied with their current levels of support, one in ten parents (11%) said they often wished they had more, and over one-third (36%) said they sometimes felt like this (see Figure 9.1).

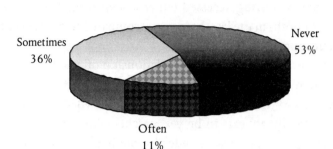

Base = 1733

Figure 9.1 Frequency of wishing for help and support with parenting

In the rest of this chapter we explore the characteristics of the 47 per cent of respondents who felt 'unsupported' in parenting to some extent (that is, those who sometimes or often wished for more help or support) as compared to those who felt 'supported' and never wished for more help, and unpack evidence about the nature of support that may help to explain why these deficits occur.

Who are the 'unsupported'?

An obvious place to start when trying to identify the characteristics of those who felt unsupported is to investigate actual levels of support reported by these parents. Did they feel unsupported because they *were* less well supported in a concrete sense, or are perceptions of supportedness in fact unrelated to actual consumption of support?

Our evidence was that perceptions of support were related, but not perhaps in the direction we might have expected. In fact, those who perceived themselves as unsupported tended, paradoxically, to be people who in fact reported receiving the most social support in an objective sense. That is, the relationship between perceptions of supportedness and actual received support was an inverse one. Parents who felt unsupported reported higher levels of enacted informal support than those who felt supported. Thus the mean enacted informal support score for parents wishing for more help was 2.62, as compared to 2.03 for those parents who said they never wished for more help ($p<0.001$). Furthermore, in terms of use of organised support services, 75 per cent of parents who felt unsupported reported having accessed either a semi-formal or a formal support service (or both) in the last three years, compared to 58 per cent of parents who felt supported ($p<0.0001$).

A further question then concerns the relationship of 'need' to perceptions of supportedness. Do parents who feel unsupported and who consume more support perhaps have higher levels of need? The answer to this questions generally appears to be yes; parents who perceived themselves to be lacking in support were indeed more likely to be 'needy' in terms of a range of objectively defined risk factors. That is, there was a positive relationship between need and perceptions of lack of support.

For example, separate cross-tabulations showed that at the level of the individual, mental and physical health problems were strongly associated with wishing for more support. For example, 65 per cent of parents with a high Malaise score felt unsupported compared to 43 per cent of other parents ($p<0.0001$).[2] Of parents with a physical health problem 52 per cent felt unsupported compared to 44 per cent of others ($p<0.01$), and in families where there was child with health problems, 54 per cent of parents wished for greater support as compared to 43 per cent of parents without a sick child ($p<0.0001$). Having a 'difficult' index child was also strongly related to feeling unsupported: 61 per cent of these parents felt this way compared to 43 per cent of other parents ($p<0.0001$).

At the level of the family, household structure was extremely strongly associated with feeling unsupported. Of lone parents, 60 per cent compared to only 39 per cent of parents with partners said they wished for more support ($p<0.0001$). Having a pre-school child in the household was also highly associated with the desire for more help,[3] (53% compared to 42% of parents without a pre-school child; $p<0.0001$). Although household income itself was not significantly associated with wishing for more help, perceptions of whether the family was managing financially were. Those who reported themselves as 'not managing' were far more likely to feel unsupported (62% compared to 43% of those who were managing; $p<0.0001$). Having high scores on the Current Problems Questionnaire was also associated with wishing for more help 'sometimes' or 'often'; two-thirds of parents with high levels of current problems (66%) felt unsupported compared to just under two-fifths (39%) of parents with fewer problems; (p<0.0001),[4] see Table 9.1. Only family size was not significantly associated with perceptions of supportedness; those with larger families were not more likely to feel in need of more support than those with smaller ones.

Table 9.1 Factors associated with feeling unsupported in parenting	
	% of parents
Parent factors	
Long-term physical health problem ($n = 684$)	52
High Malaise score ($n = 353$)	65
High level of current problems ($n = 519$)	66
Lone parent ($n = 667$)	60
Not managing financially ($n = 389$)	62
Child factors	
Pre-school child in household ($n = 823$)	53
Child with health problem in household ($n = 702$)	54
'Difficult' index child ($n = 210$)	61
All respondents ($n = 1733$)	47

Of course, as we showed in Part II, many of these risk factors are strongly associated with one another. So, in order to identify which of these variables were independently associated with wishing for more help, a logistic regression model was tested. In fact, once all other factors were taken into account, the only factors independently associated with wishing for more help were: having a high level of current problems on the CPQ, being a lone parent, having a high Malaise score, and having a pre-school child at home. Parents in these circumstances were between one and a third and two and a half times more likely to express a desire for more help and assistance than other parents. (See Table 9.2.)

Table 9.2 Role of various family and individual level risk factors in predicting wishing for more help with parenting

	Odds ratio
High level of current problems	2.52***
Lone parent	2.40***
High parent Malaise score	1.51*
Has pre-school child	1.34*
Not managing financially	1.41(n/s)
'Difficult' index child	1.40 (n/s)
Child with health problems in household	1.14 (n/s)
Parental physical health problem	1.11 (n/s)

Base = 1399. * $p<0.01$; *** $p< 0.0001$; n/s = not significant

What explanations can we offer for the support deficits described above? Why should some parents – and especially more needy parents – feel less well supported than others? How can we account for the finding that some parents who feel unsupported (for example, those with high levels of current problems on the CPQ) nevertheless reported more enacted support at the informal level and greater use of both semi-formal and informal support services, when intuitively we would expect to find the reverse pattern: that those consuming the most support would feel the most supported? Below, we discuss some of the existing theories that speak to these questions and assess them against the evidence gathered from this study. We consider first explanations for deficits in informal social support and then deficits in support provided by the organised sector.

Explanations for informal social support deficits

In terms of understanding informal social support deficits, the existing literature divides, broadly speaking, between two theoretical stances. One prioritises the role of environment and community; the other stresses family and individual level factors as being at the root of failures in support.

Community-level factors

As we discussed in Part II, there is a wealth of literature that points to the interrelationship between neighbourhood or community characteristics and social support (Seagull 1987). Furstenburg (1993), in particular, has stressed that in neighbourhoods with limited social capital, which tend to be materially as well as socially impoverished, residents are disinclined to engage in reciprocal support relationships with other local people. The results are families who are socially insular and disengaged from the wider community, and parents who receive – and give – little in the way of enacted support.

Of course, as we explained earlier, we cannot compare our sample of poor parenting environments directly with a contrasting sample of parents from 'good' (that is, affluent) parenting areas. We are therefore unable to comment on whether parents in poor environments in Britain do in fact report less social support than parents living in other areas. However, we did have a range of environments within our broad group of 'poor environments'. Thus, we were able to explore the effect of community-level factors within this more limited context. Given the overlap in demographic characteristics between what are characterised in the literature as 'socially impoverished areas' and our conception of 'poor parenting environments', we hypothesised that we might pick up variations in social support levels according to PPE-Index score so that, within poor parenting areas, the poorest areas would tend to have the greatest numbers of parents who reported themselves to be 'unsupported'.

We have already shown in previous chapters that the relative poverty of an area, as measured by the PPE-Index, was not related to enacted informal social support, even although parents in the poorest areas tended to report smaller informal support networks overall. Nor was area of residence significantly associated with use of organised services. In fact, in this study the PPE-Index score also did *not* discriminate between those who felt supported or unsupported. Those who wished for more support were not significantly more numerous in the poorest of our areas.[5] Thus, *within the context of poor environments,* desire for more support with parenting in a broad sense is not associated with where parents live. Those who lived in the poorest of the areas in our sample were no more likely than others to say they felt unsupported. Community-level explanations – at least in terms of objective measures of neighborhood poverty as captured by the

PPE-Index – cannot account for the patterns in support deficits found in this study.

However, although community-level indicators may not predict levels of social support, levels of support certainly appear to be instrumental in shaping parents' views of their neighbourhood. For example, we found a strong relationship between feeling supported or unsupported and our more subjective measure of whether a neighbourhood was 'a good place to bring up a family'. Those who felt supported were far more likely than those who reported a support deficit to rate their neighbourhood as 'very' or 'fairly' good (58% compared to 42%; $p < 0.0001$). As far as respondents were concerned, 'good' neighbourhoods, therefore, are those in which there are higher levels of social support. Nevertheless, levels of social support alone do not define a good area. In a multiple regression model to predict perception of the area as a place to bring up a family,[6] both the PPE-Index band of the area, and whether the parent felt unsupported were independently significant.

Collectively then, this pattern of results suggests that although perceptions of the community are strongly associated with levels of social support, we cannot identify where there will be deficits in informal, community-based social support with reference to measures of neighbourhood poverty alone. Levels of social support may help us understand why some areas within the category of poor environments are preferred to others as places to raise a family, but we cannot, as it were, 'blame' certain areas for the low levels of social support that some families report.

Individual-level factors: attitudes to support

If community-level factors do not fully explain informal social support deficits, what then are the roles of individual or family level factors? Perhaps not surprisingly, much of the existing literature in this area focuses on parents 'at risk', since failures of support in this context often have the most dramatic and disturbing consequences. There is relatively less work on social support and the individual or family characteristics of parents 'in need' more generally, and this makes it hard to find comparable studies against which to judge the results reported here. Nevertheless, the literature on why support often fails parents at risk gives us some hypotheses that may help us understand the patterns visible in this study of parents in need in a more general sense.

Much early writing that tried to identify why some families fell through the support 'net' while others did not more or less attributed the cause to the parents themselves. It was suggested that in the case of at-risk parents, their socially unsupported or isolated state was at least partly due to their own negative attitudes to support, which were in turn shaped by personality and temperament. High levels of need (in terms of the existence of multiple, overlapping risk factors) were seen both as antecedents and outcomes of negative attitudes. They were seen as antecedents in that the severe and chronic levels of disadvantage they faced led them to feel pessimistic about the ability of external support to solve their problems. They were viewed as consequences in that negative attitudes reinforced their isolation from support and assistance. However, personality factors were definitely seen as the most powerful explanations for lack of social support, manifested through a lack of social competence in making and sustaining supportive social relationships. The work of Polansky and colleagues (Polansky *et al.* 1981; Polansky *et al.* 1985) based on detailed, controlled studies of severely neglectful parents in deprived rural and urban areas of the United States was especially influential in this respect. In these studies, parents were described as not only beset by multiple psycho-social problems, but as temperamentally disadvantaged by an inability to engage in reciprocal exchanges of support. They were shown to be prone to feeling threatened rather than supported by close relationships with neighbours, more likely to construe offers of help as interference than assistance, and to be generally difficult to befriend. In these studies, therefore, the deficits lay not in the quality or availability of support within the community but in the inability of certain individuals to mobilise and draw on that support.

The hypothesis that unsupported parents (albeit unwittingly) contribute to their situation has been a powerful influence on work on informal social support and parenting, and in many ways continues to set the agenda for understanding how informal networks may operate to support families in need within the community (see Thompson 1995). 'Parental insularity and isolation', for example, continues to be highlighted as a significant correlate of parenting difficulties and child maltreatment in major texts on child abuse (for example, Briere *et al.* 1996). To what extent did our study find evidence to support or contest the idea that some parents – and especially those with multiple and overlapping problems – contribute to their own isolation through negative attitudes to social support? First, we did indeed find a range of views within the sample about the nature of informal support networks, demonstrating that parents with higher levels of need were more negative in their views than others. However, we also found considerable evidence to suggest that negative attitudes were widespread within poor environments and not confined purely to those with higher levels of psycho-social problems.

Barriers to asking for, or accepting, informal support in the sample as a whole
As we discussed in Chapter 6, substantial proportions of parents claimed they would never ask for help or support with certain aspects of parenting or family life. Borrowing money was especially unpopular in this regard, but as many as one in ten respondents would not even ask for a lift to an important appointment or to borrow an ingredient for a family meal. One in 12 parents (8%) would not ask anyone to mind their child, even for a couple of hours in the daytime. What might underlie this reluctance to call on family or neighbours for assistance? Data on parents' attitudes to support across the sample as a whole suggested that, even when support was available, there may be strong barriers to uptake connected with negative attitudes to asking for, or receiving, support. This applied both to support within the immediate family and external to it. Indeed, problems with perceptions of informal support as potentially threatening or undermining, and discomfort with the expectations of reciprocity embedded in informal support relationships were widely evident in this normative sample, and not by any means confined to those with more severe levels of personal problems or parenting difficulties.

Although earlier we showed that family members could provide important help and support to parents, asking for help and support from family members also had disadvantages. In qualitative interviews, many parents talked about the problems associated with this. A dominant concern was that in recruiting family supporters to tackle problems, individuals might have to relinquish some of their own control in the situation. First, parents considered that they would lose their privacy to the wider family, with requests for help leading to relatives 'poking their noses' into personal difficulties.

> I know it sounds wicked. It's a case of if family wise, if you go to family to ask them for help or anything like that they poke their nose in, 'well why what's the problem?' and everything else. So you have to sit down and tell them all what's going on. So I don't go to family, and he [partner] doesn't go to family.
>
> *(Mother, reconstituted family, large family)*

Second, parents explained that family members found it difficult to know where to draw the line between 'support' and 'interference'. Parents described how, although usually well-meaning, helpers tended to take over.

> I suppose my mum can ... take over, sort of thing. You'd think it was her that was the mother, and they were her children.
>
> *(Mother, low income, lone parent, difficult child)*

A further dimension was a concern not to 'put upon' other members of the family. Parents commented that once they had left home and had their own children, they felt they ought to be able to tackle their own problems without turning to their parents for assistance.

> I don't like asking my mum and dad and I don't like asking anyone because it feels as if I'm putting on to them, if you know what I mean ... No, I feel they're my kids, it's my life, my independence, so I've got to get on with it. It's not very nice asking my mum and dad; my mum and dad have had their life, they've looked after me, if you know what I mean?
>
> *(Mother, difficult child, lone parent, bad accommodation)*

This combination of concerns about family involvement led some parents to make a conscious effort to turn to other sources of support. For example, some parents deliberately avoided relatives in favour of help from friends.

> You wouldn't say anything to your family what you would say to a friend. Just that, I wouldn't like to ... because I wouldn't like to put my family through the worry. That's what you have got your pals for.
>
> *(Mother, lone parent)*

However, some parents also perceived disadvantages in seeking informal support from non-family within the wider community (that is, friends, neighbours and acquaintances). For example, despite the fact that, as we showed earlier, respondents said they generally felt they 'knew' their neighbours in the local community, only half the sample (51%) strongly agreed or tended to agree with the statement 'People round here help each other out in a crisis.' Well over half (57%) would not divulge personal information because of worries about lack of confidentiality and gossiping among local people, and agreed with the statement 'I prefer not to discuss my family with people round here because you can't trust people to keep things to themselves.' Nearly one-third of parents (31%) agreed that 'if you ask friends or neighbours for help, you can end up feeling in debt', and over one-fifth of the sample (22%) felt that 'asking for help outside the immediate family is a sign of not coping' was perhaps stigmatising.

BARRIERS TO ASKING FOR, OR ACCEPTING, INFORMAL SUPPORT AMONG
UNSUPPORTED AND HIGH-NEED PARENTS

To what extent did we find a relationship between lack of support, high levels of need and negative attitudes to informal social support? First, attitudes to informal support from within the wider community and overall perceptions of 'supportedness' were strongly related to one another. When we constructed a scale measuring attitudes to informal social support based on the four statements listed above,[7] the less supported the respondent felt, the lower the score on the scale. Thus, when the average scores for those who felt supported were compared with those who felt unsupported, there was a highly significant difference. The mean score for those who wished for more help (that is, felt 'unsupported') was 11.54, whereas those who felt adequately supported had a mean score of 12.39 ($p<0.0001$). Qualitative interviews illustrated well how this might impact upon some parents' tendency to seek or accept support. Although respondents tended not to be so concerned that friends would interfere and 'take over' as they were in relation to family, they often focused on anxieties about feeling obligated to friends and neighbours if they accepted help. Some, for example, considered that the expectation of reciprocity that accompanied the receipt of support was an additional stress that was best avoided altogether.

> Friends help; friends do help but in such a way you have got to give them a favour back and I don't agree on that.
>
> *(Mother, large family, sick child, difficult child)*

Second, negative attitudes to informal support were also significantly associated with the level of problems that parents reported on the Current Problems Questionnaire, and Table 9.3 shows how these higher need parents with high level of current problems differed substantially from those with average or low levels of problems on all but one of the statements that made up our measure of attitudes to informal social support.

Table 9.3 Attitudes to informal social support by level of current problems			
	% of parents agreeing with the statement		
	Low/average levels of current problems ($n = 1224$)	High levels of current problems ($n = 522$)	All ($n = 1,746$)
I prefer not to discuss my family with people round here because you can't trust to keep things to themselves	51	69***	57
People round here do not help each other out in a crisis	21	28***	23
If you ask friends or neighbours for help, you can end up feeling 'in debt'	27	40***	31
Asking for help outside the family is a sign of not coping	22	22 (n/s)	22

*** $p<0.0001$; n/s = not significant

Looked at another way, analysis of variance showed a clear and significant trend for decreasing mean scores on the attitudes to informal social support scale with rising CPQ score ($p <0.0001$); see Figure 9.2.

Last, in a logistic regression model in which levels of current problems and attitudes to informal support were used to predict wish for support, both variables were significantly independently associated with feeling unsupported. The higher the levels of current problems, the greater the wish for support but, at the same time, the more negative the attitudes to this support; see Table 9.4.

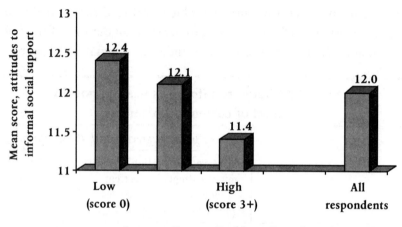

Base = 1745

Figure 9.2 Mean score on the attitudes to informal social support scale, by level of current problems

Table 9.4 Role of level of current problems and attitudes to support in predicting feeling unsupported in parenting	
	Odds ratio
Attitudes to informal support (scale score)	0.949**
Level of current problems (CPQ score)	1.38***

Base = 1732. ** = $p<0.001$; *** = $p<0.0001$

INFORMAL SUPPORT: THE DOUBLE-EDGED SWORD

What do we make of these results? In line with the literature on at-risk parents and social isolation, they appear collectively to provide strong evidence that the neediest parents in the community (who also declare themselves to feel least well supported) are simultaneously the most likely to be hostile to the concept of support. These parents have higher needs, perceive themselves to be in 'support deficit', and yet also seem to hold attitudes that militate against being able to enter whole-heartedly into the give and take of informal social support relationships.

Still, as Table 9.2 also showed, in this representative sample of parents in poor environments even those parents with low or medium levels of need were not always overwhelmingly positive about the nature of informal social support in their area. Negative attitudes were widespread throughout the sample; it was simply that 'higher-need' parents were even more negative than others. What these results seem to be telling us is that there may be intrinsic limits to the support provided by local networks of family and friends. Although valued when it is offered, informal social support is also widely perceived to have disadvantages. Specifically, many parents report that it has the capacity to threaten family privacy and undermine autonomy. It comes 'with strings attached' – carrying an expectation of reciprocity that may itself be onerous or stressful. It is not always reliable. In short – despite the optimistic assumption of most academic, policy and practice literature that social support must by definition be a positive thing – *informal social support is not a concept with purely positive attributes.* Our study was certainly not the first to pick up on this negative side of social support; Thompson (1995, p.29), for example, points out the 'liabilities of kin relations', and Hobfall (1988) provides a good discussion of how social exchange research and family systems theorists highlighted the negative side of social support long ago. However, this study is unique in having quantified the wide extent of negative attitudes within a representative sample of parents in poor environments. When we consider these findings, it then seems unsurprising that parents with higher needs – who are greater consumers of social support by their own report – register even more negative attitudes to support. Their greater dependency on, and exposure to, social support, would lead us to expect this. For example, it may be that parents with high levels of current problems were more negative about asking for or accepting support because they had more 'to hide' (that is, they had more problems, or more stigmatising problems) and more to lose from the intrusion of others into their lives. They may be more worried more than others about accepting support, perhaps because they were least in a position to return favours. When we accept that social support may not necessarily be the 'good thing' it is generally assumed to be, explanations for rejecting or hostile attitudes to support that turn on individual characteristics such as personality, temperament, or social competence seem perhaps less compelling.[8] Individual social circumstances, on the other hand, do seem to provide a ready explanation. We return to this important point at the end of this chapter.

Explanations for deficits in semi-formal and formal support

Turning now to explore deficits in semi-formal and formal support, while the literature on informal social support has highlighted both community- and individual-level explanations for support deficits, writing on gaps in organised services has placed more emphasis on the failure of services themselves to pick up effectively on the needs of vulnerable and isolated families. As with studies of failures in informal support, much of the work in this field has focused on at-risk and dangerous families and how services do – or don't – meet the needs of parents and children in extreme difficulties. For example, in the child protection field there is a substantial literature that has scrutinised practice and has highlighted deep structural fault-lines in terms of the way services are organised and delivered. Failures of multi-agency working, inadequate supervision of workers under pressure, failures in communications, problems with risk assessment procedures, difficulties in weighing up the relative needs of parents and children, and the 'defensive' and highly politicised contexts in which services are delivered have all been highlighted by various commentators in this context (for example, Dingwall, Eekelar and Murray 1983; Parton 1985; Reder, Duncan and Gray 1993; Parton, Thorpe and Wattam 1997; Fitzgerald 1998).

Studies about families more generally 'in need' rather than specifically 'at risk', and studies that have canvassed the views of parents themselves, rather than practitioners, are rather thinner on the ground. Nevertheless, the body of work in this area is growing, and several recently published UK studies have explored support deficits from this perspective. Three strong themes are emerging in this developing literature. One is about 'inclusion', and relates to both semi-formal and formal services. Several studies have revealed that many non-users (or 'lapsed' users) of family support services do not take up the support on offer because they feel themselves to be excluded from the constituency at whom they assume services are aimed. For example, black parents may feel excluded from services they perceive as aimed at white families (Butt and Box 1999), and men often feel excluded from services they assume are designed for women (Ghate, Shaw and Hazel 2000a). A related theme is that of relevance. Previous studies have revealed that non-users often regard services as irrelevant to their needs, or as not offering what they themselves define as useful. For example, families in the wider community have described services perceived as 'for families with problems' (that is, at-risk families) as unlikely to provide anything appropriate to their more 'ordinary' needs (Smith 1996; Ghate, Shaw and Hazel 2000b; Pithouse and Holland 1999). Studies of fathers have shown that they feel services do not offer things that are salient to their interests as men (Ghate, Shaw and Hazel 2000a). Last, the third major theme is about power and control, and relates especially to formal services with statutory powers. These are often viewed as threatening to self-determination or, at least, as offering little in the way of benefits to offset the considerable costs of allowing professionals into one's personal life (Cleaver and Freeman 1985). Professionals are seen as taking a different view of family life and talking a different language to parents (Mayall 1990; Sefi 1988), and as undermining parents' sense of self-efficacy in the parenting role.

What did parents in this study of poor environments have to say about how well existing organised support services meet their needs? As we showed earlier, although the majority of users of both semi-formal and formal support services gave positive reports of their experiences and had found the services generally helpful, those actually using services were in the minority. Despite the substantial levels of need in the sample, large proportions of parents were not in touch with services currently and had not used organised support services in either the recent or distant past. To assess why this might be, we asked parents who were not using services about their reasons. We also asked former users of services what had disappointed them about the services in their area. Consonant with evidence that many parents in poor environments feel they are managing the demands of parenthood well and do not require external support, the most common reason for non-use of both semi-formal and formal services was in fact a fairly positive one: that parents hadn't felt the need for any help, support or information about being a parent from services of this kind (37% of those not using semi-formal services, and 56% of non-users of formal services). However, other parents gave responses to the question that are open, perhaps, to a more negative interpretation, and did indeed echo the themes emerging from previous studies. Substantial proportions of the parents we interviewed mentioned issues of inclusion, relevance and autonomy, and – especially where formal services were concerned – there was a widespread perception of services as 'missing the mark' in terms of providing timely, practical and above all unthreatening help.

Missing the mark: services that fail to meet parents' needs

When we asked parents who had not used semi-formal support services and those who had not used formal services for their reasons, over a quarter (28%) in both groups said that 'none of the services on the list offered anything they were interested in'. On the same theme, a further one in ten (11% and 10% respectively for the two groups) thought that 'none of the services on the list is suitable for someone like me'. Smaller proportions (8% of non-users of semi-formal services and 3% of those not using formal services) said it just hadn't occurred to them to contact such a service. Other reasons cited included 'not having the time' and being 'too embarrassed or shy'. All of these responses suggest, perhaps, that services may not always offer the kind of help parents might welcome or recognise as appropriate or worthwhile. Consistent with the themes of 'inclusion' and 'relevance', they suggest that people may be dissuaded from approaching services for support because they do not see themselves as part of the natural constituency of that service.

Table 9.4 shows these data.

Table 9.4 Reasons for not using semi-formal and formal family support services		
	% of parents	
	Non-users of semi-formal services (*n* = 863)	**Non-users of formal services (*n* = 687)**
Haven't needed any help, support or information	37	56
None of services offers anything of interest	28	28
None of services is suitable for someone like me	11	10
Haven't ever thought about it before	8	3
Haven't had the time	5	2
Don't know how to get in touch with services	5	3
Too expensive (charges or travel costs)	3	–
Too embarrassed or shy	2	1
Too difficult to get to	1	1
Don't want child to mix with other children who use services	1	–
Don't want to mix with other adults who use services	1	1
Other reasons	19	11

Note: Respondents could give more than one reason.

More detailed discussions with parents who had in fact used services, but who had less positive experiences than the majority of users, were also illuminating in elaborating these issues. Parents who rated a formal service as 'very' or 'fairly' unhelpful were asked their reasons[9] (see Figure 9.3).

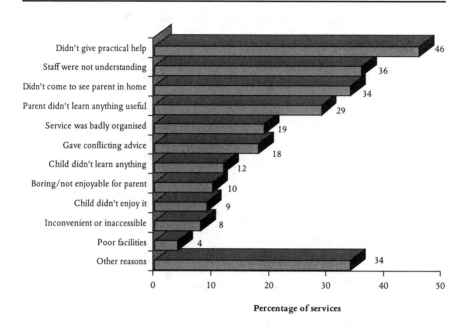

Base = 114 instances of rating formal services as 'unhelpful'

Figure 9.3 Reasons for finding formal services unhelpful

As can be seen from the figure, lack of practical value was a common complaint; nearly half of those who found a service unhelpful (46%) felt like this because the service 'did not give practical help'. In over one-third of cases (36%), the fact that the service did not make home visits was cited as unhelpful. In 29 per cent of cases, parents rated the service as poor because they hadn't learned anything useful. In terms of relevance to parents' own self-defined needs, some respondents thought that the practical value of help given by organised services was limited because service providers had an agenda for support that did not necessarily correspond to their own. Parents doubted that their self-assessed needs would really inform the action taken by professionals. As a result, some commented that they didn't think it was worth contacting services because the support offered was unlikely to be on the terms most appropriate to them.

> It's sort of like … say if you were moving into a house and it was all decorated and you needed help to move the furniture in and somebody came along and said, 'Well, I've come to help, but I'm going to paint that wall' –

it'd be of no use to you. Basically sometimes social services and things are a bit like that. Rather than saying, 'I'm here to help, you've got me for an hour, what do you want me to do?' (so that I could say), 'Well … (if I've got you for an hour I could do with you to sit with [child] while I go down town and pay bills what need to be paid, and do this, that and the other', [instead] they'll come and say 'We'll do blah and blah' And you're thinking, 'Well, great, but none of it is relevant to my situation.'

(Father, difficult child, sick child)

Sometimes the lack of relevance to families' lives lay mainly in the insufficiency of the resources offered by helping agencies. Often, these were so paltry it didn't seem worth the effort involved in asking for help in the first place.

So, I had a new-born baby which was tiny, Jack [child who had an accident] with body plaster on, and I broke my leg. And I lived in an upstairs flat and I asked for help from social services and they offered me (a home help) an hour a week. An hour a week! … Now, it took me that (long) to go to the bus stop. So I told them to stuff it … because I thought that was taking the Mick.

(Father, poor health, bad accommodation, lone parent, low income, sick child)

GPs in particular were criticised for this.

He (the GP) just makes me feel a bit uneasy. It's just as although he can't get me out of there (quick enough). I mean I was only in there a space of two minutes when we went last time.

(Mother, low income)

We have had some doctors who don't give you the time of day. I know they have a lot of patients to get through, but when you are talking to them they just don't want to know. They just say, 'Oh well, I'll prescribe this.' They don't even examine [the children].

(Father, difficult child)

Not surprisingly, then, dissatisfaction with lack of professionalism of some services also featured in the list of complaints: in just under one in five cases (19%) services were described as badly organised and, interestingly, one in six parents (18%) had found services unhelpful because 'they gave conflicting advice on different occasions'.

Last, some parents cited the inconvenience, or expense of services as a problem. Services were seen as aimed at those in higher income brackets, or at people who lived elsewhere. Although direct criticisms of semi-formal services were not prominent, when parents had decided not to utilise particular community-based services that they knew were available, the decision was usually explained in terms of these issues. For instance, one parent commented that an after-school club open to her son was too far away for him to come home from late in the evening.

> That [after-school club] is quite far (away), it's not here. It's quite far on the other side (of town), where their school is.
>
> *(Mother, large family)*

Another noted that although she had heard good things about a particular playgroup and felt that it would help her child's social and educational development, she couldn't justify the expense.

> If it's a full week – nine to five – it is expensive. It's like a full week's wage … It would be nice if we … could afford to do it.
>
> *(Mother, large family)*

Services that undermine autonomy, control and self-determination

Of all the issues that were perceived as problematic about the way in which services are currently delivered, one concern stood out: the fine dividing line between 'support' and 'interference', echoing the concerns that were raised in connection with accepting support from family members. This was particularly an issue when formal helping agencies were mentioned, where anxieties about autonomy and threats to self-determination (and self-respect) were uppermost in parents' minds.

We noted earlier that over one-fifth of parents (22%) agreed with the statement: 'Asking for help outside the family is a sign that a parent is not coping.' Apart from the possible social stigma that might attach to being labelled as 'not coping', some parents also felt that allowing professionals to get involved in family life carried a risk of losing control of what happened at home. Almost one-third of the sample (29%) agreed that 'if you ask for parenting advice from professionals like doctors or social workers, they start interfering or trying to take over'. On a similar theme, one in eight parents (12%) did not think that local professionals such as teachers or social services staff could be 'trusted to keep the things I tell them confidential'.

When a scale measuring attitudes to formal social support was derived by combining scores on these two statements,[10] scores ranged from 1 to 10, with a higher score indicating a more positive attitude towards formal support. The sample mean was 6.57. Unlike informal social support, however, although there was a slight substantive trend for parents with high levels of current problems to have more negative attitudes than those with lower levels,[11] the relationship between level of need (as measured by score on the Current Problems Questionnaire) and attitudes to formal support did not reach statistical significance.

Although in qualitative interviews parents criticised existing services for offering too little help, too much help (that is, interference) could also be problematic. Parents talked at length about worries that asking for help or assistance from support services could lead to being labelled as a struggling parent and result in unwanted attention. Social services were particularly feared in this regard.

> I think if you complain to them [social workers] too much they'll think you can't look after your children ... They'll keep coming up then (to the house) and making themselves a nuisance.
>
> *(Mother, difficult child, low income)*

> You hear all the stories about social services, 'They only come round to take your kids away because you're an unfit mother' and everything else. So I refused point blank to let them come in my house and take my kids, because as far as I was concerned I was their mother, and I was bringing them up the best way I could. I've seen how the social services work, (I knew) a family in my situation (who) have had social services in and they tried taking their kids ... And of course when someone turned round and said 'Well, we can get the social services in to help give you what you need', I refused point blank because of the stories that I've heard about them.
>
> *(Mother, reconstituted family, large family)*

Related to these comments, another major factor cited as unhelpful reflected respondents' feeling that services sometimes lacked understanding and respect for the realities of parent's lives. For example, in over one-third of cases in which formal services were found to be unhelpful, a reason given was that staff were 'not understanding or sympathetic' (36%). Parents found service staff could be patronising and lacking in respect for their situation. In qualitative interviews, a dominant theme was how professionals from formal helping agencies often failed to treat respondents as adults and as responsible parents. Complaints focused on parental concerns not being taken seriously, not being listened to, and on being patronised by service staff.

> I knew there was something wrong with [child], but it was just getting anyone to listen to me.
>
> *(Father, sick child)*

Sometimes professionals 'closed ranks' in the face of parents' concerns, as happened to this father with a two-year-old son whose problems were later labelled as severe 'global development delay':

> You go see your GP and that is where you seem to hit this barrier … We were getting the GP saying 'oh everything's okay', and feeling very frustrated because we knew things weren't okay … We saw several GPs in the same practice (and) one of the doctors said, 'It would be unprofessional to criticise a colleague, and after all he's your first child', which was infuriating. You couldn't get past this first step.
>
> *(Father, sick child)*

Feeling 'talked down to' was experienced as particularly undermining, and was apparently not an unusual experience when dealing with family support professionals. For example, it was suggested that some health visitors could be rather didactic, undervaluing the knowledge and abilities of parents, and there was definitely a perception among some parents that engaging formal support services could be a thoroughly demeaning experience.

> If they [health visitors] talked to you properly rather than *telling* me, it would be better … They think that you don't know [anything]. They seem to talk down to you as if to say 'You should be doing this'. They [think they] know better … They think that because you're young that you're stupid and don't know what you're doing.
>
> *(Mother, reconstituted family)*

> You don't want to sponge off the social. But, I tell you something, they make you feel degraded ... I went down there with my daughter a couple of weeks ago and I felt like saying to them 'Stick it, keep it' – because they talk to you ... like they're giving it out of their (own) pockets, not the Government's ... You get on the phone to them ... and their attitude is disgusting ... They make you feel ... belittled.
>
> *(Mother, lone parent)*

Some parents also reported that they were made to feel like 'bad parents' when contacting formal support services. They described professionals as undermining rather than supporting them when they sought help with a problem.

> I think they could have been more reassuring that they were acting on our behalf ... but you get the feeling that everybody is treated as if they are potential child abusers until they have proved otherwise. And then when they find out you are not, you are severely dumped and left to it.
>
> *(Mother, bad accommodation, lone parent)*

Because some parents felt that there might be negative consequences arising from involving support services, some preferred to battle on alone, without support.

> When I were first on my own, I were thinking 'Well, if anybody gets involved they're going to think I can't cope ... They're going to want to take (the) kids away from you.' Thinking things like that makes you decide that you don't *want* to have any help from anyone. And you've got nobody saying to you 'Well, that won't happen, they're just there to sort of give you a bit of help and somebody to talk to or whatever', so all sorts go through (your) mind: I know they did mine. I think that's why I mainly try to cope on my own.
>
> *(Mother, large family)*

Thus, the findings of this study in relation to deficits in support services provide very clear evidence that key issues, as far as parents in poor environments are concerned, are practical relevance, timeliness, autonomy and control. Unfortunately, many parents reported that their perceptions of semi formal – and especially formal – helping agencies were negative in these respects. They described services as providing too little help, of too little practical relevance, too late, and with such a heavy hand that parents felt undermined, belittled and even threatened. These are strong disincentives to seeking support from services.

However, while some of these perceptions were the direct result of personal contact with services, some appeared to have been formed at second and third hand and perhaps reflect the bad press that agencies get as much as agencies' actual records. It was interesting that although we found a strong relationship between high levels of need and negative attitudes to informal social support, the same clear relationship did not obtain for attitudes to semi-formal and formal social support. In other words (and perhaps contrary to how it may seem on the ground to hard-pressed agencies), in the case of service-based social support, those in greatest need were no less well disposed to services than anyone else. Services may perhaps be pushing at a door that is more open than they think.

Conclusions

What does this study tell us about the nature of support deficits for parents in poor environments? Since most parents reported relatively low levels of support at both the informal level and the organised level, perhaps what it tells us most clearly is that, in general, much parenting in poor environments is taking place as a relatively unsupported activity. Not that this is necessarily perceived as problematic: slightly less than half the sample overall said they were conscious of wishing for more help – perhaps a surprisingly low proportion given the demands that parenting can place on the most resilient and affluent individuals. However, this is only half the picture. Some parents definitely do feel unsupported and wish for more external help.

Community-level explanations for support deficits turning on the concept of social disorganisation and lack of social capital in poor environments have been given much prominence in the literature since the early 1980s. They may perhaps explain differences in social support (if they exist) between 'poor' and 'affluent' neighbourhoods – we cannot comment from the results of this study. What we can say is that, within poor environments, the type of area, as measured by our PPE-Index, does not appear to explain variations in actual or perceived support levels. Parents in the poorest neighbourhoods do not report getting less enacted support, nor do they feel less supported than parents elsewhere. Put simply, in our study, social support deficits did not appear to be explained by community-level poverty. If not to community, then, where do we look for explanations for support deficiencies within the sample? The answer – strongly evidenced by both survey and qualitative data – appears to lie in the affiliative aspects of support: in how support feels, what it implies, and how it defines and constructs relationships between individuals and within communities.

Much of what has been written about social support (whether informal, or provided by organised agencies) assumes without question that support must be an entirely good thing – especially for families living in the sorts of disadvantaged neighbourhoods covered in this study. Our data demand that we question this assumption – we picked up strong indications that in fact many parents perceived a definite downside to asking for or receiving support. Although undoubtedly valued by many, parents were also aware that support could have a negative valence. Accepting informal social support, for example, could lead to loss of privacy, loss of control over what happened in one's home and, if friends or neighbours were involved, immediately involved the recipient in a chain of reciprocal favours that could be stressful to maintain. Semi-formal and especially formal support potentially exposed one to social stigma as well as the risk of professional interference. This could lead to being patronised and undermined and, at worst, to loss of control over one's children. Support, viewed from this perspective, looks distinctly disempowering. No wonder, then, that half the sample said they did not want any external help with parenting.

Our findings were particularly interesting, however, in relation to the association between 'need' and 'support'. The study showed that those who did express a desire for more help tended to be the parents with the highest levels of need, as measured by multiple indicators of risk. These results are consistent in most respects with other studies exploring the characteristics of parents who report feeling socially unsupported; for example, Quittner, Glueckauf and Jackson (1990) reported that chronic parenting stress (that is, exposure to risk factors such as the ones we measured) was associated with low perceptions of emotional support, and in Garbarino and Sherman's important study of high and low risk areas for maltreatment (1980), parents who described low levels of social support in their area, although comparable in terms of income to other parents, were in fact experiencing higher levels of stressors across a range of dimensions. The study also showed that parents who wanted more support were, paradoxically, the greater consumers of support at both the informal and organised levels. Again, these results are consistent with other studies that have explored the relationship between consumption of services and perceptions of social support; Telleen (1990), for example, reported that mothers seeking help by participating in a family support programme in the United States were more likely to express a need for social support with parenting than mothers not using support services.

Compared to other parents, then, although needy parents reported receiving more enacted support at the informal level and greater use of organised support services, they nevertheless reported that they did not feel well supported in a general sense. They also tended to have more negative attitudes to support, at least where informal support was concerned. Although these findings echo those in the wider literature on at-risk parents and social isolation in that high-need parents appear to be less positive about support than other parents in the community, we have suggested different explanations for this than some previous studies. Rather than necessarily implying some deficiency in personality or social competence on the part of high-need parents, our data seem to suggest that the association between need and negative attitudes may equally well be explained by levels of exposure to the unpleasant side effects of social support, as by personality or temperamental disposition. Because high-need parents are more dependent on, and greater consumers of social support, they are also more likely to experience its negative aspects. It is perhaps an understandable – if intractable – fact that those with multiple problems may be the least able to be supported within the community by naturally occurring networks. Paradoxically, high-need parents have the most to gain, and the most to lose, from accepting social support. In a context in which many parents are unsure about the relative benefits and costs of accepting support, needy parents perhaps feel even more exposed than most and are also less able to cope with the reciprocity clearly implied in informal social support relationships.

More encouraging, perhaps, from a policy perspective, is our finding that, as a group, needy parents did not appear to be as hostile (relatively speaking) to organised support as they were to informal support. This may be precisely because this is a form of social support in which there are greater expectations of confidentiality and no expectations at all of reciprocity. It appears, then, that these families are the natural constituency of organised support services. They have the greatest need, and are the least likely to be able to get their needs met from within their own personal networks. Services, however, both in health and social welfare, often let these families down, as the many stories told to us in depth interviews attested. In poor environments the reputation of some services as agents of control rather than sources of support, with their own agendas and a lack of respect for parents' own skills and views, preceded them. It is this credibility gap that perhaps presents the greatest barrier to providing adequate support to those who need it.

In Part V, we return to the findings on services to explore from a more constructive basis what parents say they want, and how they would prefer organised services to be delivered. First, however, we focus in more detail on the balance between risk and resilience in poor environments. We explore the role of support in coping with parenting in poor environments, to try and understand what distinguishes those who cope, and those who do not.

Notes

1. We asked parents: 'Thinking about your current situation, do you ever wish you had some additional help or support in being a parent?'

2. A differences of means test showed that the mean Malaise score for parents who felt unsupported was 5.56 compared to 3.81 for those who felt well supported ($p<0.0001$)

3. Whereas having a teenager in the household was significantly associated with not wanting more help.

4. Analysed in a different way, the mean CPQ score for those who felt unsupported was 2.46 compared with 1.33 for those who felt supported ($p<0.0001$).

5. Two by three cross-tabulation of the three-way banding (Index Band) by wish for support/no wish for support: $p = 0.321$. Difference of mean Index score for two groups (wish for support/don't wish for support): $p = 0.189$.

6. Response categories for the outcome/dependent variable (rating of the area) were: Very good, fairly good, neither good nor bad, fairly poor and very poor. Independent variables were PPE-Index band, coded as 1 = poor, 2 = very poor, 3 = extremely poor ($p<0.0001$); and whether wishes for support (i.e. feels unsupported) coded as 1 = feels unsupported, 0 = feels supported ($p<0.0001$.)

7. See Appendix 3 for details of how the scale was constructed.

8. As noted earlier, we did not measure temperament or personality in this study, and so we cannot of course comment conclusively on how they might contribute to

negative attitudes to social support. It may be that evidence in this regard might modify the picture, for example by showing that temperament operates alongside social circumstances to influence attitudes to support. Further research would be necessary to explore this hypothesis.

9. There were very few cases of finding semi-formal services unhelpful ($n = 32$), therefore only responses in relation to formal services were analysed.

10. Response categories were: strongly agree, tend to agree, neither agree nor disagree, tend to disagree, or strongly disagree (plus don't know/no opinion); see Appendix 3 for further details of how the scale was constructed.

11. Mean attitude scores for the three CPQ bands were as follows: low = 6.67; medium = 6.54; high = 6.49. $p = 0.351$.

Part Four
Risk, Support and Coping

You just deal with things. It might be hard … but you just deal with it. There's nothing I'd like more than for me to say [to the children], 'Right, I'll give you better things in life and [let] you know a better life'. But that'll never happen.

(Mother, lone parent, difficult child, low income)

Sometimes you are just scraping through.

(Mother, lone parent, large family, difficult child, health problem, low income)

One of the aims of this study was to explore how parents in poor environments cope with the challenges and stresses of parenting in less than ideal circumstances and to determine what factors within parents' personal and social circumstances are most closely associated with coping better or worse. The data reported in Part II testify to the wide prevalence of disadvantage for both children and parents in this sample as compared with nationally representative samples in the UK. Yet, as we showed in Part III, although some parents admit to struggling under a burden of problems and actively wish for more help, others report that they are managing fine. We hoped, therefore, to find out more about what influences parents' perceptions of whether or not they are coping.

'Coping' – both conceptually and operationally – proved one of the most challenging issues to explore within the study. Although the term is used with some frequency in both lay and professional discourses about parenting, conceptually, the definition of coping in relation to parenting is ill-defined and has received comparatively little theoretical or empirical attention in the literature. There is, for example, no widely accepted definition of what constitutes 'coping' as a parent, nor even a consensus on what specific dimensions of parenting or child care would be taken account of in determining whether an individual was coping or not. In the context of parenting, coping – or rather, not coping – often appears to be defined, by default, in relation to a specific, negative outcome. Evidence of child maltreatment, for example, or a breakdown in parental mental health may be taken as an indication of failure to cope. In child protection work, for example, practitioners are making implicit judgements about coping every day: if a child is fed, clothed, clean and seemingly well-adjusted, the parent is probably 'coping'. If, on the other hand, the child is dirty, undernourished or displaying emotional or conduct problems, the parent may not be coping and intervention may be required.

When coping is defined in terms of outcomes, the concept becomes more or less interchangeable with the concept of 'resilience': the maintenance of good outcomes despite a background of adversity commonly associated with the reverse. Luthar, Cicchetti and Becker (2000) for example define resilience as 'a construct connoting the maintenance of positive adaptation by individuals despite experiences of significant adversity', a definition that has much in common with what Lazarus and Folkman (1984) have described as a 'vernacular' conception of coping which says that if a person has coped, the demands of a particular situation have been successfully overcome, whereas to say a person did not cope suggests ineffectiveness or inadequacy. Although writers such as Lazarus and Folkman have been critical of the conflation of 'coping' with 'outcome', it must be said that, in the context of practice in parenting support and child care, outcome as an indication of coping efficacy remains of obvious value in identifying situations where intervention may be helpful and is critical for monitoring the effectiveness of interventions designed to enhance coping skills.

Alternatively, coping can be defined more in terms of a strategy or a style than as an measurable outcome. Thus 'coping with parenting' may refer to how families or individual carers respond to a particular set of stressors or risk factors. To build on an ethological concept, coping is here defined as a dynamic process of adaptation to stress – something that promotes survival in the face of a changing, and threatening environment. However, the added 'human' context implies that active, effortful cognitive processes are involved in addition to the automatised adaptive behaviour of animals. In fields such as health psychology that have studied coping in far more detail than is the case for research on parenting, coping has been fruitfully conceptualised in this way. This has led to the development of instruments for measuring strategies or 'coping styles' such as the 'Ways of Coping' scale (Lazarus and Folkman 1984), and a helpful distinction between 'problem-focused' forms of dealing with stress (that is, coping that is directed at managing or altering the problem causing the distress) and 'emotion-focused' forms (that is, coping that is directed at regulating an individual's emotional response to a problem). Importantly, these models for thinking about coping have helped to press home the message that coping style is context and situation dependent and that it is not necessarily stable or trait based. Thus, although individuals may be predisposed to certain coping styles by virtue of personality attributes particular to them, coping styles may also shift with time and context. This body of work has also elucidated the difference between 'cognitive style' and 'coping style', allowing consideration of how social context (environments, resources) may influence capacity to cope in addition to the influence of individual attributes such as personality, temperament or personal history.

In the chapters that follow, therefore, we address the issue of coping with parenting in poor environments both in terms of both 'outcomes' *and* 'strategies'. We explore what risk factors or stressors are associated with poor coping outcomes, but also try to identify what protective or buffering factors appear to be operating in the lives of copers. In terms of outcomes, was 'coping' merely the reverse of 'not coping', predicted by a lower level of risk, or was there something additional involved? In terms of strategies, what approaches did parents report when dealing with the stresses they faced – for example, low income, poor housing conditions, challenging child behaviour, high levels of emotional stress, and of course living in a poor neighbourhood? To what extent were their strategies problem focused or emotion focused? Does social support enhance coping at all, and if so, how? In Chapter 10, we explore the risk and protective factors associated with different coping outcomes, and in Chapter 11 we describe the strategies that parents reported for dealing with the challenges they faced. Last, in Chapter 12 we revisit social support to explore how support – or aspects of support – interact with coping.

It should be noted that we have taken a very broad, 'global' approach to defining and describing coping in relation to parenting. The measure of coping that we used, which is described in the next chapter, was intentionally a simple and summative one. However, by using a condensed measure like this rather than unpacking coping into its component dimensions, we inevitably lose much of the richness that would be captured by a more fine-tuned exploration. The 'global' quality of our measure inevitably conflates the many and varied dimensions of parenting into a single 'overview' measure, and it is possible that had we focused in on specific, separate dimensions of the parenting role, we might have produced different results. Moreover, the study was not intended to be an in-depth study of coping style and coping outcomes, and the cross-sectional design of the study and its intentionally wide focus do not allow us to comment on the direct relationship between coping strategies or styles and the outcomes for parents and children. For example, we are unable to comment, from our data, on how coping styles may shift over time and in response to changing circumstances. To do this would require a more detailed exploration so that strategies and outcomes could be meaningfully related within specified contexts and situations. It would also, ideally, require prospective follow-up of cases to establish the temporal sequence in families' lives, in terms of onset of risk and the development of strategies for coping, before we could comment definitively on what 'causes' coping or not coping with parenting. Indeed, good instruments for measuring coping with the specific challenges of parenting (either in terms of outcomes or strategies) have not yet been developed in this field, and until they are, our understanding of this area will remain somewhat sketchy. Coping style, for example, is likely to be related to endogenous factors (such as personality or temperament) as well as learnt, and in the particular context of parenting can be expected to develop as a dynamic process in response to a wide range of factors connected both with the child and with the external environment. To define and measure the key dimensions properly is therefore a challenging theoretical and methodological task beyond the scope of the present study, and thus our attempts to explore coping in this study must be seen in the context of a new and still developing field of enquiry.

CHAPTER TEN

Coping and Not Coping

In this chapter we explore the background factors associated with coping outcomes. The measure of coping that we chose was a subjective, 'macro' one: parents' own judgement of whether and to what extent they were managing the demands of parenting in a global sense. Asked almost at the end of the survey interview, after respondents had reflected in detail on their personal circumstances and experiences of parenting, the question was intended to sum up parents' overall sense of how they were performing in this most challenging of all roles. We asked them to choose between four statements that best described 'how you are coping with parenthood these days'.[1] The statements were selected to recognise a range of possible situations, from generally coping well, to generally not coping well, and were as follows:

- I am coping pretty well with being a parent; things rarely get on top of me.
- Sometimes I feel I'm coping well, but sometimes things get on top of me.
- I hardly ever feel I'm coping well.
- I'm not coping at all these days.

Overall, the results showed that just under half of the sample (46%) thought that they were generally coping well, and only a very small proportion admitted to generally coping badly or not at all (2%). A slight majority of parents (52%) put themselves somewhere in the middle; sometimes coping but sometimes not, suggesting that for many parents, sense of coping is a fluid rather than stable attribute; a finding very much in tune with the work of key writers on coping such as Lazarus and Folkman (1984) (Figure 4.1).

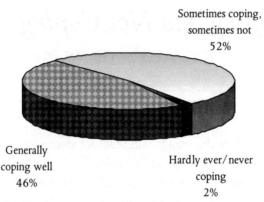

Sometimes coping,
sometimes not
52%

Generally
coping well
46%

Hardly ever/never
coping
2%

Base = 1736.

Figure 10.1 Coping with being a parent

For the purposes of subsequent analysis, we grouped parents who said they were generally coping well under the label 'coping well' (or 'coping more'). We grouped parents who said they were only sometimes coping, or hardly ever or never coping, under the label 'coping less'. Occasionally, for brevity, we also refer to these two groups as 'copers' and 'non-copers'.

Factors associated with coping

Several distinct groups of variables discriminated significantly between those who were coping well and those who were not. Located across all levels of the ecological model, we found these were most meaningfully grouped for analysis as: factors that were directly poverty related; factors that were related to child characteristics; and those related to parent characteristics. Factors related to social support variables are not discussed here, but are analysed separately in Chapter 12.

Factors related to poverty at the community and household level

Poverty and disadvantage at both the community and at the family and household level significantly discriminated between the two groups.

Those coping less well were living in areas that had a higher mean score on the PPE-index (mean score 184 compared to 178; $p<0.001$), and a group had a lower median household income than those coping more (£6508 compared to £7934; $p<0.0001$).[2] By way of illustration, Table 10.1 shows the proportions of parents who were coping well or coping less in the very poorest areas and in the very lowest income quintile. As the table also shows, rating the area as a 'bad' place to bring up a family, having accommodation problems and feeling that the family was not managing financially were also particularly powerful as indicators of coping less.

Table 10.1 Coping well or coping less, by poverty-related, child-related and parent-related risk indicators		
	% of parents	
	Coping well	Coping less
Poverty-related indicators		
Lives in extremely poor area (PPE-index band 3, $n = 569$)	41	59*
Rates neighbourhood as poor ($n = 308$)	36	64**
Low income (lowest quintile in sample, $n = 288$)	37	63**
Family 'not managing' financially ($n = 387$)	32	68**
Accommodation problems ($n = 711$)	41	59**
Child-related indicators		
Large family ($n = 428$)	37	63**
Pre-school child at home ($n = 820$)	42	58*
Sick child in household ($n = 702$)	41	59**
'Difficult' index child ($n =211$)	22	78**
Parent-related indicators	39	61**
Lone parent ($n = 668$)		
High Malaise score (score 8+, $n = 355$)	25	75**
High level of current problems (CPQ score 3+, $n = 521$)	29	71**
All respondents ($n = 1736$)	46	54

* = $p<0.01$; ** $p<0.001$.

Child factors

Cross-sectional analysis also showed that a number of child-related factors at both the individual and the family level were consistently significantly related to how the parent was coping. For example, the fewer dependent children in the household, the more likely to be coping well. Those coping well had a mean family size of 1.83, compared to 2.10 for those who said they were coping less ($p<0.001$). Chi-squared tests also showed that having a 'large family' (three or more children under 16 in the home) was related to coping less. Parents with pre-school children in the home were more likely to report problems in coping, as were those who had a long-term sick child in the household. Having a 'difficult' child was the most strongly discriminating factor of all, with only 47 out of 211 of these parents reporting coping well.

Parent characteristics

A number of parent characteristics also showed a significant relationship to our global measure of coping. For example, lone parents were far less likely to be coping than parents with partners, and self-reported mental or emotional health problems were indisputably a key indicator of not coping: the mean Malaise score for those generally 'coping well' was 3.34, compared to a much higher 5.79 for those 'coping less' ($p<0.001$).[3] Following a similar pattern, the mean score on the Current Problems Questionnaire (CPQ) for copers was 1.33, compared to 2.33 for others ($p<0.001$), indicating that the more numerous were parents' personal and family problems, the less likely they were to feel they were coping. It is worth commenting that there were no differences between parents according to ethnic group, however; minority ethnic parents were no less likely to be coping than white parents.

The 'key' predictors of coping

The highly compound nature of all these variables requires us to try and disentangle which are the key factors and which show statistical associations with coping primarily due to some other, shared, underlying factor. Therefore, in order to determine which of these many factors were independently associated with coping, we built a series of logistic regression models in which the groups of variables were entered as co-variates, with coping as the dependent or outcome variable.[4] This enabled us to control for 'overlap' between highly correlated variables (for example, accommodation problems and household income) in order to determine how each factor contributed to the chances of a parent experiencing difficulties with coping over and above the other significant factors that affected coping.

In the 'poverty' group of variables, only whether managing financially or not, and household income, were independently significant at the 99 per cent confidence level, with the odds of not coping well being nearly doubled if the parent also felt the family was *not* managing financially (see Table 10.2).[5] Community level variables (area of residence, and rating of the area as a place to bring up a family) ceased to be independently significant once household poverty was controlled for.

Table 10.2 Role of poverty-related risk factors in predicting not coping with parenting	
	Odds ratio
Whether family managing financially	1.85***
Household income	1.00*
Accommodation problems	1.25 (n/s)
Area of residence (PPE-Index score)	1.00 (n/s)
Rating of area as place to bring up family	1.18 (n/s)

Base = 1448 * = $p<0.01$; *** = $p<0.0001$; n/s = not significant

Among the group of child-related factors, family size (entered as a continuous variable – the number of dependent children in the home) and having a 'difficult' index child emerged as the strongest predictors of not coping. Effectively, what the results tell us is that for each additional dependent child in the home, the odds of not coping rose by a fifth.[6] Strikingly, having a difficult index child meant that the parent was nearly three and a half times more likely to feel they were not coping than would be the case were the child not displaying conduct or emotional problems. (See Table 10.3.)

Table 10.3 Role of child-related risk factors in predicting not coping with parenting

	Odds ratio
'Difficult' index child	3.45***
Number of children in family	1.23**
Pre-school child in household	1.21 (n/s)
Sick child in household	1.21 (n/s)

Base = 1404; ** = $p<0.001$; *** = $p<0.0001$; n/s = not significant

In the case of parent characteristics, being a lone parent, having a high Malaise score and having a high level of current problems all contributed independently to not coping (Table 10.4). The odds of not coping were two and a half times greater for a parent who reported high scores on either the Malaise Inventory or the Current Problems Questionnaire than for a parent who did not. Lone parents were one and a half times more likely not to be coping than parents with a partner. Moreover, the additional 'risk' to coping added by being a lone parent was not explained by the fact that lone parents are also more likely to be poor parents. When we ran marital status together with household income in a separate logistic regression model to predict not coping, both variables remained independently significant, and being a lone parent still increased the odds of not coping by 40 per cent (odds ratio = 1.41; $p = 0.0033$).

Table 10.4 Role of parent characteristics in predicting not coping with parenting

	Odds ratio
High Malaise score (score 8+)	2.53***
High level of current problems (CPQ score 3+)	2.51***
Lone parent	1.53**

Base = 1729 ** = $p<0.001$; *** = $p<0.0001$

To determine the significance of all these independently important factors relative to one another, we put them together in a further logistic regression model. A striking result was that, at this point, the two most directly poverty-related variables – household income and whether managing financially – 'dropped out' of the model as significant predictors of not coping. It appears, then, that although income is very strongly associated with all five key risk factors when individual cross-tabulations or differences of means tests are carried out, the fact that it so strongly underlies other risk factors means that, of itself, it ceases to be a useful predictor of coping as we move further and further along the 'pathway' to coping. In other words, within poor environments, relative poverty appears to act as a distal more than a proximate indicator of coping.

Table 10.5 Role of key risk factors in predicting not coping with parenting	
	Odds ratio
'Difficult' index child	2.75***
High level of current problems (CPQ score 3+)	2.30***
High Malaise score (score 8+)	2.01***
Lone parent	1.45*
Number of children in family	1.33***
Whether family managing financially	1.47 (n/s)
Household income	1.00 (n/s)

Base = 1167; * = $p<0.01$; *** = $p<0.0001$; n/s = not significant

In summary then, although a number of factors were associated at some level with differential coping outcomes, certain key factors appeared to be critical. Put another way, although many variables were part of the 'pathway' to not coping, as we progressively controlled for the overlaps between them the number of key variables that remained independently significant was reduced. The final results indicated that the odds of not coping well in poor environments were particularly increased for parents if they had greater numbers of dependent children, had a 'difficult' child, exhibited a tendency to depression as measured by high Malaise Inventory score, reported high levels of personal and family difficulties on the Current Problems Questionnaire, or were parenting alone.

Moreover, although each of these factors independently heightened the likelihood that a parent would feel they were having difficulties in coping, in combination, the effect of having more than one of these problems could be considerable. While only just over one-quarter of parents with none of these problems (36%) reported that they were not coping well, among parents with just *one* of these problems 47 per cent were not coping, and among those with *three* problems, the proportion not coping rises to 79 per cent. Although the bases become small for the latter groups (those with four to five problems), it can be seen from Figure 10.2 that the proportion of parents who were not coping rose dramatically with increasing burden of problems ($p<0.0001$). Risk factors included: difficult index child, high Malaise score, high CPQ score, large family, lone parent family. Note that numbers for four and five factors have been combined due to small bases ($n = 62$ respondents with four risk factors, $n = 7$ with all five factors).

Further, in a more sophisticated and finely calibrated logistic regression analysis of the effect of the total number of problems on 'not coping' as an outcome, the odds ratio was 1.99 ($p< 0.0001$), indicating that for each additional problem experienced by parents, the chances of not coping were almost doubled. Of course, this analysis does not control for problems other than those on this list that affect coping, but it gives us a vivid indication of how problems can 'pile up' to reduce parents' sense of being able to manage their lives.

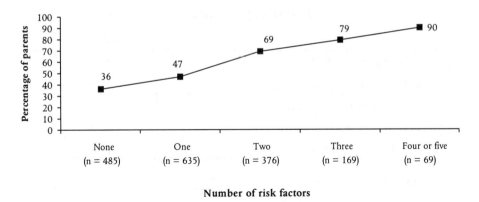

Figure 10.2 Not coping with parenting, by cumulative burden of problems

Protective or positive factors, versus risk factors

Next, to explore whether the factors that predicted coping were the same as, or different to, the key factors that predicted not coping, we also calculated the odds of coping when the factors were reversed or recast as 'protective' factors. By 'protective' we mean not that the presence of these factors would altogether prevent a parent having difficulties in coping, but that their presence might enhance the odds of coping; that is, we use 'protective' in the sense of stress-*buffering*, not stress-*preventive*. Thus, we entered into a logistic regression model with 'coping well' as the outcome:[7] having a partner as opposed to parenting alone; having an 'easy' or average child as opposed to having a 'difficult' child; having a 'small' family (two or less children) rather than three or more children; having a low rather than a high Malaise score (score of 4 or less); and having a zero rather than a high score on the Current Problems Questionnaire. As can be seen in Table 10.6, each of these factors positively and significantly contributed to the odds of coping in a pattern that more or less mirrored the results in relation to coping difficulties:

Table 10.6 Role of various 'protective' factors in predicting coping with parenting	
	Odds ratio
Easy or average index child	2.84***
Low Malaise score (score 4 or less)	2.40***
Low level of current problems (CPQ score 0)	1.71***
Small family (two or less children)	1.70***
Parent with a (resident) partner	1.63***

Base = 1402; *** = $p<0.0001$

In much the same way that risk factors accumulated to heighten the likelihood that a parent would report difficulties in coping, so positive factors accumulated to increase the likelihood of coping well. The proportions of parents who were coping rose substantially with increasing number of positive factors, so that while less than one in four parents with *none or one* of these positive factors (18%) reported that they were coping well, getting on for twice as many parents with two of the factors (31%) were coping, and the figures for those with three and four protective factors were 49 per cent and 63 per cent respectively. Among those with all five protective factors nearly three-quarters of parents (73%) said they were coping well with parenting ($p<0.0001$). Looked at using a logistic regression analysis in which total number of positive factors was used as the independent variable and 'coping' was the outcome variable, the odds ratio was 1.89 ($p<0.0001$), indicating that for each additional positive factor present in parents' lives, the chances of coping with parenting were almost doubled.

We also tested for a number of additional variables that might potentially have a positive effect on coping with parenting, based on previous literature. However, we found no evidence from our data that any of these factors independently enhanced coping (other than support factors, which are discussed in Chapter 12). For example, some writers have suggested that working – providing it is reasonably satisfying and not overly stressful in itself – may be protective against parenting difficulties, not only because it raises the family income but also because it enhances the general psycho-social well-being of parents (see Belsky and Vondra 1989 for a discussion). Other studies, finding that low maternal educational attainment is associated with elevated rates of maltreatment of children, appear to suggest that higher educational attainment might protect against parenting difficulties (Garbarino and Kostelny 1992). In our study, both working full- or part-time and educational level ('A' level equivalent or higher) indeed showed a significant association with coping when cross-tabulated individually against coping, using the chi-square test. However, once these factors were added into a logistic regression model that included the key protective factors identified in Table 10.6, and which controlled for household income (likely to be a key correlate of educational attainment and working status), neither factor reached significance as an independent predictor of coping.[8] Thus in this sample, any 'pro-coping' effect of working or higher educational attainment could not be disentangled from the fact that working and more highly educated parents were also those with higher household incomes. Once we controlled for income, neither working nor better educational levels seemed to add anything to the odds of coping well with parenting in a poor environment.

Conclusions

In this chapter we have explored the relationship of various factors to coping with parenting, other than those factors connected with support. Our results showed that a relatively small group of key factors, all connected with the attributes of parents or their children, acted to increase the risk that parents would report difficulties in coping. Conversely, the same factors, when absent or reversed, acted in a 'protective' or positive way to enhance the chances of reporting coping well. Despite exploration of the effects on coping of other potential risk and protective factors, after controlling for the underlying commonalties that variables shared, these same few variables consistently showed up as most strongly related to coping or not coping. Parenting alone, having a larger family and having a 'difficult' index child all increased the likelihood that a parent would not cope well, as did being in poor emotional health and having a high tally of current problems as measured by the CPQ. However, the relative poverty of the area in terms of our PPE-Index, parents' rating of the area as a good or bad place to raise a family, and families' own household income did not increased the odds of not coping once other factors were taken into account.

It is important to note that these results do not disconfirm any relationship between coping with parenting and poverty. On the contrary, although within poor environments relative poverty becomes gradually less significant as we dig deeper into the factors associated with coping as an outcome, poverty, as we showed in detail in Part II, is nevertheless strongly related to many of the risk factors – such as having a difficult child or having an elevated Malaise score – that appear as more proximate to coping in the analyses shown in this chapter. In other words, quantitatively speaking, within poor environments poverty appears to be important as a distal factor at an earlier point in the pathway to coping with parenting, although it may be less significant as a proximate indicator. Of course, if we had been able to compare these results with those from a sample of parents living in more affluent areas, we might have been able to say more about the threshold beyond which poverty 'kicks in' as a predictor of coping. Moreover, as we pick up in the next chapter, there may also be things to say about the qualitative rather than the quantitative relationship between poverty and coping that help to elaborate our understanding of the role of poverty-related variables.

We must of course acknowledge the possible limitations of our exploration of risk and protective factors in coping with parenting. In not measuring parents' personality, temperament, social competence, past history or a wealth of other individual or circumstantial characteristics we may of course be missing pieces of what is clearly a complex picture. The strong association between Malaise scores and perceptions of coping, for example, could be at least partially explained by the sense of helplessness that is characteristic of depression. It could also be the case that those who feel they cope less well do so because they are temperamentally or attitudinally more likely to have a negative outlook on life (known in the psychological literature as 'negative cognitive set'), and such a correlation might, for example, explain the very strong relationship between reporting having a 'difficult' child and coping less. In fact we had evidence in the study to suggest that the overlap between our global measure of perceptions of not coping with parenting and being generally more negative about other aspects of life was not necessarily very strong, even on purely attitudinal measures that we would expect to be sensitive to cognitive set.[9]

Moreover, the fact that we included a number of more 'objective' indicators of risk in our analyses (for example, household income, area of residence, marital status, number of children in the family) helps us to be more confident that negative cognitive set is not biasing our results and confounding our measure of coping. Therefore, we can say with some confidence that *within the context of poor environments*, the factors that we have highlighted in this chapter stood out very clearly as important indicators of coping and not coping. Moreover, the results concerning cumulative burden of problems and rising odds of not coping (and *vice versa*, for positive factors and odds of coping) follows a classic 'dose response' pattern, in the language of the natural sciences. The higher the level of problems (the 'dosage'), the greater the chances of a particular outcome or response (in this case, the likelihood of not coping). We can therefore also say with some confidence that not only are the risk factors highlighted in this chapter prejudicial to coping with parenting but also that a greater burden of problems may of itself lead to difficulties with coping. By the same token, the greater the number of positive factors in a parent's life, the more likely they are to be protected against difficulties with coping. We return to these results to consider their wider implications in terms of need in Part V. Before that, however, in the next chapter we explore qualitative data on parents' coping strategies, to flesh out these quantitative survey results.

Notes

1. The actual question read: 'Most people find being a parent has its ups and downs. Taking everything into account, which of these statements best describes how you are coping with parenthood these days?'

2. Mann-Whitney test.

3. Parents with physical health problems were also more likely to report not coping than those without health problems (57% compared to 51%), although the result just missed statistical significance at the 99 per cent level of confidence; $p = 0.011$.

4. 'Coping less (i.e not coping)' was coded as 1; 'coping well (i.e. coping)' was coded as 0.

5. Note that the odds ratios for some continuous variables (e.g. household income) are 1.00, despite being significant, as a function of the scaling (i.e. they consist of large numbers of closely spaced values).

6. When number of children was entered into the same model as a dichotomised variable ('large family' – 3 or more children – versus 'small family'), the odds of not coping were one a half times greater for parents with large families.

7. That is, 'coping well' was coded as 1; 'coping less' was coded as 0.

8. Working full- or part-time: $p = 0.8677$. 'A' level or higher qualifications: $p = 0.6705$. Household income: $p = 0.1695$.

9. For example, strikingly, there was no significant association between reporting having difficulties in coping with one or more children in the family and perceptions of coping with parenting more globally.

CHAPTER ELEVEN

Coping Strategies

Having identified some of the key factors associated with differences in coping outcomes in poor environments, we now turn to explore not just what makes a difference, but why. In particular, we were interested not just in enumerating the key risk and protective factors in poor environments but also in trying to understand more about why particular factors did or did not distinguish between the groups of parents who coped well and those who struggled. Such questions inevitably touch on the territory of coping styles, at least part of which are likely to be endogenous (for example, related to personality and temperament), and which were not formally measured as part of this study. However, our data do allow us to explore aspects of parental coping responses and strategies, and in this chapter we report on what parents did in response to the difficulties raised by their personal circumstances.

In fact, qualitative data that we collected on how parents dealt with life's daily challenges shed some interesting light on the quantitative findings reported in the previous chapter, and it became apparent that our earlier results in fact tell us as much about parents' coping skills as they do about the effects of life in a poor environment. We asked parents to tell us about what caused them most difficulties in daily life and how they dealt with problems. Did they have any special strategies that they used to get round difficulties or to deal with the stresses they encountered? What were their strengths, and what did they think they were particularly good at, in terms of parenting? What did they feel they did least well? What sorts of things really got them down, and what happened when they felt like this?

Space does not, of course, permit us to discuss the full array of data that was collected on coping strategies, which varied widely from one parent to the next and from one set of personal or family circumstances to the next. In this chapter, therefore, we focus only on the key themes that seemed to contribute most to an understanding of the more general issues facing parents in poor environments, and that enhance our understanding of the findings reported in Chapter 10. What we uncovered was considerable evidence of parents' resourcefulness and impressive coping skills in some respects but less successful coping strategies in others.

Coping with poverty

We reported in Chapter 10 that community and household-level poverty were distal but not proximate indicators of coping. However, qualitative data showed it would be wrong to assume that it is 'just as easy' to cope in a poor area, or on a low income, as it would be in more favourable circumstances. What we found, in fact, was that, on the contrary, it can be very hard work.

Coping with life in a poor environment

Parents adopted a range of active coping strategies to deal with the stresses that living in a poor neighbourhood entailed. For example, as we saw in Chapter 5, dog fouling was nominated as the single most pervasive nuisance for parents in poor areas. To get around this, parents described how, rather than taking children to play in public areas, they tried to find friends and neighbours with private gardens in order to let their children play outside safely and cleanly:

> I go to a friend's house most of the time.
>
> *(Mother, bad accommodation, ethnic minority)*

To circumvent the dangers to personal safety and to property of crime-ridden neighbourhoods, careful preparations were made and money was spent to keep family members safe.

> We go by the main roads, we travel on the main roads even if it's longer to get there. I have warned [child] about personal safety. I bought her a personal alarm. My mum bought both of us a mobile phone so that I can

now ring her [child] when she is late. And I encourage her when she can to get cabs.

(Mother, lone parent, low income, bad accommodation)

[We've] great big iron, thick bars across the windows so that if [burglars] did smash the window, [they wouldn't] be able to get in bodily, to get anything out.

(Mother, bad accommodation, large family)

And children, in particular, were given restrictions on where they could go unattended in their local neighbourhood.

My kids don't go out; my kids have got to stay on my street. We've got a football green and woods [nearby] [but] they're not allowed near them, they've got to stay at the top of the street ... It's sad, but there you go – this is the times we live in.

(Lone father)

Nevertheless, as we reported earlier, it was striking and perhaps rather surprising that the majority of parents in the sample were generally rather positive about their area as a place to live, with two-thirds (66%) saying their area was 'very' or 'fairly' good as a place to bring up a family. Although parents were well aware of the problems that existed around them, and often felt personally affected by them, problems were normalised and rationalised by respondents, many of whom accepted these deficiencies as an unavoidable part of life. Parents reconciled themselves to a variety of defects in their own familiar neighbourhood, reckoning that other areas in which they might live would be the same, or worse. For example, this mother expressed a commonly-held view that it was fanciful to expect to live in a crime- and drug-free environment.

It don't matter where [I could] go, there's drugs everywhere. Ideally I would like to live where there is no drugs, where there is no violence, no gangs, thugs – but that's living in my own fantasy world. There is nothing like that.

(Mother, low income, reconsitituted family)

Coping with poor accommodation

A common feature of life for families in poor neighbourhoods was substandard housing conditions, as we showed in Part II. However, although problems with accommodation loomed large in the study as a source of stress, many parents reported developing creative strategies to cope with the difficulties that poor housing created. For example, some parents undertook extensive, if amateur, remedial work on their homes.

> I've had to put sheets of wood around the wall where the [children's] beds are because the wall's soaking wet and it's black [from damp]. I've put a sheet of wood under one of the beds because the carpet's wet.
> *(Father, lone parent, bad accommodation, low income, sick child, poor health)*

Problems with inadequate or expensive heating were difficult to deal with on a low income, but respondents were thrifty in making the most of any heat in the home.

> I have to leave the kitchen door open, that's why the [child safety] gate's up in the kitchen, so if I'm cooking, the heat comes into [the living room]. While the tumble dryer is on, the door is open sometimes.
> *(Mother, bad accommodation)*

When all else failed, at a more fundamental level, for example, parents tried to cope by making children wear extra layers of clothing to combat cold and draughts, or encouraging children to share beds to keep warm at night.

> They was wearing coats day and night, jumpers, vests, coats, hats, scarves. You name it, they had it on. Blanket upon blanket on their beds. I mean these were only babies. It was just a case of wrapping them up and putting as much on them as you could … that's how cold it was, it was freezing.
> *(Mother, bad accommodation)*

> They all three sleep in with each other because they don't like it [in their own rooms] … it's too cold.
> *(Lone father)*

Coping with low income and financial strain

In addition to living in a poor area, the majority of the households in the study were living on incomes well below the national average. Given this fact, and the generally high levels of anxiety about financial matters, the fact that over three-quarters of the sample (77%) claimed to be 'managing very or fairly well', or 'getting by all right' financially itself suggests that the majority of families in the sample were 'copers' in this respect, and were implementing successful strategies for making a little go a long way. Indeed, parents in the sample considered themselves, by and large, highly successful in this regard. For example, when parents who said they were managing well or getting by all right were asked why they thought they were surviving financially, the most popular reason given was that the respondent considered herself or himself 'very good at managing money' (46% of those who were managing), followed closely by being careful 'not to waste things' (45%). Less than one-third of those who were managing financially attributed their success to having an adequate income; much more important in respondents' perceptions was the ability to juggle funds and exercise caution with money (see Table 11.1).

Table 11.1 Reasons for managing financially	
	% of parents
I am very good at managing money	46
We are careful about not wasting things	45
Income is enough for needs/ to cover commitments	29
Partner is very good at managing money	16
We get help from other members of the family	8
We have savings/investments to draw on when things get difficult	4
Some other reason/don't know	3

Base = 1362 parents who were 'managing financially'. Respondents could cite more than one reason

In part, parents' success at financial management could be attributed to the careful prioritisation of expenditure that we discussed in Part II. Given that, in total, nearly two-thirds of parents (62%) said that they could not afford at least one of the items of basic expenditure on our list in Chapter 4, not surprisingly, a lot of careful manipulation of limited funds went on in families in the sample. As we showed earlier, in poor families the first things to go are leisure and recreation activities, followed by heating and equipment, followed by clothing, followed by food. Parents overwhelmingly put children's needs first, so that the majority of the children in the sample were, despite low incomes, warmly clothed and adequately fed.

This was reflected in qualitative interviews. Parents were clear that they had to form financial priorities and organise their income accordingly.

> When I get my Family Allowance on a Monday, you just learn to sort of pull in your strings and think of the children. I make sure I pay my bills, get the food for the children and then whatever money is left, then perhaps I go out. If I've got no money left, I just don't go out.
>
> *(Mother, lone parent, low income, sick child)*

Some parents reported that it wasn't just luxury items that the adults in the family were expected to forgo. The order of priorities in families when it came to food and clothing was clear. Adults preferred to go without, or improvise, to ensure that the children were looked after properly.

> My husband hasn't even got a coat because I just haven't been able to buy him one. That's not fair I know, but it just means him having to wear two or three jumpers when he goes out in the winter just so they [children] can have school shoes.
>
> *(Mother, bad accommodation, large family)*

Many of the poorest parents were experts at controlling limited budgets. Some described careful systems that enabled them to meet all their necessary family costs.

> I'm very organised to be truthful. I've a tin upstairs, it's a big old biscuit tin that I've had for years. It's got envelopes in it and on every one I've got like 'gas', 'electric', 'rent', all things like that. And every week when we get paid that's the first thing I do. Jim goes to the bank and gets his wages, and I put money in the envelopes, [assigned] to what we have to pay out every week.
>
> *(Mother, large family, reconstituted family)*

Other parents explained how they 'juggled' the timing of when bills were paid to ensure that essential items could be afforded when necessary. As well as paying in small instalments for as many goods as possible, usually using mail order catalogues for this purpose, parents described how they helped to keep on top of finance by prioritising the most pressing expenses and stalling payment on others.

> You've got to juggle the bills so you can afford it. You just don't pay one bill and you leave it for a couple of weeks, so you can get [other] stuff that they need.
>
> *(Mother, low income)*

In addition, parents clearly spent a great deal of time and effort on getting to know where to pick up bargains in basic items – food or clothing – indeed, this was discussed at some length. Many parents could cite to the last penny the relative cost of a tin of baked beans or a pound of potatoes at different shops in their area.

> I get the Asda cornflakes because they're quite cheap and I get the big 750 gram [packet] ... and I get my milk from down there. I'm always looking around for bargains, because you can't always afford the expensive stuff. You have to go around and look ... I'll go around and I'll look for the [cheap clothes] that are around and about.
>
> *(Mother, bad accommodation, low income, poor health)*

Parents' strategic comparisons of shop prices meant that they were aware and taking advantage of different supermarkets' special offers. This mother describes how, with the help of her sister, she managed to stock up on essential food items when she realised that they were discounted for a limited period:

> We buy more of it because it's cheap, and we know that it's only going to be cheap this week. Instead of buying like four which lasts us like two weeks, we'll buy eight packets because we've got my sister's chest freezer as well as my fridge freezer ... that's going to stop me buying it at full price for the next few weeks.
>
> *(Mother, bad accommodation)*

Some parents also described how they took advantage of the second-hand market where possible, typically buying essential furniture or younger children's Christmas toys.

> With buying furniture, well, I never have new stuff. I only have second-hand stuff, say £50.00 for a settee. You can't buy new stuff.
>
> *(Father, lone parent, poor health, low income)*

In addition, parents described a host of inventive ways to help stretch low income in a variety of different parenting situations. For example, one mother outlined how she managed to deal with her child's unaffordable birthday request to take all his friends out for tea, by 'recreating' McDonalds at home:

> They wanted to go to McDonald's or something like that and I go, 'I can't afford it'. It's a lot of money. But what we did, we went to Farm Foods and bought the microwave chips and the burgers and the chicken burgers and done it like that [ourselves].
>
> *(Mother, bad accommodation, low income, poor health)*

Finally, qualitative interview data suggested strongly that, as with poverty and disadvantage at the community level, parents often tried to cope personally with the stresses of balancing the budget by facing household-level poverty as a part of a reality they 'just had to deal with'; in other words, by rationalising or normalising their experiences.

> You get a bill, you just deal with things. It might be hard, and I know I'm in debt and I've got catalogues, but you just deal with it. There's nothing I'd like more than for me to say [to the children], 'Right, I'll give you better things ... and (let) you know a better life'. But that'll never happen.
>
> *(Mother, lone parent, difficult child, low income)*

Coping with problems at the child and parent level

Coping with 'difficult' children

Parents often described themselves as coping reasonably successfully with the stress of living in a poor area or having a low income. However, as the results of Chapter 10 suggested, stressors connected with parent and child-related characteristics emerged as somewhat more challenging to parents' ability to cope. In particular, Chapter 10 showed that having a 'difficult' child was strongly predictive of difficulties with coping, and further survey data on living with difficult children confirmed this. Parents of difficult children were more likely to say they found their child 'hard work all or most of time' (30% compared with 9% of other parents; $p<0.001$). They were also less likely to feel able to solve problems with their child than other parents (39% said they 'rarely or never' felt they were able to solve problems with the index child compared to 17% of parents who did not have a difficult child; $p<0.001$). Not surprisingly, then, in qualitative interviews parents described difficult children as more fatiguing to care for. The strain of living with a child with emotional or behavioural problems seemed particularly intractable, and parents often said they felt they were not entirely successful at dealing with it. For example, many parents of younger children with behaviour problems suffered from chronic lack of sleep at night. This mother of a young hyperactive boy described how she was exhausted on the day of the fieldwork interview because he had kept her awake from the early hours of the morning:

> He was tapping like this (on the bedstead) and I said 'stop tapping', and he started clicking and making noises in his mouth. In the end then, you've just got to get up because he keeps on like that until you get up … it doesn't matter what time it is. If you don't, you've got the neighbours knocking the wall because of the noise.
>
> *(Mother, lone parent, low income, sick child, difficult child)*

Another mother of an extremely difficult child aged eleven years described how, in desperation, she would sometimes physically restrain her daughter from getting up in the night and wandering around the house:

> Some nights I tie my leg to her leg and stay in her bed all night to make her go to sleep, … to make sure she don't go downstairs to help herself to the food. I am actually learning about herb(s) to put around the room to help her relax … I tried heather in the bedroom, fresh heather that did relax, I changed the light bulb to blue and everyone looked at me suspicious. It's supposed to relax your mind.
>
> *(Mother, large family, sick child, difficult child)*

For parents of difficult teenagers, although, fatigue was generally less of an issue, behaviour problems were also described as especially intractable. Problems were often multiple and overlapping, and furthermore could bring conflict with external agencies such as schools, the police and courts, thus multiplying parents' sense of stress:

> The police station had got [15-year-old daughter] locked up for shoplifting. She should have been at school but she'd been shoplifting in Boots and they'd picked her up. Of course they wanted me to go … I was sitting waiting to go in to see her while they were interviewing her and I just

happened to say (to the policewoman) 'What did she shoplift?' 'Pregnancy testing kit ' [they said]. That's how I found out [she was pregnant]).

(Mother, large family)

Many parents described a sense of futility in trying to deal with older children's behaviour problems, which could be overwhelming at times.

> The issue was that she couldn't see why she couldn't come in at three o'clock in the morning, or half past five in the morning, and sometimes would take an hour to get from the gate to the front door, because either she was drugged up or drunk.
>
> *(Mother, sick child)*

> I spoke to him, told him he cannae do this. But it didnae make any difference, he just kept doing it. He was spoken to at the school, he was spoken to by me, and it didnae do any good.
>
> *(Mother, poor health, low income, difficult child, line parent)*

> Once or twice a week I burst into tears with him. When he don't listen ... and he just keeps on and on and in the end you just explode ... and I've got that wound up, sometimes, that frustrated, that you just burst into tears...
>
> *(Mother, difficult child, low income, sick child, lone parent)*

Coping with stress and depression, and multiple problems

In addition, although having a difficult child was definitely a threat to coping, as we showed in the previous chapter, having multiple personal problems was also strongly associated with coping difficulties. Qualitative interviews revealed that although parents described a range of coping strategies to deal with high levels of emotional stress due to problems in a number of areas of life, most had bad days and good days on this front. As one mother put it, beginning to cry during the interview as she talked about her financial problems, her truanting teenager, her absent partner and her desperate wish for a holiday:

> You have good days and bad days, don't you? I do have good days. I'm not always like this – you've just caught me on a bad day.
>
> *(Mother, difficult child, low income, lone parent)*

By far the most common strategy for dealing with intolerable levels of stress was to take time out for a short while. Parents described isolating themselves to give vent to stress in private or more safely, or distracting themselves by focusing on something other than the source of stress.

> I find it's better shutting yourself off sometimes from them ... otherwise it could really drive you crackers ... I go into the kitchen very often and scream. I lock the door [to stop the kids coming in]. And it's better really because I say to myself, 'If you did hit them, you could really go a bit stupid'.
>
> *(Mother, poor accommodation)*

Others concentrated on calming down when they felt especially stressed.

> You can't just walk out when you're stressed out ... with the children, you just have to find some other way. Normally I go out in the garden and wander round for a little while, and then come back in and try to start again ... We just start again.
>
> *(Mother, low income)*

> [When I'm really stressed] I just sit down and unwind and have a cup of tea ... that's the only way, just shut yourself off and unwind. I'll tell you what I do – puzzle books. It's surprising, you just unwind, just doing them.
>
> *(Mother, low income, lone parent, sick child, difficult child)*

> I have hypnosis tapes, actually ... I put them on when I go to bed, or in the afternoon if I've come home from work before the kids get home from school ... it's very, very relaxing.
>
> *(Mother, difficult child, lone parent)*

However, these strategies were often only partially effective, especially when problems were multiple and chronic, as the mother quoted above went on to explain:

> My average night's sleep is about three hours or so ... I went to the doctor actually – not just because of the sleep but because I was in agony with my arms, my legs – everything just hurt. He said it was all due to the fact that I was totally exhausted and had too many emotional problems ... It's a horrible feeling. I just feel totally washed out.
>
> *(Mother, difficult child, lone parent)*

And another parent with chronic health problems of his own, a large family and at least one child with clear behavioural difficulties said this of the 'pile-up' effect of multiple stressors that our quantitative analysis so clearly illustrated in Chapter 10:

> I've been waiting nearly two years for an operation (shoulder replacement). It's terrible ... and I get angry with the children because I'm in pain. It's all stress ... it's all stress.
>
> *(Father, poor accommodation, sick child, lone parent, poor health, low income)*

Last, in the face of multiple stressors, many parents described their coping strategy as simply to keep problems to themselves, soldiering on, and reminding themselves that others faced the same, or worse, problems.

> *Interviewer:* Is there anyone you can talk to when you're feeling stressed?
>
> *Respondent:* No. I just do it on my own ... I just go to bed, wake up and start again. It's a strain ... but there's thousands of blokes out there that don't even get to see their kids. I'm the lucky one.
>
> *(Father, poor accommodation, sick child, lone parent, poor health, low income)*

> I mean most kids from the age of 13 up until they're about 16 are hard work. Every parent I've talked to from the age of 13, they've all got problems with their children. They go through that stage – like I said, a bad stage – and you've just got to ride it out.
>
> *(Mother, lone parent)*

As one mother summed up this essentially pragmatic approach:

> Sometimes it gets you, but you accept it really don't you? You've got to really, because no matter how much you let it get you down, it don't get you anywhere.
>
> *(Mother, low income, lone parent, sick child, difficult child)*

Conclusions

How do the data reported in this chapter add to our understanding of the patterns identified in Chapter 10? To what extent can we speak of there being an interface between coping strategies and the relative contribution of different risk factors to poor coping outcomes? Although just a fraction of the extensive information that was collected on individual coping strategies, the data reported in this chapter do help us to take a more rounded view of the quantitative findings reported in Chapter 10.

First, the data reviewed in this chapter show that parents in poor environments adopt a wide range of strategies – both problem focused and emotion focused – for dealing with life's daily hassles. Our qualitative data showed that in a wide range of situations, a problem-focused approach was adopted by many parents, who tried hard to grapple in a very direct way with the source of a given problem. Parents' creativity, resourcefulness and willingness actively to tackle difficulties was a striking feature of this study. Many described huge amounts of time and energy devoted to, for example, shopping around for bargains to stretch the family budget, dealing with substandard housing, protecting themselves from crime or findings ways round other hazards in the local area. However, not all problems were amenable to change by an individual's efforts. In this respect, parents also reported emotion-focused strategies for coping, either working on lowering their own stress levels, or rationalising, normalising and minimising the problems as general to their area and perhaps even to all parents.

Second, the data on coping strategies described in this chapter may help to elucidate the 'pathway' to coping or not coping that we suggested on the basis of the results in Chapter 10. We spoke there of a possible model in which poverty-related variables acted as distal risk factors underlying, and contributing to, other stressors that act as proximate triggers for coping difficulties. The data reported in this chapter lend some support to that model, and offer some insights for the specification of process in this respect. In particular, they suggest that if certain risk factors (for example, poverty variables) show more distant relationships to coping than others, this may reflect the relative success with which parents deal with different kinds of stressors. For example, parents reported a wide range of active, problem-focused strategies for dealing with poverty that allowed them to feel some sense of mastery and indeed pride in their ability to cope with life in a poor environment. On the other hand, effective problem-focused strategies for dealing with child behaviour problems or the cumulative effects of multiple personal problems seemed more elusive, often leaving parents struggling with emotion-focused responses that were palliative but short lived. It may be, therefore, that when directly poverty-related stressors such as low income are superseded, in statistical models predicting coping, by factors related to the characteristics of individual children and parents, an underlying explanation may be that parents are better able to diffuse the direct effects of poverty at the household and community level than they are able to manage other kinds of strains.

Alternatively, another way to understand the pathway to coping problems for parents in poor environments may be to consider the cumulative effects of strain at different dimensions of the ecological model. Material poverty – low income, poor neighbourhoods, bad housing – was the permanent backdrop to the lives of most of the families who were part of this study. It was clear that a great deal of 'coping energy' was expended in dealing with the challenges this presented although, by and large, parents claimed success in this respect. However, it is not unreasonable to speculate that when parents are faced with other problems – a difficult, tiring child, fatigue, emotional stress and so on – on top of the demands already presented by raising a family in conditions of material poverty, they may have rather depleted personal resources upon which to draw. Graham (1994) suggests that this can create a conflict of demands 'when parenting is structured around an unending conflict between caring enough and economising enough', and it was clear from our data that the individual costs of a constant struggle against multiple adversity could be substantial, characterised for many by high levels of emotional and physical stress, depression, fatigue, and occasional feelings of desperation. Small wonder, then, that dealing with a difficult or demanding child could feel like the last straw for struggling parents.

In the next chapter we explore the effects of social support and support deficits on coping, to complete our picture of the various risk and protective factors that impact on parents' sense of how well they are managing the demands of child rearing in a poor environment. However, we return to the implications of the data reported in this chapter in Part V, to discuss what messages we may draw for policy and practice about how best to enhance parents' ability to cope.

CHAPTER TWELVE

Social Support and Coping

Does Support Make a Difference?

Having identified the key risk and protective factors that are associated with different coping outcomes and highlighted some of the coping strategies that parents use in poor environments, we now turn our attention to exploring the role of social support in coping. As we discussed in detail in Part III, social support is consistently cited as an important factor in parents' functioning and has been a central focus of studies that have tried to understand the determinants of parenting problems. In the context of work on coping, social support is often described as one of the key 'resources' on which individuals can draw when managing stress which may enhance natural coping skills and buffer against the deleterious effects of adverse conditions. Having investigated the extent of social support earlier in this report and highlighted the groups who appear to be most in need of support, in this chapter we re-examine our data in relation to coping, to see whether those who lack support are also those who experience coping difficulties and, conversely, if those who are coping better are also those who are better supported. Is support protective and stress buffering, as much of the literature claims and, if so, can we identify which particular types of support (informal or organised) or which dimensions (structural or affiliative) appear to be most protective for those parenting in poor environments?

'Feeling supported' and 'coping': overlap and divergence

An important finding of the study was that feeling unsupported, defined in Part III as a 'wish for more help and support with parenting', was extremely strongly related to coping difficulties, as Table 12.1 shows. Whereas 60 per cent of parents who felt adequately supported felt they were also coping well with the general demands of parenting, only 32 per cent of those who wished for more help reported coping well ($p<0.001$). Of course, these two variables – feeling supported and sense of coping – are conceptually related, since they both measure parents' subjective perceptions of their general situation. Thus, we might expect them to show a statistically significant relationship to one another. However, the results tell us three important things. First, despite being conceptually related, the results in Table 12.1 show that the two variables are not measuring exactly the same thing, since a substantial number of those who said they did not need further support (40%, $n = 366$) nevertheless said they were sometimes or often not coping. Some of those who are coping less well, therefore, clearly do not see support as the solution to their problems. Second, Table 12.1 alerts us to the fact that nearly one-third of those who would like more help nevertheless say they *are* coping, suggesting that, in spite of a sense of inadequate support, many of those who feel unsupported still remain basically confident about their ability to function and do a 'good enough' job as parents. This said, however, Table 12.1 tells a third important story – that, on the whole, parents who express the need for more external support tend to do so with good reason; over two-thirds felt their ability to manage the demands of parenting was compromised to at least some extent. In summary, then, although feeling supported or unsupported as a parent does not map precisely on to perceptions of coping or not coping, the two variables are clearly strongly related to one another.

Table 12.1 Wish for more support with being a parent, by coping		
	% of parents	
	Coping well	Coping less
Wish for more support	32	68
No wish for further support	60	40

Base = 1724

Informal social support and coping

To what extent did informal social support act to bolster parents' sense of coping? Taking first the structural aspects of informal support (here, network size and extent of enacted support), a picture emerged that was strikingly similar to that discussed in Chapter 9. In terms of network size, 'copers' reported significantly more extensive networks than 'non-copers' ($p<0.001$, see Table 12.2), suggesting that a larger personal support network may be protective against coping difficulties to some extent. Qualitative discussions certainly showed how wide networks provided important and accessible support for parents and friendships for both parents and their children.

> I think it makes a difference when you know a lot of people around the area ... You know you've always got your friends, and they ... have got their kids which become your kids' friends. In that way this area is good for me and for my children.
>
> *(Mother, sick child)*

On the other hand, enacted (received) informal support was lower for those who were coping well and higher for those coping less well. For those who were coping well, the mean enacted support score on our scale was 2.10, compared to 2.51 for those who were coping less well ($p<0.001$; see Table 12.2). Indeed, perceptions of coping with parenthood showed a strongly inverse (that is, negatively associated) relationship with levels of enacted support as measured by our scale, and parents who were coping less were the greater consumers of actual support. As Figure 12.1 shows, the more enacted informal support that was reported, the more likely parents were to also report problems with coping.

We interpret this to mean not that the less support, the better parents were coping (that is, that support was somehow detrimental to coping) but that those who are coping well are less like to ask for, or accept, help from others, presumably because they have fewer support needs. On the other hand, those who recognise that they are not coping well are more likely to seek (and, it would seem, find) support from their informal networks. Consonant with the findings reported in Part III, where we showed that those who felt unsupported received more enacted support, analysis by perceptions of coping also indicated that enacted informal support was, at least to some extent, reaching those who reported greater needs.

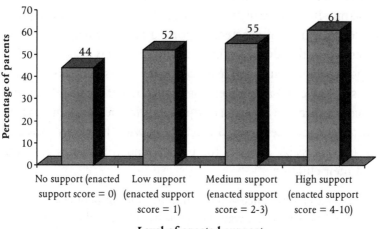

Base = 1736

Figure 12.1 Not coping with parenthood, by actual support received in last four weeks

In terms of the affiliative aspects of informal support – how support feels as opposed to the shape it takes – once again we found a pattern similar to that reported in Part III in relation to parents who wished for more support. The less well respondents were coping, the less positive their attitudes to informal social support on the scale described in Chapter 3.1 and the more attuned they were to the downsides of seeking and accepting support from naturally occurring networks ($p<0.0001$; see Table 12.2).

Table 12.2 Mean informal support scores for network size, enacted support and attitudes to support, by coping		
	Coping well	*Coping less*
Size of network	6.71	5.49
Enacted informal support score	2.10	2.51
Attitudes to informal support	12.34	11.69

Base = 1736

Evidence that perceptions of, or attitudes towards, informal support were positively associated with coping is even more clearly revealed when we examine the composite elements that contributed to our overall measure of attitudes to informal social support. For example, those who were concerned about disclosing personal information to other local people (that is, those who strongly agreed or tended to agree with the statement 'I prefer not to discuss family issues people round here because you can't trust people to keep things to themselves') were more likely than other parents to be in the 'coping less' group (61% of parents in the coping less group felt like this compared with 52 per cent in the coping more group; $p<0.001$). Similarly, those who worried about the reciprocation implied by asking friends or neighbours for help (that is, those who strongly agreed or tended to agree with the statement 'If you ask friends or neighbours for help you end up feeling in debt to them') were also much less likely to be coping (35% compared with 26%; $p<0.001$). As with parents who felt unsupported, those who were coping less were much less positive towards informal social support, in spite of – or indeed, as we suggested in Chapter 9, perhaps because of – their greater consumption of actual support.

Other factors in informal support: coping and relationships

We showed earlier that lone parenting was consistently and strongly prejudicial to coping with parenting – and not just because of the stress of low income that commonly accompanies single parenthood. As we discussed in Part II, the loneliness of lone parenting was a strong theme in depth interviews, with the impact on coping being described not just in terms of having less practical support with child care within the home, but having less emotional support. In this context, informal social support became extremely important. Supportive friends, in particular, were vital to coping, not necessarily to provide instrumental assistance but also to act as a listener and sounding board.

> I talk to my friend, and after I had a talk I'd be alright. As long as I had somebody to talk to, tell them my problems … it's like a weight lifted off your shoulder … I've got to be honest – when you're on your own and you're bringing up children, you need somebody like that. You need somebody there just to talk to. Not to help you, just somebody there to

listen to you. I think if you've got that you can cope. If you've got somebody to sit there and you can pour your heart out to them ... Although you haven't resolved anything, you feel better in yourself and you can cope a little bit better. It gives you that bit more energy then to think, 'Right. I know what I've got to do.'

(Mother, lone parent)

A particularly 'therapeutic' strategy, stressed especially by lone parents, was going out socially to 'have a laugh' and a talk to other adults.

If you didn't have your friends you would crack up ... Sometimes the mothers in school get together and we have one night a month where we all go round to one girl's house ... and we all take a bottle of wine and literally sit around the table and talk and have a laugh. It's a release from the children, so you just talk about yourself, about men, the usual – little tales of what's gone on.

(Mother, lone parent, poor health, sick child, low income)

And supportive family members as well as good friends were vital to many lone parents' sense of coping.

I'm fortunate – I've got a good supportive family. I've got a dad and brothers that help. A lot of the time (when I've got a problem) I phone my dad up. My dad is my lifeline, you know.

(Mother, lone parent)

However, as we noted in Part II, even although not having a partner was difficult, having a partner could also be a source of stress. Although we did not explore the quality of respondents' adult relationships in great detail, some parents reported high levels of family conflict and difficulties with partners that contributed to, rather than ameliorated, the stress of being a parent in a poor environment. For example, of those parents with partners, one-quarter (26%) reported that 'lack of support or help' from their partners caused them 'difficulties or stress' in their daily lives. Of these, nearly one-fifth (or 4% of all parents with partners) reported that this was the situation 'all or most of the time'. Having a supportive partner is often suggested in the literature as an important protective factor against parenting difficulties. In our study, cross-tabulation of supportiveness of partner against coping revealed that having a supportive partner was indeed strongly related to coping well whereas, conversely, having an unsupportive partner[1] was associated with coping difficulties ($p<0.001$, see Table 12.3). Indeed, as a group, parents with resident but unsupportive partners were more similar to lone parents than to those who were supportively partnered in terms of the proportions who were coping well or coping less. Whereas, as we showed earlier in Chapter 10, 61 per cent of lone parents were in the coping less group, a similar proportion of parents with unsupportive partners put themselves in this category (65%) compared to only 43 per cent of those with supportive partners.

Table 12.3 Presence of supportive partner (married or cohabiting respondents only) by coping		
	% of parents	
	Coping well	Coping less
Supportive partner (Lack of support causes difficulties 'rarely or never'; $n = 762$)	57	43
Unsupportive partner (Lack of support causes difficulties 'all or most of the time', or 'sometimes', $n = 265$)	35	65**
All with a partner ($n = 1027$)	51	49

** = $p<0.001$

Organised support and coping

What did our data tell us about the relationship between organised support (semi-formal and formal services) and coping with parenthood? First, looking at the structural aspects of support, those who said they were coping less well with the demands of being a parent were significantly more likely to have used these kinds of services recently, once again reflecting the pattern that was revealed in relation to wish for more support. For both types of services, nearly three out of five users were parents who reported that they were coping less well with parenthood (see Table 12.4).

	% of parents	
Table 12.4 Use of semi-formal and formal support services in the past three years more or less, by coping		
	Coping well	Coping less
Used semi-formal services in past 3 years (n = 705)	42	58**
Used formal services in past 3 years (n = 942)	40	60***

** = p<0.001; *** = p<0.0001

Looked at another way, those who were generally coping less with parent-hood were significantly more likely to have accessed a semi-formal support service in the last three years than those who were coping more (44% compared with 37%; p<0.01), and even more likely to have accessed a formal service (61% compared with 47%; p<0.001). Furthermore, nearly three-quarters (72%) of those who were having difficulties in coping were 'in the system' and reported that they had used at least one organised service in the past three years, compared with 60 per cent of those who were coping well (p<0.001). Again, this provides clear evidence that support – in this case, the organised variety – is at least to some extent reaching those in greater need of help.

Second, in terms of the affiliative dimensions of organised support, although as we commented earlier those who reporting difficulties in coping were substantially more negative about informal support in their attitudes as measured by our 'attitudes to informal support' scale, they were not significantly more hostile to organised support. Thus, the mean score on our scale measuring attitudes to formal social support for those coping less was 6.69, compared with the score for those coping well, which was only slightly lower at 6.47. Again, these results follow the patterns we identified in Part III in relation to parents who felt unsupported, who were more hostile to informal support, but not significantly more negative about organised forms of social support.

Social support, protective factors and coping

How did social support modify our initial picture of protective factors described in Chapter 10? To explore whether positive support factors added anything to the model predicting coping with parenting, we ran a further logistic regression model that included the five key protective factors identified earlier plus the two 'pro-coping' support factors that applied to the whole sample and were shown to be positively associated with coping better in cross-sectional analyses, that is, having a larger than average support network (defined as having seven or more supporters) and feeling supported. The results are shown in Table 12.5.

Table 12.5 Role of key protective factors, plus positive support variables, in predicting coping with parenting	
	Odds ratio
Easy or average index child	2.73***
Feels supported	2.59***
Low Malaise score (score 4 or less)	2.17***
Small family (2 or less children)	1.63**
No current problems (CPQ score = 0)	1.45*
Parent with a (resident) partner	1.28 (n/s)
Large network (7 or more supporters)	1.27 (n/s)

Base = 1393; * = $p<0.01$; ** = $p<0.001$; *** = $p<0.0001$; n/s = not significant

As can be seen from Table 12.5, feeling supported proved to be very significantly independently associated with coping. Those who felt supported were over two and a half times more likely to be coping well than those who did not feel supported. Finding that feeling supported superseded the protective effect of having a partner again suggested that the quality of the relationship between parents matters more than the simple presence of a partner. This is a conclusion borne out by previous studies. For example, Belsky (1981) noted that 'a positive marital relationship is a major component of competent parenting', and a study by Crnic *et al.* (1983) concluded that the quality of marital relations was the strongest predictor of positive effects on parenting compared with a range of other potential social supports. In a similar way, having a large network added nothing to the model once perception of being supported was accounted for: the quality of support, then, mattered more than the quantity in terms of how many supporters were within one's personal network. These findings concur with those of some previous researchers, for example Henderson (1981), who found that the perceived adequacy of available support was more important than availability *per se*. However, the other key factors – having an easy or averagely behaved child, being in good mental or emotional health, having no current problems on the CPQ and having not more than two children – remained important in the model as predictors of coping. This indicates that, even in the presence of feeling supported, these factors continue to act positively to offset coping problems. Feeling supported, therefore, is important but is not by any means the only key to coping well with parenting.

Conclusions: does support make a difference to coping?

To what extent, then, did we find evidence that social support, in its various forms, enhances the ability of parents in poor environments to cope with the challenges of parenting? Our results were mixed. First, tending to support the 'buffering' hypothesis, it was clear that those who said they were coping well were also, in the main, those who felt socially supported in a broad sense. These parents reported more extensive networks of friends and family in their personal networks and claimed not to wish for additional help or support in being a parent. Feeling supported contributed positively and significantly to a model predicting coping with parenting and was clearly an important component of the extent to which respondents rated themselves as coping better or worse.

According to our data, however, there was also evidence that raised questions about the 'buffering' role of social support. It was not true to say, for example, that a larger social network protected against coping difficulties once other factors were controlled for. In this respect, our findings tend to concur with Cohen and Wills' (1985) conclusion that

> embeddedness in a social network is beneficial to well-being, but not necessarily helpful in the face of stress … social integration influences well-being in ways that do not necessarily involve improved means of coping with stressful events.

It was also not true to say that the consumption of support, in a practical sense, necessarily protected against difficulties in coping. Indeed, our results suggested the reverse as far as both informal social support and use of organised services were concerned: the parents who were coping least well were also the greatest consumers of enacted informal support, and were the most likely to have used an organised support service in the recent past. This is not of course the same thing as saying that support is a bad thing, or that it does not enhance coping. Since we already know that parents who were the greatest consumers of support were also the most needy on a number of criteria, the inevitable question we must ask is, would these more needy parents be coping even less well were it not for the support they receive? We cannot answer this question from cross-sectional data, and in any case the complex, overlapping nature of need and use of support that we uncovered in the study suggests that it may in fact be difficult ever to disentangle one from the other, statistically speaking. What the data do tell us is that actual support – both practical and emotional, and both informal and organised – looks to be especially important to the more needy families who are coping less well. Clearly, there is reassuring evidence from this study that in poor environments, enacted support of all types is reaching those with higher levels of need to some extent, whether measured using objective criteria or on the basis of self-perceptions. However, by the same token the facts that over one-quarter of non-copers were not accessing any kind of organised support service and that two-fifths did not report any enacted informal support in the recent past also means we cannot be complacent about the extent to which support is reaching those who perhaps need it most.

It is apparent, then, that there is not a straightforward relationship between social support and coping with parenting. Our data show that while the majority of non-copers also felt unsupported, not all non-copers felt this way and, by the same token, not all copers reckoned they were well supported. In the same way, then, that support does not necessarily 'solve' problems with coping, lack of support need not necessarily imply that we should expect to see difficulties in coping. However, most importantly, there are clear messages that what does matter most about support in terms of coping with parenting in a global sense is not the quantitative, structural aspects of support but the qualitative, affiliative aspects. *Feeling* supported emerges as the critical factor, and turned out to be more significant than the number of supporters in the network or how much enacted support was received. If parents feel supported in a general sense, this acts, together with other 'protective' factors, as an important stepping-stone on the pathway to coping.

Note

1.   That is, a partner with whom 'lack of support or help' was sometimes or often a problem.

Part Five

Summary of Key Findings, Implications and Messages for Policy and Practice

This study was the first to have taken place in Great Britain involving a nationally representative sample of parents living in objectively defined 'poor environments'. The sample was selected from among households living in the most disadvantaged areas of the country, using a specially created scale, the 'PPE-Index', to rank districts according to their relative levels of social deprivation. Households were then randomly selected from among areas with scores in the upper 30 per cent of the national distribution. All selected households were screened for the presence of a parent of a child aged less than 17 years and interviews were carried out with 1754 parents in total. All parents who participated in the study took part in an extensive face-to-face survey interview, and data from these were supplemented by 40 in-depth follow-up qualitative interviews with parents in especially difficult circumstances.

The aims of the study were threefold. First, we aimed to ascertain the extent to which families in poor environments are subject to stressors known to increase the risk of experiencing difficulties with parenting. To explore these risk factors, we drew on the widely respected 'ecological' model of parenting, which conceptualises risk and protective factors in family functioning in terms of a nested, overlapping ecological system with various levels, including the level of the individual, the family or household, and the community or local environment. Second, we wanted to explore the interface between stress factors, social support and coping with parenting. What social supports are available to and used by parents, and how do support factors interact with risk factors? Which factors are most prejudicial to coping, and why? Last, we aimed to throw light on how social support to parents in poor environments can be enhanced. What do parents really want from social support?

In the final part of this book, we focus on this last aim, drawing together the key messages from the study for policy makers and service providers in respect of supporting parents in poor environments. In Chapter 13 we summarise what we learned from the study about existing patterns of need and social support in poor neighbourhoods, and identify the groups of parents who might, according to our data, benefit most from pro-active policy and practitioner attention. In Chapter 14, we then turn to messages for improving social support to parent in poor environments. We describe parents' views on what specific improvements to existing support services would they like to see and draw out some general principles arising from the study on how support should be delivered to be most acceptable, and useful, to families in poor environments. We draw some overall conclusions in relation to the nature of social support in poor environments and what support services in the UK might do to better meet the needs of parents and children in future.

CHAPTER THIRTEEN

Patterns of Need and Support

Priority Groups for Policy and Practice Attention

Patterns of need

The results of the study confirmed that parents living in poor environments are typically exposed to high levels of risk factors at all levels of the ecological model. Whether we explore stressors at the level of the individual, the level of the family and household or at the level of the community and environment, we find clear evidence of elevated levels of adversity for parents and their children relative to the wider population. Based on the data we gathered, there can be little doubt that parenting in a poor environment is a particularly difficult job.

Stressors at the individual, family and community level

At the level of the individual, we found that parents in poor environments experience considerably worse physical and mental health than adults in the wider population. They were substantially more likely to suffer from a long-term, limiting, physical health problem than other adults and had extremely high scores on the Malaise Inventory, a measure of tendency to depression. Although differences between our sample and the wider population were not so stark in relation to child health (either in terms of physical health or emotional and behavioural difficulties as measured by one of three widely used scales), we did find that the two sets of problems were likely to go together; that is, parents in poor physical health tended to have high Malaise scores, and tended also to be those parents who had a child with physical health problems. Those with poor emotional or mental health were more likely to have a child who was behaviourally challenging to care for.

At the level of the family and household, the stressors faced by parents were many and various. Low income was a critical stress factor, with only one in six of the families who were interviewed reaching the national average for household income. Only half of all households contained an adult in paid employment. Nearly two-thirds of families were unable to afford at least one basic necessity of family life and, unsurprisingly, parents reported chronic levels of anxiety about financial matters. Hand in hand with low income went accommodation problems of varying severity, with some parents living in housing conditions that posed a serious health risk to adults and children alike. In terms of family structure, the study revealed that families in poor environments are disproportionately likely to be headed by lone parents and, as other studies have found, lone parents reported especially low incomes and limited financial resources. This often meant they went without a number of basic necessities; most lone parents, for example, could not afford to take their families on an annual holiday away from home. Furthermore, the study showed that in poor environments lone parenting is a chronic stressor, with the vast majority of lone parents reporting that they had been alone for at least three years and many for much longer periods. Moreover, unlike lone parents in the wider population, lone parents in this sample were as likely to have three or more dependent children as couple households. Large families were affected by a 'double whammy' in terms of material resources: not only were there more mouths to feed and bodies to clothe, but they tended to have lower disposable incomes than smaller families, even once household incomes were 'equivalised' to reflect family size and composition. Last, family conflict emerged as a serious stressor for some, although overall the levels of serious conflict (for example, incidence of physical assault by current partners) were approximately the same as those reported in the wider population.

At the level of the community and the environment, the study confirmed that poor environments are generally considered by parents to be physically dirty and degraded, and prone to crime and antisocial behaviour. Environmental problems were reported to have more frequent personal impact on families than crime and related social problems, and even seemingly trivial hazards (for example, dog fouling) can have quite far-reaching effects – for example, preventing parents from allowing children to play freely in public spaces. Indeed, parents were widely concerned about the hazards to health and to physical safety to which children were exposed as a result of living in poor neighbourhood. Moreover, in terms of these environmental stressors, we identified a 'hierarchy of risk' in respect of poor environments. By using the PPE-Index score to measure relative levels of neighbourhood disadvantage within the sample, and subdividing sample areas into three bands – 'poor', 'very poor' and 'extremely poor' – we were also able to show that, in general, the poorer the area the higher the reported levels of environmental hazards and social problems, and the more likely it was to be rated as a bad area in which to bring up a family. We concluded that living in poor neighbourhood adds additional, environmental, stresses to the already demanding job of being a parent, and that families in the very poorest areas of the country face the greatest numbers of environmental challenges.

Last, a key finding of the study was the extent to which stressors are multiple, overlapping and cumulative in their adverse effect, with risk factors in one domain almost always highly associated with risk factors in another. Thus, for example, within the sample, the poorer the area according to its PPE-Index score, the lower the mean household income and the greater the concentration of families with poor accommodation, lone parents and parents with high Malaise scores. Similarly, when we used a composite measure of specified risk factors at the family and household level – the Current Problems Questionnaire, or CPQ (which measures stressors connected with family finance, accommodation, relationships and work–life balance, among other things) – we found that parents with the highest scores on this measure were disproportionately likely to be lone parents to have poor mental health and have problems with child behaviour. Also, in terms of 'coping' with parenting in a global sense, we found that certain of the risk factors we explored were more closely associated with coping difficulties than others. In particular, the 'key five' factors that were independently associated with coping difficulties were having a difficult child; having a high Malaise score; having a high CPQ score; having three or more dependent children; and being a lone parent. Moreover, there appeared to be a 'dose-response' effect on coping of these problems: the more problems, the greater the odds of reporting coping difficulties. Conversely, an increasing tally of 'protective' factors (that is, having an easy or averagely well-behaved child, having a low Malaise score, having a low CPQ_score, having a partner and a small family) appeared strongly to enhance the chances of reporting coping well with parenting.

Priority need groups

As discussed in Part I, by definition, all parents in this study could be said to be 'in need' to some extent. However, it was also the case that many were coping well with parenting. If we had to identify which groups of parents could be considered 'priority need groups' on the basis of the findings of the study, the key indicators would be those summarised in Box 13.1.

Priority needs:

- parents living in the very poorest neighbourhoods
- parents on the lowest incomes
- lone parents
- parents with high Malaise scores
- parents with high levels of current problems
- parents with 'difficult' children
- parents with accommodation problems
- parents with large families.

Box 13.1 Priority need groups within poor environments

In part, the factors we have highlighted as indicating priority need have been selected because they underpin so many other problems. Low income is perhaps the most obvious of these, and it was clear from both quantitative and qualitative data that the financial strain under which so many families lived was a huge strain on coping resources. Much emotional energy – and not a little effort – went into trying to make ends meet on a tight budget. As we showed in Part IV, coping with low income was clearly an area of strength for many parents in the sample. However, we can reasonably speculate that parents whose coping resources were not so strained by managing life in poverty might experience fewer poverty-related problems (such as poor accommodation, for example), and might also be better able to cope with those problems that did remain. Material poverty underpinned so many other risk factors in this study that our data suggested lifting the very poorest families out of this situation could have a knock-on effect on a wide range of other adverse life circumstances. Similarly, although 'coping with parenting' in a general sense was not predicted by the area in which a parent lived, and parents in the very poorest areas were no less likely to be coping than those in the least poor areas, it was also the case that those living in the very poorest areas faced an increased burden of environmental and social hazards. Again, improving the physical quality of poor neighbourhoods and tackling crime and antisocial behaviour in these areas were confirmed by this study as priority areas for policy attention.

In part, however, our selection is based on the 'diagnostic' implications of the overlap between factors. For example, by screening for parents with high Malaise scores as a priority need group, one would at the same time pick up a substantial proportion of parents with high levels of current problems, 'difficult' children and so on. According to our data, offering services routinely to all parents in poor environments with a high Malaise score would also net 36 per cent of parents with high levels of current problems, 35 per cent of those with difficult children, 31 per cent of those with longstanding health problems, 28 per cent of those with accommodation problems, and so on. The factors in Box 13.1 are those that were shown to be the most considerable obstacles to coping with parenting in a general, global sense, according to parents' own reports. For example, parents found behaviourally difficult children especially challenging to deal with, and often lacked effective strategies for coping with them. Furthermore, cumulatively, the more problems the less the chances of coping well, and our analyses demonstrated that each risk factor tackled could represent a significant enhancement to the chances of parents coping better. Targeting services at parents with these particular needs might, then, represent particularly good 'value for money' in the context of distribution of limited resources.

Patterns of social support

The study revealed a complex network of issues relating to social support within poor environments. Not only did it prove important to distinguish between sources of support (informal, arising out of respondents' own natural networks of family, friends and neighbours, and organised, provided by community-based and statutory agencies), but it was also clear that both structural and affiliative aspects of support were important components of the overall picture. In order to make sense of the relationships between risk, support and coping, we needed to explore not only the form that support takes but also the way it is experienced by respondents and the extent to which parents felt supported or unsupported in a general sense.

Overall, for example, most parents reported reasonably extensive networks of supporters at the informal level, with only a tiny minority regarding themselves as completely without anybody to turn to for help, advice or support. However, despite the relatively reassuring picture for the sample overall, some groups of parents reported more restricted social networks than others. Minority ethnic parents, for example, tended to have smaller networks, as did lone parents, those with high scores on the Malaise Inventory and those living in the poorer areas within the sample. Moreover, when we explored the extent of actual, enacted support that parents had received in the recent past we found that low levels of help and support appeared to be the norm. At the informal level, one-fifth of all parents reported that had received no support at all – emotional or practical – from family and household members, friends or neighbours in the four weeks preceding the survey. Of course, not all parents may have felt the need for support during the period we asked about, but parents' expectations of help should they perhaps need it in a crisis were also, in general, strikingly low. There was a particular dearth of emergency or respite child care – leaving children for longer than a couple of hours was deemed impossible by one in five parents, and one in ten thought they could not depend on someone else to look after a child even for a couple of hours. Similarly, in terms of organised support, only two in five of the sample had been in touch with any kind of semi-formal service in the past three years and only just over one in two had used a formal service in the same period.

There was some relationship between need and enacted informal and organised support, so that, for example, some particularly needy groups were especially likely to have received informal support recently, and organised services were also much more likely to have accessed by high need groups. For example, lone parents and those with high levels of current problems reported more enacted informal support than parents with partners or those with lower levels of problems. Parents with elevated levels of current problems and parents of children with a long-term health problem were more likely to have used a semi-formal service, and formal services were also more likely to have been accessed by these parents as well as those with poor mental health, difficult children or large families. All types of organised services were used more often by parents with pre-school children than those with older children. This does, reassuringly, indicate that at least to some extent, support is reaching those most in need. However, there were still substantial minorities of high-need parents who were not receiving much support, and organised services were not, for example, significantly more likely to be used by those on the lowest incomes or those living in the poorest areas in the sample, or indeed by lone parents – all of whom might be expected to have much to gain from using an organised family support service. It was also noticeable and worrying that minority ethnic parents were significantly less likely than other parents to have used an organised service in the recent past. Last, there were also some striking gaps in awareness of organised support, even for 'universal' services such as health visiting, with substantial minorities under the impression that no such services existed in their own local area.

Of course, take-up of support with parenting and child care, be it informal or organised, has to be examined in relation to the extent to which parents themselves want or feel they need extra help with these things. For example, it might be argued that parents did not call on informal support or use organised services because they did not perceive a need for them. For some parents, this did appear to be the underlying explanation, and the pride that many parents took in self-sufficiency in family life was a notable feature of this study. However, low enacted support levels were not wholly explained by absence of need. There were substantial proportions of parents who did express a wish for more help and support with parenting but who were not receiving this help, while parents who felt unsupported were, paradoxically, also the parents who were receiving higher levels of actual support of both informal and organised kinds. Perceptions of 'supportedness', rather than actual levels of support *per se*, therefore, emerged as a critical indicator in the study. Indeed, of all the types of support indicators that we explored, whether a parent felt supported or not was the critical factor in the relationship between support and coping with parenting. Thus, our analyses showed that while the actual level of support a parent had received did not in fact predict coping, feeling supported did. Groups who tended to feel inadequately supported (and more likely to say they were not coping well with parenting) were those with high levels of current problems, lone parents, those in poor mental or emotional health and those with a pre-school child in the home.

Priority support groups

Thus, based on the findings of the study in relation to existing patterns of support, it appeared that there were a number of key groups who might be considered a priority for enhanced support with parenting, in that they appeared less well supported than other parents in similar areas. These groups are summarised in Box 13.2.

Priority support groups:

- parents who feel they are 'not generally coping' with parenting
- minority ethnic parents
- lone parents.

Parents with high levels of current problems:

- parents with high malaise scores
- parents with pre-school children
- parents with conflicted or unsupportive relationships with partners.

Box 13.2 Priority support groups within poor environments

It will be noticed that while there is some overlap between these groups and those we singled out as priority need groups, the list is not identical. This is because the groups in Box 13.2 reflect not levels of risk factors or stressors, but a combination of patterns of access to support, patterns of support uptake and perceptions of support availability. For all of the groups we have singled out as candidates for extra support of one kind or another, a common factor was either that they reported restricted sources of support, or had more limited enacted support, or had a sense of being inadequately supported (despite in some cases relatively high levels of enacted support or relatively extensive networks). Thus, although minority ethnic parents did not on the whole emerge as a high-need group within the overall context of poor parenting environments, and also did not report feeling any less well supported than other parents, they did nevertheless emerge as a group with substantially more restricted social networks and significantly lower uptake of enacted support on both informal and organised dimensions. Lone parents, on the other hand, reported the same levels of enacted support in most respects to parents with partners, but they got this support from comparatively more limited networks. Critically, of course, lone parents generally lacked support from a partner (only one-quarter named an ex-partner as part of their current support network) and cited a more restricted 'wider family' network. Moreover, they tended to feel unsupported more often than other parents. Parents with high Malaise scores reported a similar pattern to lone parents, and parents with a high levels of current problems, although they in fact reported more enacted support than other parents, nevertheless had smaller networks and a strong sense of wishing for more support.

Drawing on our data on coping with parenting, we have added to the list of those who could be regarded as high priority for more support the 'non-copers' – parents who expressed a sense of not generally coping well with parenting – as this group overlapped substantially with those who felt 'unsupported'. We have also picked out those with unsupportive partners or from families in conflict, since our analysis of the key predictors of coping indicated that the quality of relationships was more important than the simple presence or absence of a partner. Last, although parents with pre-school children were consumers of relatively high levels of enacted support and were not less likely to feel they were coping than other parents, they were nevertheless significantly more likely to express a wish for more support with parenting. Thus the common factor linking the groups in Box 13.2 is some deficiency in support levels, either as interpreted by us, or reported by parents themselves. This is not to say that other groups would not also benefit from enhanced support; however, in policy and practice terms, the study indicated that these groups could well be considered as having a 'priority' case for greater support with parenting.

CHAPTER FOURTEEN

What Do Parents Want from Support?

Messages for Policy and Practice

What specific messages were there for policy and practice from this study, in terms of improving social support in poor environments? Having identified the particular groups of parents who might draw especial benefits from policy and practice attention, we now turn to the ways in which this might be best deployed. In this concluding chapter, we spell out the implications of the study for those planning and providing services to families in need. We begin with some additional data on parents' views of what specific improvements to existing family support services they would like to see. We then draw out some broad principles of what parents want in terms of the delivery of family support. Last, we review the key messages we learned about the general nature of social support in poor environments, since these form an important backdrop to the policy and practice-oriented conclusions that we reached.

What do parents want from family support services?

We saw in Chapter 9 that parents identified a range of shortcomings in existing support services. What did the findings of the study suggest in terms of concrete ways of improving family support services as they currently exist within poor environments?

Improving the accessibility and quality of services

Suggestions from parents with previous experience of using organised support services – both semi-formal (in general open to all and provided by community-based organisations) and formal (usually provided by statutory agencies on the basis of need) were helpful in unpacking how existing services could be built upon or improved in order better to meet the needs of parents in poor environments. We asked parents to indicate what aspects of services were most in need of improvement, selecting from the list of areas shown in Figure 14.1. Although the order of priority attached to different suggestions for improvements varied between semi-formal and formal services, the main themes could be summarised in terms of:

- improved accessibility (for example, extending opening hours, reducing waiting lists and charges for use)

- expansion of services (for example, increased range of activities, improvements to facilities, increased numbers of staff)

- improvements in the quality or training of staff (have more understanding staff, have better training for staff)

- expanding the social profile of users, and

- supplying written information for parents to read at home.

Taking semi-formal support services first, despite generally positive experiences of these services, parents who had used them nevertheless had a wide range of views about how they could be improved. The most popular suggestions were about expanding or increasing various aspects of service provision – for example, extending or increasing the hours that services were available (two in five respondents, or 41%). A relatively large proportion of respondents also wished for an 'increased range of activities' (29%), for 'better equipment or facilities' (26%), and 'increased numbers of staff or volunteers' (24%) at semi-formal services. In Part III we showed how parents use semi-formal services for primarily social reasons, to meet other local families. It was therefore interesting that in terms of suggestions for improving services nearly one-third (31%) of parents wanted an expanded, more heterogeneous profile of users, defined as a 'wider range of people, or more parents and children' using services. This reflected a feeling (endorsed by some of the parents who were interviewed for the qualitative part of the project) that community-based services are some-times not well attended or are dominated by small cliques of regular users. Other suggestions concerned making services more accessible and more informative. Nearly one-quarter of users wanted lower charges for use (23%), reflecting the poverty in the sample as a whole. Last, one in ten services (11%) would have been improved, according to respondents, by providing written information for people to take away with them – a recurring area of concern for parents that we pick up again below.

Similarly, a range of potential improvements were suggested for formal services. Again reflecting respondents' main reasons for using these services as discussed in Part III, practical, instrumental issues were to the fore. The most frequent improvement suggested related to the need for greater ease of access to services. Nearly one-third of users (30%), wanted reduced waiting lists or waiting time to use the service, closely followed by increased number of staff (29%). A further quarter (25%) wanted service opening hours extended. Last, over one-quarter of respondents (27%) also thought that providing additional written information – such as leaflets – for service users to take away would have improved the service. Figure 14.1 shows the full range of views on potential improvements to organised services.[1]

The lack of accessibility, in particular, of certain key services was stressed by some respondents in the qualitative phase of the study.

> It would have been much easier [to deal with child's health problems] if there had been much easier access to the health experts to sit down and really talk about the [problem].
>
> *(Mother, lone parent, sick child)*

> She [daughter] needed to have had [help] right for the outset, not three or four months later when we finally got the social services interview.
>
> *(Mother, difficult child, low income)*

> He [nine-year-old son] does do my head in sometimes. Last year he started being a problem ... he sort of goes [mad] – he's hyperactive – he's always doing one thing or another ... stupid things. One time he went on a phase of lighting matches ... one time he got a knife and he was going to kill himself ... and then one time he tried to jump out of the bathroom window ... stupid things – but at the same time they could be dangerous. I've seen my doctor, and she referred me to the [child psychologist], and

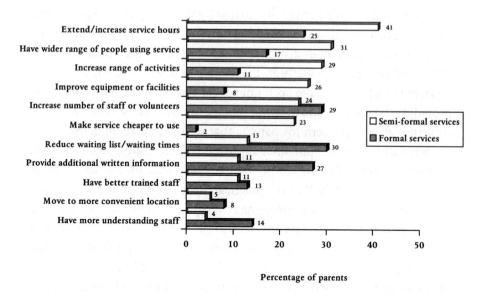

Base = 683 respondents using a semi-formal service in past three years, and 838 using a formal service. Respondents could suggest more than one improvement.

Figure 14.1 Suggestions for improving organised support services

> I've had a letter this week saying do I want to go on the waiting list. But the doctor told me it was about two years. It's disgusting, really. I mean, waiting two years. Anything could happen in them two years.
>
> *(Mother, large family, difficult child)*

Another parent, this time with a truanting child who also had severe health problems, told a similar story.

> He's been truanting from school, playing around in the classroom, causing disruptions – silly things like that. Which has led to expulsions – three of them in the last 12 months. But I'm annoyed more than anything about the school because no one has sat him down and talked to him and asked him what's going on in his head. I've approached the school about it and they're supposed to be getting a psychiatrist to see him ... but for the last six weeks nobody has come ... he's got cancer, and he's just had to go through it all on his own ... and I think that's pretty sad, and the school is a bit sad for not getting involved.
>
> *(Father, lone parent, poor accommodation, poor health, low income, sick child)*

That key services should be so lacking in certain areas is clearly a matter requiring particularly urgent attention from service planners and providers.

Making services more informative

That parents stressed the need for more written information when identifying ways of improving existing services was a key finding of the study that bears more comment. In fact, we found substantial evidence that that there is a large information deficit as far as parents in poor environments are concerned. Many parents reported that they felt inadequately informed about key aspects of parenting and child rearing, and wanted to know more. For example, when we showed parents a list of 14 topics and asked if they had ever felt they would like to know more about these things, a substantial proportion of the sample (over two-thirds – 68%) said they would like to have more information in at least one general area. In total, the mean number of areas about which parents felt ill informed in was two, and one in five parents (19%) wanted information in four or more areas. Table 14.1 shows the specific aspects of family life that parents said they would like to know more about. Three out of the four most common topics of information requested by parents concerned the behaviour of children. A quarter of parents said that they would like more information on 'what to expect as "normal" behaviour for children at different ages' and wanted to know more on 'how to deal with problems in children's behaviour'. One-fifth of parents wanted more information on 'the pros and cons of different ways of disciplining children'. Other common requests included information about education or schools, and parenting teenagers. As can be seen from Table 14.1, however, the information most wanted by parents varied substantially according the ages of their children. As might be expected, parents with teenagers in the household (defined as children aged 12 years or more) were particularly eager for information on parenting teenagers, but although almost one-third of parents with pre-school children wanted to know more about dealing with problems in children's behaviour, less than one-fifth of those (more mature and experienced) parents with teenagers wanted more information on this topic.

Table 14.1 Topics on which parents would like to have more information				
	% of parents			
	Parents with pre-school children ($n = 832$)	**Parents with primary school children** ($n = 1032$)	**Parents with teenagers** ($n = 628$)	**All parents** ($n = 1754$)
What to expect as 'normal' behaviour at different ages	30	27	18	25
How to deal with problems in children's behaviour	31	28	17	25
Education or schools	24	21	16	22
The pros and cons of different ways of disciplining children	24	23	15	21
Parenting teenagers	10	20	30	18
Problems between siblings	13	21	21	17
How to talk to children about physical and sexual development	14	18	12	16
How children learn	22	15	6	16
Children's diets	15	7	3	9
Problems with children's or babies' sleeping or crying	14	6	3	8
Child/baby health	13	5	2	7
Normal stages of child and baby development	10	4	1	6
How parenthood affects relationships with partners	7	5	4	5
Something else	1	1	1	1

Note: Respondents could name more than one topic of information. Age groups are not discrete – parents could have children in more than one age range.

We also asked about how parents would most like to receive information on each of these different topics. We gave parents a wide range of methods to choose from, ranging from self-administered methods of communication (leaflet, booklet, video to watch at home, TV or radio programme) through semi-formal methods (informal discussion group with other parents; telephone helpline or advice line) to formal (personal visit to a professional at a hospital, clinic or GP surgery; home visit from a professional, or a formal parenting education class). We asked parents to tell us, for each topic they had indicated they would like to know more about, 'How would you prefer to receive this information?' Parents could nominate as many methods as they liked.

Based on the results of this question, Table 14.2 summarises the 'top three' methods by which parents in the sample said they would prefer to receive information, across the range of topics. So, for example, of those wanting more information on what to expect as 'normal' behaviour at different ages ($n = 448$), over one-half (57%) said they would like to access this kind of information through a written leaflet or booklet, over one-quarter (28%) chose a video to watch at home, and one-quarter (25%) said they would find an informal discussion group with other parents a suitable format for learning more about this.

Table 14.2 How parents prefer to receive information about parenting

Topic of information	Top three most popular methods of receiving information about specific topics % of parents citing method as appropriate		
	First	Second	Third
What to expect in terms of 'normal' behaviour at different ages (*n* = 446)	Leaflet 57%	Video 28%	Group discussion 25%
How to deal with problems with children's behaviour (*n* = 435)	Leaflet 46%	Home visit 30%	Video 26%
Education or schools (*n* = 379)	Leaflet 60%	Home visit 26%	Group discussion 23%
The pros and cons of different ways of disciplining children (*n* = 362)	Leaflet 49%	Group discussion 30%	Video 30%
Parenting teenagers (*n* = 311)	Leaflet 50%	Video 29%	Group discussion 28%
Problems between siblings (*n* = 290)	Leaflet 49%	Group discussion 27%	Video 25%
How children learn (*n* = 274)	Leaflet 56%	Video 32%	TV/Radio 29%
How to talk to children about growing up, bodies and sex (*n* = 271)	Leaflet 59%	Video 39%	Group discussion 23%
Children's or babies' diet (*n* = 157)	Leaflet 63%	Visit to professional 36%	Video 26%
Problems with children or babies sleeping or crying (*n* = 141)	Leaflet 50%	Video 31%	Home visit 29%
Children's or babies' health (*n* = 124)	Leaflet 65%	Visit to professional 36%	Video 24%
The normal stages of baby or child development (*n* = 101)	Leaflet 64%	Video 32%	Parent class 25%
How parenthood affects relationships with partners (*n* = 95)	Leaflet 47%	Home visit 24%	Video 23%

Key =	Self-administered delivery	Semi-formal delivery	Formal delivery

As can be seen from Table 14.2, the order of popularity for methods of receiving information varied relatively little depending on the topic at issue. What was striking, across all the different topics, was the popularity of methods of information transfer which did not involve face-to-face contact with other people or with professionals, but which parents could peruse in private, at home, and in their own time. In other words, there was a strong preference for 'self-administered' support, irrespective of the topic at issue. Thus leaflets or booklets were, across the board, the favoured method of information delivery of most parents, followed in many cases by videos to watch at home. Home visits from professionals or personal consultations with site-based professionals were never the most popular option, although in some cases (where the information that would be most useful was, perhaps, likely to vary according to the personal circumstances of the individual parent) these were cited as the second most appropriate method of gaining information. Informal discussion groups with other parents were selected by some parents, although these were by no means as popular as home-based methods of receiving information.

How do parents want family support services delivered?

What, then, did the study tell us about key principles of how support services should be delivered to parents in poor environments? Below, we highlight the main messages.

Services that allow parents to feel 'in control'

Making parents feel listened to and respected, and acknowledging that they are also 'experts' in their own lives seems to be as important – if not more important – as providing them with access to specific types of practical help. As we saw in Chapter 9, the issue of who has the control is critical in family support: parents defined 'good' support as help that nevertheless allowed them to feel 'in control' of decisions and what happened to them and their families. The fear of loss of autonomy was a strong theme throughout the study, whether parents were discussing informal or organised support, and there is clearly a delicate balance to be struck between 'help' that genuinely supports (or as some would term it, 'empowers') and help that in fact undermines, disempowers and de-skills. Busy professionals often gave out messages that parents found disempowering – that parents were over-anxious, inexperienced, or ignorant, for example. Making the time to listen and engage seriously with parents' concerns seems a top priority for services wanting to improve the way they support this section of the community. Parents' strong preferences for self-administered modes of information delivery tended to confirm this general picture: written information or information from videos, television and radio can be digested in private and without compromising confidentiality. Reading leaflets and watching television or videos is of course also easier and more convenient for busy parents than going out to services; furthermore, the information can be saved and re-visited at times of particular need, when certain problems come to the fore and parents want to refresh their understanding of specific issues. Thus, what may underlie this strong preference for self-administered forms of information and advice is that this is a way of acquiring knowledge or getting support with parenting problems that allows parents to stay firmly in control, choosing when and where they access it. As one parent indicated:

> It's much easier for people to relate to Kilroy-type programmes and agony aunt type situations than to make approaches to officials for help.
>
> *(Mother, poor accommodation, lone parent, low income)*

Given this, it might surprise some that telephone (or indeed internet) helplines were not cited as preferred sources of information and support in the survey interviews. Our view was that this probably reflected the 'newness' and unfamiliarity of these methods at the time of the survey, because when we probed in qualitative interviews there was some evidence that these could also offer substantial promise for providing parenting support in a timely, individually tailored and suitably confidential, 'hands-off' format.[2] Some were familiar with the concept of a telephone helpline from publicity about services such as ChildLine, and could see very real potential in a method that would offer direct access to professionals without risking overstepping the boundary between help and interference.

> There's no-one that [parents] can just pick the phone up to and say, 'I could really do with a chat', 'I'm tired' or 'I'm lonely' or something like that. There's no one you could really phone up and talk to about that, without feeling that they're going to pry too far or check your children over or do something.
>
> *(Father, low income, difficult child)*

What would be really good for parents would be something [where] they know they could pick that phone up, and there would be someone on the end. And you'd be able to say to them, 'Oh. I got so close to whacking him today because he did this …'. And they could say, 'Well we understand that, we know how you're feeling, just tell us all about it. Scream and holler at us' – someone on the end of a phone similar to the Samaritans. You've got ChildLine for children but you've got nothing for adults. You haven't got an AdultLine.

(Mother, low income)

And as one parent said, summing up what many parents felt in relation to the need for advice:

[What I'd like is] a phone number you can ring at any time of the day for support, advice, whatever … someone that you can contact at any time of day.

(Mother, large family)

Practical, useful services to meet parents' self-defined needs

Parents set great store by the practical value of services, but often only insofar as they met their own self-defined needs. We quoted earlier one father who likened the help he was offered by social services at a time of crisis to having somebody offer to redecorate his house when what he really wanted was help moving furniture. That is, the help was well meant, but irrelevant to his actual needs at the time. The implication is that it is important that family support services pay more attention to parents' perception of the support they provide in terms of the manner in which the support is delivered and parents' feelings about how useful and appropriate the service is. Matching what is delivered to what parents themselves identify as their needs is likely to be critical here, because the study suggested that services and professionals sometimes do not listen to parents. Service agendas for provision of support sometimes seem to reflect what is available rather than what is needed, and do not always match well with parents' own support agendas. A key principle is that services need to pay more attention to assessment of need in partnership with the families to which they cater, so that what is provided does more closely match what is wanted. A related point is that, particularly where formal services are concerned, parents do not necessarily expect to 'enjoy' the experience of seeking help: on the contrary, parents described largely instrumental and rather businesslike approaches to help seeking from formal agencies. They are unlikely, therefore, to be much impressed by superficial attempts to make services seem more friendly, approachable or concerned with 'customer satisfaction' and so on unless these are also accompanied by clear practical outcomes.

Timely services

Finally, a major issue that stood out in terms of how the delivery of support to families in poor environments could be improved was that of timeliness. By far the most frequently cited suggestion for improving services was, for semi-formal services, 'extend or increase the service hours' and, for formal services, 'reduce waiting lists or waiting times' and 'increase the number of staff'. Respondents pointed to the need for greater access to services when parents decided they needed it, stressing that there were times when they needed help or advice quickly but that existing services were slow to respond, if indeed they responded at all. Some parents described long waits for essential services. Another key principle, then, is that what parents want from support is help when *they* feel they need it, not weeks, months or even years later.

Concluding thoughts: key messages about the nature of social support for parents in poor environments

We draw this book to a close by taking an overview of the key messages about the nature of social support as described to us by parents in this study: what it is, what it is not, and the relative importance of different sources of support bearing in mind the diverse needs of families in poor environments. These key messages are important because they caution against simplistic approaches to the provision of services, reminding us of the complex and subtle ways in which social support manifests itself in parents' daily lives.

The importance of diversity in support provision

A first 'overview' message from the study concerned the way in which we conceptualise support and its various manifestations. We have tended to treat the various sources of support (informal, semi-formal, formal) as discrete types in order to make it possible to measure support inputs and attitudes more accurately, an approach that seems to be borne out by our findings on how and why parents utilise different types of support. Certainly, it is important to note that different forms of support do seem to fulfil different functions for parents, according to our data, and this may be important for deciding how to market and target services. One size does not fit all, and what may work well for one service may not be appropriate for another. For example, there was clear evidence that parents expect and receive different things from semi-formal, as opposed to formal, services. Semi-formal support services tend to be accessed for social reasons, giving both children and their parents an opportunity to broaden their social networks. On the other hand, parents report going to formal services for more instrumental reasons, to get professional advice and help with specific problems. Some formal services are also seen as providers of crisis or emergency support (for example, social services), whereas no-one expected this of semi-formal services. Diversity of provision is therefore essential to meet diversity of need.

The continuing importance of the formal support sector

A related issue, then, concerns the relative importance of community-based, as opposed to statutory, services. In these days of constant criticism of both health and social services, anyone picking up almost any Sunday newspaper might be forgiven for questioning if statutory services have much to offer on the child welfare and family support front. Might not wholesale reform, involving a move to more community-based and community-delivered services, be the answer? Should we not be bolstering informal social support networks rather than continuing to fund expensive and perhaps ineffective formal agencies? Perhaps, but our data strongly suggested that since community-based and formal services appear to perform different functions and cater to different levels of prevention, both types of support are important precisely because they meet different needs. Indeed, although we did pick up plenty of criticism of the statutory sector, our findings tend to re-confirm the vital importance of getting these sorts of services 'right', in particular for the neediest families in the community. Those families in our sample who had the highest levels of needs also had, in general, the highest 'consumption' levels of support across the board. They also held the least positive attitudes to naturally occurring support. This was not, we argued, necessarily because they were temperamentally incapable of sustaining healthy social relationships, but because their greater reliance on support of various kinds coupled with their greater vulnerability exposed them more than others to the downsides of informal support. These were the families, we suggested, that were least able to engage in the reciprocal give and take of informal social support relationships. They were also the families with the most to lose, socially speaking, in terms of being exposed to the scrutiny of neighbours and others in the local community. Thus, these parents can be seen as the natural constituency of formal support services, which can offer help without expecting reciprocation and advice without breaching confidentiality. It was not therefore surprising to find that high-need families were more likely to use formal services than other sorts of support and, despite their vulnerability, were actually comparatively positive in their attitudes to formal support. The message we take from this is that services in this sector continue to have a vital role to play in supporting those at greatest risk. The drive to develop better community-based support services and to strengthen families' informal networks should not be allowed to freeze out resources for the formal sector, and the undoubted need for universal support services should not obscure recognition that there are families who, in addition, require special, targeted services.

Multiple problems need multiple solutions

A third key message from the study in relation to the general nature of support was that we need always to bear in mind the multiple and overlapping nature of risk factors among parents in poor environments. Many parents reported that they were subject to two, three, four or even five distinct risk factors, and in many cases sets of stressors seemed to go together – for example, lone parenting, low income, accommodation problems and high levels of current family problems; poor mental and physical health, and so on. Thus, support to families in poor environments needs to operate on a number of dimensions, tackling stressors simultaneously at the individual, the family and the community level. Typically, for example, a parent in our study with poor mental health as measured by a high Malaise score is also quite likely to be struggling with one or more problems in the areas of child behaviour, financial strain, poor housing and physical ill health. In an 'ideal support world', such a parent would receive a thorough assessment of all the areas of difficulty they faced, and then be offered as many services as were appropriate to tackle these various issues.

The results of this study therefore add to the already substantial body of evidence that indicates the importance of careful and holistic preliminary assessment of need at the family level, followed by multi-agency working, partnership across as well as within sectors, and partnership between communities and agencies in order to deliver comprehensive and 'joined up' services.

The concept of negative support

Another key message was that an appreciation of the downside to social support is also important in helping us to understand the limitations of support, as it currently exists, in terms of enhancing parenting. Although we are by no means the first commentators to assert that support may not always be the good thing practitioners, policy makers and researchers often assume it to be, the downside of social support was a loudly voiced theme in this study. We concluded that the concept of 'negative support' may be very useful in understanding why parents do and do not access different sorts of help and support in parenting. Many parents reflected on the disadvantages as well as the benefits of accepting informal help from family, friends and neighbours, as well as being sensitised to the potential problems inherent in accessing organised services. There were strong indications that 'support' is not always perceived in an entirely positive light: there is a fine dividing line between help and interference, and losing control over one's life (and one's children) was perceived to be a possible consequence of asking for help or support. Confidentiality and control loomed large as issues underlying parents' willingness to accept support provided by agencies, especially those in the statutory sector. In terms of accepting informal social support, parents were anxious about loss of privacy, and about reciprocity, indebtedness and having to 'return favours'. Furthermore, the more problems in parents' personal circumstances, the more negative the perceptions in this respect, so that the neediest parents were also the least likely to feel positive about asking for or accepting informal support. Although it is clear that support is vital to many, we should be wary of assuming that measures aimed at enhancing the level of support available will always be welcomed by all parents.

Support is not a universal panacea for parenting problems

A further critical message we learned from this study was that social support as it currently exists – whether informal or organised – cannot be regarded as the universal 'solution' for parents who are experiencing difficulties in coping. Some parents reported relatively extensive support networks of high affective quality and reliability, high levels of enacted informal support, high levels of organised service use, and yet still said they felt unsupported and that they were not coping well. Not everyone who was experiencing problems with parenting welcomed the idea of extra help or support, and conversely some parents who reported relatively restricted networks and minimal enacted support nevertheless felt adequately supported and said they were coping well. Although feeling supported was an important indicator of coping, it was not the only one. Again, this leads us to conclude that we should be wary of assuming that providing extra family support services, or working to bolster informal support networks, is necessarily the solution to all parenting difficulties. It also reminds us that genuine 'primary' prevention of parenting problems means finding ways to enhance parents' ability to master their own problems before they set in and without external assistance, as well as helping to reduce underlying risk factors in families' lives as a way to avoid problems with coping.

Build on the existing strengths of parents and their communities

On a positive note, the study showed that parents in poor environments, despite often living in circumstances of considerable stress, were on the whole remarkably resilient and positive. Many took pride in their local neighbourhood and, despite a keen awareness of its deficiencies, continued to feel committed to staying and making a life for their families. Although parents were often wearily resigned to the environmental and social hazards their neighbourhood presented, it was clear that a sense of community was by no means dead in many of the areas we studied. This has important implications for those interested in supporting families in need. Subject to the caveats arising from the 'uncontrolled' nature of the study, as discussed in Part I, we found that poverty – either at the area level or at the household level – was not strongly related to social support for parents. In general, with the exception of a significant relationship between area-level poverty as measured by PPE-Index and size of social network, we found no evidence that degrees of poverty within the sample of poor environments were related to levels of enacted support either at the informal level or in terms of organised services. Neither the type of area (poor, very poor or extremely poor), nor household income were associated with differing levels of support or with perceptions of being 'supported' or 'unsupported'. Thus, apart from an indication that parents in the poorest areas may have somewhat more restricted social networks from which to draw informal support, within the context of poor environments we could not find any clear data that led us to conclude that the poorest areas or families were less well supported than other areas or families. Although the popular image of the poorest environments, as portrayed by the media covering stories of 'sink estates', is one of social fragmentation and disintegration, and although there is a body of academic literature on support deficits that describes poor areas as frequently lacking in sense of community and social cohesion, our study did not confirm these pictures. Parents were certainly well aware of the deficiencies of their neighbourhood but, by and large, most were rather positive about their local community and their own support networks. Support deficits, in this study, were not a function of community-level stressors arising from living in a poor environment but rather of a complex web of individual and family-level characteristics. We cannot therefore say that poor areas are necessarily prejudicial to social support for parents. For policy makers and those interested in strengthening communities, the heartening message may be that, despite external appearances, even in the poorest areas many parents take pride in their local community and may be surprisingly receptive to initiatives to strengthen and build support networks. The study showed that parents in poor environments are resourceful and that many are coping remarkably well with the strains they face. Perhaps at a community level those coping better could be mobilised to help those coping less well. For example, parents of older children report coping better, on the whole, than parents with younger children, and are more experienced and confident about parenting than those with babies and pre-schoolers. Finding ways to involve these parents in befriending and supporting newer parents could be a potentially powerful way of boosting families' own naturally occurring social support networks.

Tackle weaknesses in the marketing and the image of services

We have already discussed parents' criticisms of existing support services at length and will not rehearse them in detail here. However, two final key issues strike us as requiring serious attention from policy makers and service planners. One is that there appear to be gaps in awareness of what services are available as well as rather low levels of use of some organised services. Even in the case of so-called universal services such as health visiting – now accorded a central role in some of the new policy initiatives such as Sure Start – some parents in poor environments were unaware of this service, and had not used it. Given the very high levels of need in this sample, there is clearly work to be done in marketing services more effectively to parents so that they know what is available and how to access it. Better marketing of services might also help fulfil parents' desire for more heterogeneous profiles of service users, in that a wider range of parents could be drawn into community-based services in particular. The study quite strongly suggested that local surveys among families might reveal useful information about gaps in service awareness that could help services promote their activities more effectively.

A related point is that there appears to be an urgent need to tackle the poor public image of many family support services – especially those in the formal sector. The bad reputation of some agencies seemed to some extent to have been earned, in the sense that parents' poor opinions were grounded in their own direct experiences of service use. Clearly, services need to improve their performance in order to remedy this. However, in many cases it was not clear to what extent the problem was one of performance or one of image, because some parents' attitudes had been formed second- and third-hand on the basis of stories they had heard and impressions they had formed without personal experience of the agencies involved. Nevertheless, wherever the attitudes come from, the end results are the same, and can be serious. This study showed that there is a high level of need for formal services among parents in poor environments but that a substantial minority of high-need parents are not in the system, and that some parents will do anything rather than seek help. Social services departments, in particular, appear to need a complete image makeover if they are to present themselves to parents as valuable sources of help rather than as threatening agents of social control. Some health services also failed to impress, being seen by parents as rushed and uncaring or else as didactic and patronising.

Perceptions of support, and helping parents to feel in control

Last, if there was one overriding message for policy and practice arising from the study it was this: that how parents *feel* about support is critical. The best services in the world will not necessarily enhance parents' ability to cope unless they are perceived as helpful and acceptable. Perhaps one of the strongest messages from this study, and the one that we conclude with, is that the best way to support parents in poor environments is to ensure that parents feel in control of the type of support they receive and the way in which it is delivered. At present, parents sometimes perceive family support services as pulling against them rather than with them. While parents do not by any means reject the concept of external support with parenting and child care (indeed, quite the reverse, in that parents very much want certain types of services), there is nevertheless a strong culture of family self-sufficiency within poor environments. External support that appears to undermine parents' autonomy and which steps over the fine line that divides 'help' from 'interference' can end up being experienced as negative rather than positive and may simply add to, rather than relieve, stress. Providers of support will, however, only discover where communities and individual families draw the delicate line between helpful and unhelpful support by asking them, and so all support services should ideally begin by consulting families about what they want and how they want it provided. This does not, of course, mean that some families will not also benefit from assistance from professionals in clarifying and prioritising their needs. Moreover, there will always be cases in which the interests of children and their parents do not coincide, and where control has to be removed from dangerous parents. But for the majority of 'ordinary' families in poor environments, struggling to do a good enough job of child rearing in the face of numerous challenges, it remains the case that parents want to feel in control of their own lives even when seeking help. We leave the last word to one mother who summed up forcefully the balance that must be achieved.

> 'Support' means that you are still in charge; the parent is still in charge and you are asking for help, advice and whatever – but you are the one in

charge. You are not handing over your kids to someone else to take over. You are still in charge of them.

(Mother, lone parent, low income, sick child)

Notes

1. Parents were asked this question in relation to each service they had used and the results shown combine figures for all cases of service use within that sector during the past three years.

2. However, it should be remembered that one in ten of the sample did not have any kind of telephone in the home, and these are also likely to be the neediest group of parents.

Appendix 1

Glossary of key terms

Enumeration District (ED)

An Enumeration District ('ED') is the smallest area on which standardised national data exist. Designed to be approximately the area of a single Census enumerator's 'walk' (approximately 150 addresses), there are around 121,000 EDs in England, Scotland and Wales. These can be mapped on to postcode sectors in order to select samples of private addresses and households within them.

The Poor Parenting Index (PPE-Index)

The Poor Parenting Environments Index, or PPE-Index was a scale, specially developed for this study, that allowed us to identify areas of high social deprivation across the country. It was composed of a 'basket' of indicators shown by previous research to be associated with parenting difficulties, and was available on the 1991 Census. The Index was used to give each Enumeration District in the country a score, with a higher score indicating a greater level of disadvantage. The eventual sample for the study was drawn from EDs in the upper 30 per cent of the national distribution (with scores in the range 124 to 295). See Appendix 2 for further technical details.

PPE-Index bands

In order to explore the effects of area-level poverty within the sample of poor environments, we further subdivided areas in the sample into three equal bands or triciles. The distribution of scores in each band and the label we applied to each band was as follows:

PPE-index score 124–157: 'Poor'

PPE-index score 158–200: 'Very poor'

PPE-index score 201–295: 'Extremely poor'

Main carer

We defined 'main carer' as: 'the person who is responsible for looking after or caring for the children in this household for the greatest amount of time. For example, the person who spends the most time doing things for the children, like shopping, cooking or laundry, or the person who spends most time with the children day to day.' A child could have one main carer or two joint-equal carers.

Index child

Parents who had more than one child aged under 17 in the home were asked to answer certain questions with one specific child – the 'index child' – in mind. For this purpose, interviewers used a randomised system to select one child from all the children in the household at the start of the interview.

Appendix 2

Sampling for the Survey of Parenting in Poor Environments

Our first step in developing a method of sampling for the survey was to develop a system for scoring areas of the country based on their relative levels of social deprivation, using indicators of particular salience to the ecological model of parenting. The scale (which we refer to hereafter as the Poor Parenting Environments Index, or PPE-Index) was composed of a 'basket' of indicators shown by previous research to be associated with parenting difficulties, and was available on the 1991 Census. Using Census data to construct such a scale has its drawbacks. In common with other indices dependent on the 1991 Census (such as the ILD 1998 and ACORN), a key limitation was that by the time work began on devising the scale (late 1997) the Census data were already somewhat old. If the geography of poverty had changed in the years elapsed since the Census, our scale would not, of course, reflect this. Furthermore, data available at the highly localised Enumeration District (ED) level – the level required for selecting a probability sample of addresses – are somewhat restricted. These limitations to the PPE-Index must be acknowledged. However, on the plus side, Census data have the advantage of being robust and reasonably complete at small-area level and in respect of national coverage, and are also readily available online.[1]

It remains to be seen, of course, if the same scale, constructed using the new 2001 Census data when they become available, would identify the same areas that were identified based on the 1991 data.

Selecting the variables for the Poor Parenting Environments Index (PPE-Index)

We began the work of selecting the variables to go into the PPE-Index by reviewing recent literature on the correlates of child maltreatment.[2] A substantial number of studies (many from the United States) have explored these, mostly in relation to rates of child maltreatment reported to the authorities, although some studies (for example, Straus and colleagues 1980), Straus and Smith (1995) have also explored the relationship of demographic characteristics and self-reported child physical maltreatment. For example, Garbarino and Kostelny (1992) found the following variables to be useful in explaining differential community rates of child maltreatment: percentage of households living in poverty; unemployed; in female-headed households; in overcrowded housing; Afro-American or Hispanic; affluent (coded negatively); resident less than five years; below median educational attainment. Together, these variables accounted for 79 per cent of the variance between different areas in the above study, and 'socio-economic status' (a composite variable) accounted for 49 per cent of the variance. Allowing for cultural differences between the US and the UK, many of these variables are also consistently found to be associated with child maltreatment and 'at-risk' status in British research,[3] and, taken as a whole, the studies we reviewed tended to give remarkably consistent findings. Isolating the variables of interest to go into our initial model of the index was therefore a relatively straightforward task. Essentially, the variables that were most consistently reported can be grouped into those connected with poverty (for example, low income, unemployment, lone parenting, living in social housing, overcrowding); those connected with low social cohesion (high mobility); and those connected with social class (socio-economic group, educational attainment).

Because not all of the variables found to be associated with poor parenting environments were directly available from the 1991 UK Census, some indicators (for example, educational attainment) were not able to be included in our model, and some 'proxy' indicators had to be used in place of key indicators.[4] For example, we used car ownership as a proxy for low income/low affluence. Thus the variables that were eventually chosen to go into the model are shown in Box A2.1.

Percentage of:

- unemployed adults aged 16 or more
- overcrowded households (defined as more than one person per room)
- lone parents
- households in social housing (local authority or housing association-owned)
- households of social class iii(n) or below (skilled non-manual occupations and below)
- households with no car
- households who had moved in the last year.

Box A2.1 Variables included in the model of 'poor parenting environments'

Testing the model

To test the Poor Parenting Environment Index model (outlined in Chapter 2), all Enumeration Districts (EDs) in the country[5] were first stratified by Government Standard Region and Scotland (excluding the Highlands and Islands); urbanity; and then ranked with probability proportionate to size in terms of the percentage of households with dependent children. This stratification was necessary to ensure a final sample that would be representatively distributed in terms of regions of the country, urban versus rural areas, and that would contain sufficient numbers of households with children to make fieldwork efficient. A pilot sample of 10,000 EDs was then selected at random.

The sample of 10,000 EDs was split into two for diagnostic purposes, and factor analytical data reduction techniques[6] were employed on each half of the sample to examine the correlation structure of the set of variables (which ranged from 0.10 to 0.72, but were mostly highly correlated, see Table A2.1); and to determine the proportion of total and shared variance explained by the combination of variables. Two factor 'solutions' were identified, and the solution explaining the greatest proportion of the total variance (55.5%), was then used to form a weighted scale. The solution provided factor loadings for the component variables that take account of correlation effects between the variables, and these factor loadings were used as the weights to be applied to each component variable in the scale. A score for each ED was obtained by multiplying the factor loading by the proportion of the population with the relevant characteristic within that ED. The scale was applied to the ED half-samples (that is, each ED in each half of the sample was scored using each of the weighted scales in turn) allowing us to view the ranked distribution of EDs using the different scales. Further tests showed that the two rankings were not significantly different, and we were thus able to finalise the scale (see Box A2.3).

Table A2.1 Correlation matrix for variables used in construction of PPE-Index: Census 1991 data at ED level

	% unemployed	% overcrowded	% lone parents	% residents social housing	% social class iii(n) and below	% households with no car	% households moved in last year
% unemployed	1.00	.59	.71	.66	.47	.76	.15
% overcrowded	.59	1.00	.43	.37	.30	.49	.11
% lone parents	.71	.43	1.00	.72	.42	.67	.12
% social housing	.66	.37	.72	1.00	.51	.82	.00
% social class iii(n) and below	.47	.30	.42	.51	1.00	.56	-0.13
% hhs with no car	.76	.49	.67	.80	.56	1.00	.10
% hhs moved in last year	.15	.11	.12	.00	-0.13	.10	1.00

(0.88532 x % unemployed adults 16+) + (0.64268 x % over-crowded) + (0.83503 x % lone parents) + (0.85986 x % social housing) + (0.65222 x % HH social class iii(n) or below) + (0.90352 x % no car) + (0.10602 x % moved last year)

Box A2.3 Factor weightings from Principal Components analysis, applied to EDs to derive final PPE-Index score

Applying the scale to select a sample

The final scale was then run against the full test group of 10,000 Enumeration Districts and the distribution examined. ED scores ranged from 0 to 307, with a sample mean of 100 (SD 58.9). The higher the score, the greater the level of disadvantage. The point on the distribution of scores beyond which we defined 'poor environments' as beginning was of course essentially a subjective and arbitrary decision but, based on the shape of the overall distribution, we chose a threshold at the 70th percentile (score = 124) as our threshold for 'poor parenting environments'; that is, we defined 'poor parenting environments' as those in the top 30 per cent of the national distribution. Figure A2.1 shows the ranked distribution of all EDs in the country according to the PPE-Index and indicates the threshold for 'poor parenting environments'.

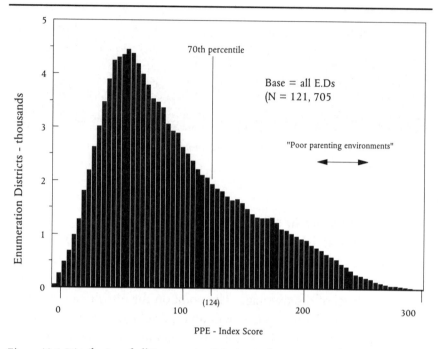

Figure A2.1 Distribution of all Enumeration Districts in the country, ranked by PPE-Index

Six Enumeration Districts and 40 addresses within them were selected from this top 30 per cent for a pilot study (see below), to verify that this system did indeed yield environments with high levels of social and economic disadvantage. Then, for the main survey, all EDs in the country whose score on the Index was 124 or more were used as the base for a further sample, randomly selected, of 135 primary ED sampling points. The maps below show the geographic distribution, first, of the 'top 30 per cent' Enumeration Districts (*n* = 37,105) across England, Wales and Scotland (Map A2.1) and, second, of the areas selected for the study (Map A2.6). It will be seen from A2.1 that, as we might expect, the high scoring areas are clustered around the major conurbations (London, Birmingham, Merseyside, Newcastle upon Tyne, Glasgow, Cardiff, etc.), although there are also more sparsely scattered areas in rural locations. Within our selected sample of Enumeration Districts, scores on the PPE-Index ranged from 124 to 295, with a mean score of 180.

Base = 37,105 Enumeration Districts

Map A2.1 National distribution of poor parenting environments

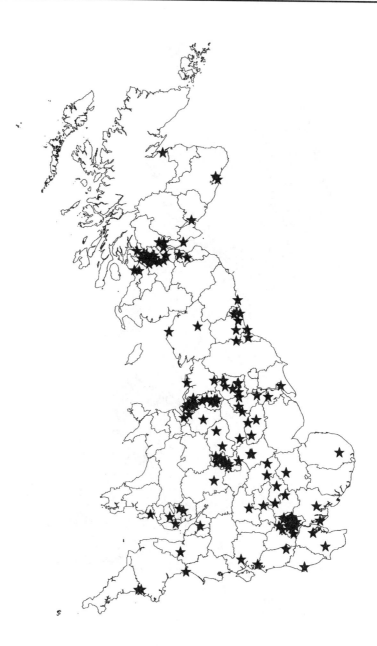

Base = 135 Enumeration Districts

Map A2.2 Distribution of Enumeration Districts selected for the survey of parenting in poor environments

The selected 135 high scoring EDs were then matched against the Postcodes Address File (PAF), maintained by the Post Office, to obtain a complete listing of private residential addresses within these EDs. A sample of addresses was then randomly and systematically selected from the listing using a sampling fraction of one in ten. The selected addresses (N = 10,500) formed the issued sample. All selected addresses were then issued to a team of over a hundred interviewers across the country who visited in person and screened each address for the presence of a 'main carer' of a child aged 0–16 years.[7] Where parents or parent figures were located, they were invited to participate in the study. Where there was more than one parent in the household who considered themselves a main carer, one carer was selected by random system and identified as the 'selected parent'.

Sample outcomes

The issued sample of approximately 10,500 addresses yielded just over 2,800 households 'in scope' (that is, occupied households containing children under 17 years old, where interviewers could theoretically have completed an interview). Nine per cent of addresses turned out to be 'dead wood' (untraceable, empty, derelict, etc.) or unavailable/excluded (for example, the eligible respondent was ill at the time of the survey, in prison, or unable to speak English). At 64 per cent of addresses interviewers were either completely unable to obtain information about the occupants despite a number of visits at different times of the day and on different days of the week,[8] or they were verified not to contain children. At a further 306 addresses interviewers were unable to contact the appropriate selected household or respondent. Of the remaining households who were identified as eligible for the survey, refusals from eligible parents (either direct, or made by someone on their behalf) constituted 31 per cent of the in-scope sample, leaving a net response rate of 69 per cent of the eligible in-scope addresses, reducing to 62 per cent if households and parents that could not be contacted are included as potentially in scope (that is, using a more stringent definition of eligibility) (see Table A2.2).

Table A2.2 Sample outcomes			
	Numbers	*Percentages*	
Issued sample	10,530	–	
Ineligible address (dead wood or unavailable)	913	–	
No children at address (*n* = 6,527) /No information about address (*n* = 246)	6773	–	
In scope (total potentially eligible)	2844	–	100
No contact at selected household after 4+ calls	166	–	6
No contact with selected parent after 4+ calls	140	–	5
Eligible households (total successfully contacted)	2538	100	–
Refusal on behalf of or by selected parent	776	31	27
Partial interview	8	*	*
Completed interview	1754	69	62

Distribution of the sample by region

Table A2.3 shows how the achieved sample was distributed by Government Standard Region. In the table, we also show response figures for households with children to the Family Resources Survey (FRS) 1996–97, for comparison. The FRS figures relate to all households with children (not just those living in poor environments) and so are not exactly comparable with our data. Still, they give some picture of how our sample of families differed in regional distribution from the national picture. It will be seen that our achieved sample was composed of a smaller proportion of parents in the Eastern region than the FRS, and that we also had fewer families in the South East. On the other hand, we had more parents in the North/North East, and a substantially greater proportion in Scotland. Because no genuinely comparable large-scale nationally representative samples of parents in poor environments exist we cannot, of course, be sure to what extent these figures accurately reflect the true distribution of parents in poor areas or whether they also reflect differences in the tendency of parents in some areas to respond to the survey. The probable situation lies somewhere between the two, although the differences between our sample and the FRS do not seem too surprising, given regional differences in poverty.

	% of parents in sample (n = 1754)	% of households in FRS 1996–7 sample (n = 7263 approx)
North/North East	10	5
North West and Merseyside	12	12
Yorkshire and Humberside	8	8
East Midlands	5	8
West Midlands	10	10
Eastern/East Anglia	2	9
London	11	12
South East	10	14
South West	5	8
Wales	5	5
Scotland	22	9

Table A2.3 Distribution of the achieved sample by Government Standard Region compared with FRS sample 1996–97

Note: FRS figures are approximate due to rounding.

Reliability and validity issues: possible sources of bias in the achieved sample

Our method of sampling and approaching potential respondents followed rigorous probability sampling procedures to minimise the chances of biases arising within the achieved sample. However, a few implications follow from these response rates, which bear on the reliability and validity of the findings of the study. First, the fact that we were unable to make contact with 9 per cent of occupied households and with 5 per cent of selected parents bears comment. Although interviewer visits to selected addresses were spread out over time in order to maximise the chances of contacting families and selected parents, it may be that the people we were unable to contact were different in some way from other families or parents – more likely to be working (or working shifts or long hours), for example.

These may also have been households which were least willing to answer the door to an unknown caller, perhaps because of fear of crime. Our final sample may thus underestimate the numbers of working parents, and perhaps may also underestimate the numbers of parents in the very poorest areas. Second, at 31 per cent of contacted households parents actively declined to take part in the survey and we have no way of knowing their reasons. Third, although differences in the distribution of our sample compared to general population samples of all households with dependent children seem explicable in terms of regional variations in poverty, we cannot verify that this was in fact the explanation.

To what extent might non-response have affected the representativeness of the final sample composition, and hence the validity of the survey data? We cannot fully answer this question. The possibility remains that parents in selected households where we were not successful in obtaining an interview may have differed from parents we *did* interview in some systematic way. If this were the case, some unknown biases could be present in our data. A standard of way of checking for bias due to survey non-response is to compare the demographic characteristics of respondents in an achieved sample with those of respondents to (other) nationally representative samples. However, this option is not easily open to us because there are no other large, nationally representative samples of parents in poor environments in Great Britain against which we can compare the characteristics of our final sample. However, what we can say is that the rate of non-response is not by any means high by contemporary research standards. Survey response rates on both sides of the Atlantic are generally thought to be declining over time (Bradburn 1992; Campanelli, Sturgis and Purdon 1997) and although response rates are often higher among households with dependent children, conversely response rates in deprived inner-city areas (which were disproportionately represented in our sample) and to surveys covering topics that might be considered to be sensitive or intimate (such as aspects of family life) tend to be lower than average (Fowler 1993; Foster 1996). Although we cannot eliminate the possibility of bias in the sample, we had no evidence to suggest that our data should not be regarded as reliably representative of parents in poor environments. Overall, our response rate appears to be in the range becoming typical for complex large-scale surveys in the UK.[9] The pilot survey (in which issues connected with response rates were investigated very thoroughly) gave no indication that refusals were related to the subject of the survey or to any other key issue that might systematically affect our results. Our final sample contained a wide range of parents. Both fathers and mothers were included, as were parents of all ethnic groups and from a range of social circumstances including many of extreme disadvantage as well as some of comparative comfort. We have no reason to think that any particular group of parents was systematically excluded from the study.[10] In qualitative follow-up interviews, parents told us that they had welcomed the chance to take part in such an important survey and that they had felt able to be frank and free in their answers in the survey interview. We are therefore confident that the sample was, as far as we are able to tell, adequately representative of parents in poor environments in Great Britain. For this reason, no weighting for non-response has been applied to the data set.

Appendix 3

The Data Collection Instruments

The survey questionnaire

A full copy of the survey questionnaire can be found at www.prb.org.uk/parenting in poor environments/data collection instruments. Box A3.1 on pages 280–281 gives an outline of the areas covered in the survey interview.

Measures of child behaviour used in the survey

Bates Infant Characteristics Questionnaire (ICQ)

The Bates Infant Characteristics Questionnaire (Bates, Freeland and Lounsbury 1979) is self-completed schedule, developed in the United States, which measures parent perceptions of child behaviour and temperament. There are a number of different versions, designed for use with infants and toddlers of various ages and comprising between 24 and 32 items in total. The ICQ breaks down into a number of subscales, but we used a modified version focussing on two subscales only – 'fussy/difficult' and 'unadaptable'. These two scales were chosen because they best predict observer-noted and parent-perceived difficulties in the pre-school years and therefore seemed to have the greatest concurrent validity. They therefore seem to be the most robust measures, as well as capturing many of the characteristics which together are thought to combine to make a baby more challenging and less rewarding to care for (Bates 1980). In addition, it was necessary to restrict the length of the instrument as much as possible.

Introduction and demographic:

- family and household structure
- ethnicity and marital status
- employment and education
- physical health
- mental health (self-completed)
- income and expenditure.

Accommodation and environment:

- tenure and housing conditions
- problems in the local area
- community relationships
- ratings of quality of area.

Current problems:

- Current Problems Questionnaire (self-completed).

The index child:

- physical health
- emotional and behavioural issues (self-completed)
- parent and child relationships
- caring for children and others.

Social support in general:

- support with child care
- areas of difficulty
- information and advice
- attitudes to support.

Informal support:

- attitudes
- support network – extensiveness and quality
- enacted support.

Organised support:

- awareness/use of semi-formal support
- perceptions of quality/reasons for use on up to three services used in past three years
- reasons for not using semi-formal support services
- awareness/use of formal support
- perceptions of quality/reasons for use on up to three services used in past three years
- reasons for not using formal support services.

Parenting in general:

- coping
- things that would most improve parents' lives.

Box A3.1 Topics covered by the survey questionnaire

Based on reviews of the different versions, piloting among UK parents and reviews of some anglicised versions of the schedule, we developed a modified version of the ICQ which was completed by all parents with a child aged from birth to 24 months. Our modified version contained 16 items, although at the analysis stage only nine of these were scored. Bates offers three versions of the ICQ (6 months, 13 months and 24 months), with various recommended ranges around these core ages. Because the scales do not overlap perfectly in terms of the age groups covered, in this sample we were not able to obtain a valid score for children who fell between two age groups. For example, the six month ICQ is not recommended for children aged under four months or over seven months. Thus children under four months and between seven months and 13 months (when the next version of the ICQ becomes valid) cannot be assigned scores with any confidence. As a result, the numbers of valid scores for some age groups in the sample were very small, necessitating combining age groups and compressing the scales to eliminate items that are peculiar to one age version of the ICQ.

The resultant scales we have used are therefore compressed versions of Bates's original scales.

The scales were composed as follows.

1. Fussy/difficult subscale (4 items)

How often does your child get fussy and irritable?

1	2	3	4	5	6	7
hardly ever			sometimes			very often

How often does your child cry?

1	2	3	4	5	6	7
hardly ever			sometimes			very often

How changeable is your child's mood?

1	2	3	4	5	6	7
hardly ever changes or changes very slowly			sometimes changeable			changes often and quickly

Taking everything into account, how easy or difficult would your child be for the average mother?

1	2	3	4	5	6	7
very easy			neither easy nor difficult			very difficult

Results: sample range 4–25, mean = 12.83; S.D. 4.62. 59 cases (42%) were above the sample mean. (Comparable Bates mean: 21.86; S.D. 6.51)

2.   Unadaptable ('Negative adaptation to change') sub-scale (5 items)

How does your child usually respond to a person that he/she does not know?

1	2	3	4	5	6	7
almost always responds well			sometimes responds well, sometimes badly (or doesn't respond either way)			almost always responds badly/fearfully or gets upset

How does your child usually respond to being in a new place?

1	2	3	4	5	6	7
Almost always responds well			Sometimes responds well, sometimes badly (or doesn't respond either way)			Almost always responds badly/fearfully or gets upset

How does your child respond to disruptions and changes in everyday routines, such as when you go shopping or on outings?

1	2	3	4	5	6	7
Almost always responds well			Sometimes responds well, sometimes badly (or doesn't respond either way)			Almost always responds badly/fearfully or gets upset

How does your child respond to new foods? (*If your child has not yet gone onto solids, go straight to question 11*)

1	2	3	4	5	6	7

almost always
responds well

sometimes responds well,
sometimes badly (or doesn't
respond either way)

almost always
responds
badly/fearfully or
gets upset

How easily does your child get used to new things (for example, people or places)?

1	2	3	4	5	6	7

almost always
responds well

sometimes responds well,
sometimes badly (or doesn't
respond either way)

almost always
responds
badly/fearfully or
gets upset

Results: sample range = 5–26, mean = 12.45; S.D. 5.13. 58 cases (41%) were above the sample mean. (Comparable Bates Mean = 12.60; S.D. = 3.80)

Valid scores were calculable for a total of 142 children (n = 130 children aged between 12 months and 23 months, and $n = 12$ children aged 24 months exactly), using a version of scale derived from a composite of the Bates ICQ scales for children aged (a) 13 months and (b) 24 months. Children were given a score on each subscale, with 'high' scores taken as those above the mean for the subsample as a whole. Eighty-two children had high scores (that is, scores above the mean) on one subscale only; 36 had high scores on both subscales and were classified as 'difficult' for our study.

RESULTS FOR THE INFANT CHARACTERISTICS QUESTIONNAIRE (ICQ)

The ICQ gives a sample mean score against which the scores for individual children can be compared. Children scoring above the mean can be said to be perceived by their parent as more challenging than the average child. Since relatively high proportions of children scored above the mean on each of the two subscales we used ('fussy/difficult' and 'unadaptable'), we took high scores (that is, scores above the mean) on both subscales as a more conservative measure of 'general difficulties'. Just over one-quarter of the children (27%) were rated as challenging using this method. See Table A3.1.

Table A3.1 Scores on the Infant Characteristics Questionnaire (ICQ; Infants aged 13–23 months)	
	% of children with high scores (above mean)
Fussy/difficult subscale (mean = 12.2)	53
Unadaptable subscale (mean = 12.5)	43
Scores on both subscales (combined)	27

Base = 147 children aged 12–23 months with valid scores

Richman, Stevenson and Graham Behaviour Check List (BCL)

This 21-item scale (Richman, Stevenson and Graham 1982) was developed for use with children aged around three years old. It has been widely used as a simple screening device, based on a clinical-diagnostic framework approach, to identify children who might need further assessment. Like the ICQ, it is designed for self-completion by parents, and measures parents' perceptions of their child's behaviour. It covers 12 potentially problematic areas of child development and behaviour (eating, sleeping, encopresis, etc.). Some items are included for completeness only, and some are combined in scoring to avoid giving undue weighting to certain related behaviours. Twelve items are included in the final score, giving a maximum score of 24. A score of 10 or more is taken to indicate risk for emotional and behavioural problems. The BCL has been shown correctly to identify children thought to be moderately or severely disturbed in clinical criteria at a rate of about 82, with roughly 12 per cent false positives and 30 per cent false negatives.

In total, because of the age restrictions attached to use of the BCL, scores were only calculated for a total of 49 children. Of these, 36 scored 9 or less, and 13 scored 10 or more (equivalent to 27% of valid scores).

Goodman's Strengths and Difficulties Questionnaire (SDQ)

We used the parent-completed SDQ (Goodman 1994, 1997) to collect information on the behaviour of children in the sample aged upwards of four years old. The SDQ is a widely used, well-validated and simple self-completed screening instrument comprising 25 items answered on a three-point scale, which break down into five subscales each containing five items or attributes: pro-social behaviour (not included in the total difficulties score); emotional symptoms; conduct problems; hyperactivity; and peer problems. The inclusion of the pro-social behaviour subscale avoids focusing entirely on problematic areas and is thought to make the SDQ especially acceptable to parents. Parent-generated total difficulty scores on the SDQ can range from 0 to 40, with bandings for 'caseness' suggested by the author (based on data from normal community samples) of 0–13 = normal, 14–16 = borderline and 17–40 = abnormal. Results by child sex and age are given in Chapter 3.

SDQ IMPACT DATA

The SDQ also contains questions additional to the 25-item checklist, known as the 'Impact Supplement'. These questions ask if the child is considered to have a problem in various areas of functioning (emotions, behaviour, concentration or being able to get on with other people), how longstanding the problems are, whether the young people themselves are distressed by the problem, the extent of the impact on general functioning and, finally, the extent of the burden on the family as a whole. Results for the individual SDQ impact supplement questions for this sample are given in Tables A3.2 to A3.6.

Table A3.2 Impact: Does your child have difficulties in one or more of the following areas: emotions, behaviour, concentration or being able to get on with other people?

	% of valid cases
No	75
Yes, minor difficulties	18
Yes, definite difficulties	5
Yes, severe difficulties	2

Base: n = 1,224 children aged 4–16 with valid scores

Table A3.3 Chronicity: How long have these difficulties been present?	
	% of valid cases
Less than a month	4
1–5 months	9
6–12 months	17
Over a year	70

Base: n = 307 children aged 4–16 with problem in one or more area

Table A3.4 Burden: Do the difficulties upset or distress your child?	
	% of valid cases
Not at all	29
Only a little	41
Quite a lot	22
A great deal	7

Base: n = 307 children aged 4–16 with problem in one or more area

Table A3.5 Impact: Do the difficulties interfere with child's everyday life in the following areas?				
	% of valid cases			
	Home life	Friendships	Learning	Leisure activities
Not at all	35	45	27	58
Only a little	43	34	35	26
Quite a lot	17	15	24	9
A great deal	4	5	15	7

Base: n = 307 children aged 4–16 with problem in one or more area

Table A3.6 Burden: Do the difficulties put a burden on you or the family as a whole?	
	% of valid cases
Not at all	30
Only a little	42
Quite a lot	19
A great deal	8

Base: n = 307 children aged 4–16 with problem in one or more area

The Current Problems Questionnaire (CPQ)

This 23-item self-completed binary scale/checklist was adapted by us from the Difficult Life Circumstances Questionnaire (Mitchell *et al.* 1998). The DLC is designed to act as a stand-alone checklist of current problems. In part to reflect the UK context of the survey, but also because some of the items covered by the 28-item DLC were covered by our survey questionnaire in more detail in other sections of the schedule, we modified the items included in the CPQ from those in the DLC both in terms of content and wording. The style, however, owes much to the DLC. The question items cover relationships with current and former partners, financial problems, problems with work and accommodation, problems with substance misuse and difficulties with children, including problems at school and involvement with social agencies such as the police or social services.

The CPQ measures what might be althought of as acute stress (things which are currently perceived as a problem to the respondent) as well as chronic stressors (things which have been present in the individual's circumstances for a long time). It does not, however, give any indication of the 'weight' or seriousness of problems relative to one another, but simply counts the number of current problems in an individual's life. Scores can range from 0 to 23 and, in our study, the sample mean was two current problems. We classified all respondents with a score of three or more problems as having a 'high' score (30% of the sample overall).

Measuring attitudes to informal social support

This scale was derived by summing the responses to four statements:

1. I prefer not to discuss my family with people round here because you can't trust them to keep things to themselves.

2. People round here help each other out in a crisis.

3. If you ask friends or neighbours for help, you can end up feeling 'in debt'.

4. Asking for help outside the family is a sign of not coping.

Statements (1), (3) and (4) were coded as: strongly agree = 1, tend to agree = 2, neither agree nor disagree = 3, tend to disagree = 4, strongly disagree = 5, don't know = missing. Statement (2) was coded in reverse (strongly agree = 5, tend to agree = 4, etc.). Values for each statement were then summed to give a total score for each respondent. The higher the score, the more 'positive' the attitudes. For the sample as a whole, respondents' scores on this scale ranged from 1 to 20, with a mean score of 12.

Measuring attitudes to formal social support

This scale was derived by summing the responses to two statements:

1. If you ask for parenting advice from professionals, they start interfering or try to take over.

2. I can always trust local professionals to keep the things I tell them confidential.

Response categories were: strongly agree, tend to agree, neither agree nor disagree, tend to disagree, or strongly disagree (plus don't know/no opinion).

Statement (1) was coded as: strongly agree = 1, tend to agree = 2, neither agree nor disagree = 3, tend to disagree = 4, strongly disagree = 5, don't know = missing. Statement (2) was coded in reverse (strongly agree = 5, tend to agree = 4, etc.). Values for each statement were then summed to give a total score for each respondent. The higher the score, the more 'positive' the attitudes. Scores ranged from 1 to 10, with a higher score indicating a more positive attitudes to wards formal support. The sample mean was 6.57.

Appendix 4

Analysis of Survey Data

All survey data were double-keyed for accuracy and manually coded, edited and cleaned to ensure a consistent and complete data set. Analysis of the survey data was conducted using SPSS for Windows.

The concept of statistical significance

In quantitative research a key concept is that of statistical significance. When they find differences between one group and another, researchers want to know what the likelihood is that the difference could have arisen by chance, as a result of random variation, as opposed to reflecting some real ('significant') difference in the data. In general, whether a result is statistically significant or not is a function of the way in which the sample was selected, the way in which key values are distributed, the size of the groups being compared and the value that is the subject of the test. Statistical procedures that give a 'p' (for 'probability') value indicating the significance level of the result take these things into account as part of the calculations that are made. Conventionally, the threshold for a 'significant' value is set at what is referred to the 'ninety-five per cent confidence level'. This means that if a given test result has a p value of less than 0.05 per cent, the result is taken to be meaningful in that it shows that there is less than a five in a hundred possibility that this result could have occurred by chance. Put another way, if p is less than 0.05, we can be 95 per cent certain that the result is not simply a result of random variation but reflects 'real' differences within the sample (that is, the 'null' hypothesis is rejected).

The problem with the 95 per cent confidence level is that it is a relatively easy test of the 'null' hypothesis and thus a fairly non-stringent estimate of significance (De Vaus 1993; Bryman and Cramer 1999). This means that the chances of obtaining what is called a 'Type I' error (obtaining a result that is a 'false positive', that is a result that is misclassified as different when it is not) are high. Thus, within large samples such as the one we had for this survey, Type I errors can mount up. Moreover, in large samples, relatively small differences between groups can emerge as statistically significant even when they may be substantively unimportant. A solution to this is to set the confidence level higher at, say, 99 per cent, requiring a p value of less than 0.01 to indicate significance. This is a more stringent test of statistical significance and the one that we have chosen for analysing the results of the study. There is, however, a drawback with setting the level at 0.01, which is that the risk of 'Type II' errors rises – that is, the chances of obtaining a false negative result and accepting that there are no differences between groups when in fact there are. However, given a choice between two statistical evils, we have preferred to err on the side of caution. Two-tailed tests have been used throughout our analysis, as recommended for more accurate testing of 'non-directional' hypotheses (Bryman and Cramer 1999). Last, it should be remembered that statistical significance does not necessarily tell us anything about practical or substantive significance (Blalock 1981). A significant test result tells us only that the result is not very likely to have occurred by chance, all things being equal, and tells us nothing about the magnitude or direction of the difference. To determine the substantive importance of statistical results we need to examine them in the context of trends in the data, patterns of other results and, sometimes, with reference to qualitative data.

Logistic regression analysis

Partly because of the sheer volume of the data and the large number of significant associations found in them, we found it necessary to use multivariate techniques in order to distil out key factors that influence parenting in poor environments. It is too difficult to untangle the overall contribution of one factor among many simply by using a series of cross-sectional comparisons. Multivariate analyses, on the other hand, allow us establish whether any single factor has an independent effect on a given 'outcome' or 'dependent' variable, over and above the effects it has a result of 'statistical overlap' with other variables. Thus, for example, we can explore the contribution of large family size to coping with parenting while controlling for the fact that large families also tend to have lower equivalent household incomes. We can tell, therefore, if it is really family size or the poverty that goes with large family size that seems to have the most impact on coping. The technique we have mainly used is binary logistic regression analysis. This technique of analysis uses a binary (either/or) outcome variable (for example, coping/not coping). Other variables to be tested are entered into the model as independent or 'predictor' variables – variables that may or may not turn out to be significantly associated with the outcome variable once the effect of all the other variables in the model have been accounted for. If a variable is significantly associated within the model, we can say that this variable is independently required to 'predict' coping. An 'odds ratio' is generated as part of the test, and this tells us what the odds or chances are that the outcome variable will be seen (relative to its chances of not being seen) if a particular predictor variable is present. Where the independent variable is dichotomous (for example, lone parent: yes/no), the odds ratio represents the extent to which a change (for example, from lone parent to parent with a partner) affects the outcome. Where the independent variable is continuous (for example, number of children in the household) the odds ratio estimates the degree of change in the outcome associated with one unit increase (in this example, each additional child) in the independent variable. An odds ratio of one indicates an even chance of the characteristic being present. An odds ratio of more than one indicates a positive relationship between the two variables, and an odds ratio of less than one indicates an inverse relationship.

It is important to note that the term 'predict' is used in our analysis in a purely statistical sense. It does not imply that the presence of one significant variable will inevitably lead to the outcome being tested. Nor does it mean that predictor variables 'cause' the outcome. Rather, it means that the test indicates that within this particular model a certain variable is strongly, significantly and independently associated with the outcome, and may therefore be viewed as influential in the 'pathway' to that outcome. Of course, the results obtained in logistic regression models (as with any model) are only a reflection of the variables that are put into it. There may be many other important variables that we cannot, or do not, measure that might influence the pattern of prediction or the pathway to a particular outcome, and this should be borne in mind when interpreting results. Moreover, it is generally regarded as difficult to determine causation based on cross-sectional (as opposed to longitudinal) data sets, such as the one we have here, since we cannot establish the chronological sequence of predictor and outcome variables.

Notes

1. We are grateful to the to Manchester Computing MIDAS service at Manchester University for their assistance with access to the small area and local base statistics.

2. We include here only physical maltreatment and neglect, as child sexual abuse is thought to have different antecedents and to be far less strongly related to environmental variables.

3. An exception is ethnicity. The make-up of the UK population is very different to that in the US, and there is an absence of community data for the UK that speaks to possible relationship between ethnicity and parenting breakdown. We did not therefore include ethnicity in our model.

4. For example, income data, data on educational attainment and data on age of mother at birth of first child are not available on the 1991 Census.

5. See Appendix 1 for definition.

6. Principal Components Analysis was used to explore total variation; Maximum Likelihood Analysis was used to explore shared variance.

7. See Appendix 1 for definition.

8. A minimum of four visits was made at each selected address, followed by at least four visits to a selected household within that address (if relevant), followed by a further four attempts to reach the selected parent before the address was abandoned as a 'non-contact'.

9. Response to the FRS 1996–7 was 69 per cent, for example, for a sample size of over 25,000 households.

10. The one exception to this is, regrettably, that parents who did not speak English could not be included in the survey, and overall 109 families were disqualified on this basis.

References and Further Reading

Albarracin, D., Repetto, M.J. and Albarracin, M. (1997) 'Social support in child abuse and neglect: support functions, sources and contexts.' *Child Abuse and Neglect 21*, 7, 607–615.

Barrera, M. Jnr (1986) 'Distinctions between social support concepts, measures and models.' *American Journal of Community Psychology 14*, 413–445.

Barry, F.D. (1994) 'A neighborhood-based approach – what is it?' In G.B. Melton and F.D. Barry (eds) *Protecting Children from Child Abuse and Neglect: Foundations for a New National Strategy*, 14–39. New York: Guilford.

Bates, J. (1980) 'The concept of difficult temperament.' *Merrill-Palmer Quarterly 26*, 299–319.

Bates, J.E., Freeland, C.B., and Lounsbury, M.L. (1979) 'Measurement of infant difficultness.' *Child Development 50*, 794–803.

Belsky, J. (1980) 'Child maltreatment: An ecological integration.' *American Psychologist 35*, 4, 320–335.

Belsky, J. (1981) 'Early human experience – a family perspective.' *Developmental Psychology 17*, 3–23.

Belsky, J. (1984) 'The determinants of parenting: A process model.' *Child Development 55*, 83–96.

Belsky, J. (1993) 'Etiology of child maltreatment: A developmental–ecological analysis.' *Psychological Bulletin 114*, 3, 413–434.

Belsky, J. and Vondra, J. (1989) 'Lessons from child abuse – the determinants of parenting.' In D. Cicchetti and V. Carlson *Child Maltreatment: Theory and Research on the Causes and Consequences of Child Abuse and Neglect*, 153–202. Cambridge: Cambridge University Press.

Berthoud, R. and Kempson, E. (1992) *Credit and Debt; the PSI Report*. London: PSI.

Blalock, H.M. (1981) *Social Statistics – Revised Second Edition*. Singapore: McGraw-Hill.

Bradburn, N. (1992) 'A Response to the nonresponse problem 1992 AAPOR Presidential Address.' *Public Opinion Quarterly 56*, 3, 391–397.

Bradshaw, J. and Millar, J. (1991) *Lone Parent Families in the UK*. London: HMSO.

Briere, J., Berliner, L., Bulkey, J.A., Jenny, C. and Reid, T. (1996) *The APSAC Handbook on Child Maltreatment*. California: Sage/APSAC.

BMJ (1999) *Growing Up in Britain: Ensuring a Healthy Future for Our Children*. London: BMJ Books.

Bronfenbrenner, U. (1977) 'Towards an experimental ecology of human development.' *American Psychologist 32*, 513–531.

Bronfenbrenner, U. (1979) *The Ecology of Human Development*. Cambridge, MA: Harvard University Press.

Bronfenbrenner, U. and Crouter, A.C. (1983) 'The evolution of environmental models in developmental research.' In P.H. Mussen *The Handbook of Child Psychology*. New York: Wiley.

Brooks-Gunn J., Duncan. G.J., and Aber J.L. (eds) (1997) *Neighbourhood Poverty Volume I – Context and Consequences for Children*. New York: Russell Sage Foundation.

Bryman, A. and Cramer, D. (1999) *Quantitative Data Analysis with SPSS Release 8 for Windows: A Guide for Social Scientists*. London: Routledge.

Buchanan, A. and Ten Brinke, J. (1997) *What Happened When They Were Grown Up? Outcomes from Parenting Experiences*. York: Joseph Rowntree Foundation and YPS.

Burghes, L. (1994) *Lone Parenthood and Family Disruption: the Outcomes for Children*. London: FPSC Occasional Paper No 18.

Burghes, L., Clarke, L. and Cronin, N. (1997) *Fathers and Fatherhood in Britain*. London: Family Policy Studies Centre.

Butt, J. and Box, L. (1998) *Family Centred: A Study of the Use of Family Centres by Black Families*. London: REU.

Campanelli, P., Sturgis, P. and Purdon, S. (1997) *Can You Hear Me Knocking: an Investigation into the Impact of Interviewers on Survey Response Rates*. London: SCPR.

Cawson, P., Wattam, C., Brooker, S., and Kelly, G. (2000) *Child Maltreatment in the United Kingdom: a Study of the Prevalence of Child Abuse and Neglect*. London: NSPCC.

Chaffin, M.J., Kelleher, K. and Hollenberg, J. (1996) 'Onset of physical abuse and neglect: Psychiatric substance abuse and social risk factors from prospective community data.' *Child Abuse and Neglect 20*, 3, 191–204.

Chan, Y.C. (1994) 'Parenting stress and social support of mothers who physically abuse their children in Hong Kong.' *Child Abuse and Neglect 18*, 3, 261–270.

Cheung, S.Y. and Buchanan, A. (1997) 'Malaise scores in adulthood of children and young people who have been in care.' *Journal of Child Psychology and Psychiatry 38*, 5, 575–580.

Cleaver, H. and Freeman, P. (1995) *Parental Perspectives in Cases of Suspected Child Abuse*. London: HMSO.

Cochran, M., Gunnarsson, L., Grabe, S. and Lewis, J. (1990) 'The social networks of coupled mothers in four cultures.' In M. Cochran, M. Larner, D. Riley, L. Gunnarsson and C.R. Henderson (eds) *Extending Families; the Social Networks of Parents and their Children*, 86–104. Cambridge: CUP.

Cochran, M., Larner, M., Riley, D., Gunnarsson, L. and Henderson, D.R. (eds) (1990) *Extending Families: The Social Networks of Parents and Their Children.* Cambridge: Cambridge University Press.

Cochran, M.M. and Brassard, J.A. (1979) 'Child development and personal social networks.' *Child Development 50*, 601–616.

Cohen, S. and Wills, T.A. (1985) 'Stress, social support and the buffering hypothesis.' *Psychological Bulletin 98*, 310– 357.

Coleman J.S. (1988) 'Social capital in the creation of human capital.' *American Journal of Sociology 94*, 95–120.

Conger, R.D., Ge, X., Elder, G.H., Lorenz, F.O. and Simons, R.L. (1994) 'Economic stress, coercive family process and developmental problems of adolescents.' *Child Development 65*, 541–561.

Connelly, C.D. and Straus, M.A. (1992) 'Mother's age and risk for physical abuse.' *Child Abuse and Neglect 16*, 5, 709–718.

Coohey, C. (1995) 'Neglectful mothers, their mothers and partners: The significance of mutual aid.' *Child Abuse and Neglect 19*, 8, 885–596.

Coohey, C. (1996) 'Child maltreatment: Testing the social isolation hypothesis.' *Child Abuse and Neglect 20*, 3, 241–254.

Cotteril, A.M. (1988) 'The distribution of child abuse in an inner city borough.' *Child Abuse and Neglect 12*, 4, 461–468.

Coulton, C.J., Korbin, J.E., Su, M. and Chow, J. (1995) 'Community level factors and child maltreatment rates.' *Child Development 66*, 1262–1276.

Creighton, S.J. (1988) 'The incidence of child abuse and Neglect.' In K. Brown, C. Davies and P. Stratton (eds) *Early Prediction and Prevention of Child Abuse*, 31–42. Chichester: John Wiley and Sons.

Crnic, K., Greenberg, M.T., Ragozin, A.S., Robinson, N.M. and Basham, R. (1983) 'Effects of stress and social support on mothers of premature and full-term infants.' *Child Development 54*, 209–217.

Danoff, N.L., Kemper, K.J. and Sherry, B. (1994) 'Risk factors for dropping out of a parenting education programme.' *Child Abuse and Neglect 18*, 7, 599–606.

Davies, H., Joshi, H., and Clarke, C. (1997) 'Is it cash that the deprived are short of?' *Journal of the Royal Statistical Society 160*, 1, 107–126.

DETR (Department of the Environment, Transport and the Regions) (1998a) *1998 Index of Local Deprivation, Regeneration Research Summary No 15*. London: DETR and www.detr.gov.uk/regeneration

DETR (Department of Environment, Transport and the Regions) (1998b) *The English House Conditions Survey 1996*. London: DETR.

DETR (Department of the Environment, Transport and the Regions) (2000) *Indices of Deprivation, Regeneration Research Summary No 31.* London: DETR and www.detr.gov.uk/regeneration

Department of Health (1995) *Child Protection : Messages from Research.* London: HMSO.

Department of Health (1998) *Health Survey for England 1996.* London: Stationery Office.

Department of Health (1999) *Health Survey for England: Health of young people '95–'97.* London: Stationery Office.

DfEE (Department for Employment and Education) (2001) *Sure Start: making a difference for children and families.* London: DfEE.

De Vaus, D.A. (1993) *Surveys in Social Research, Third Edition.* London: UCL Press.

Dietz, T.L. (2000) 'Disciplining children: Characteristics associated with the use of corporal punishment.' *Child Abuse and Neglect 24,* 12, 1529–1542.

Dingwall, R., Eekelaar, J. and Murray, T. (1983) *The Protection of Children: State Intervention and Family Life.* Oxford: Basil Blackwell.

Drake, B. and Pandey, S. (1996) 'Understanding the relationship between neighborhood poverty and specific types of child maltreatment.' *Child Abuse and Neglect 20,* 11, 1103–1018.

DSS (Department of Social Security) (1998) *The Family Resources Survey Great Britain 1996–1997.* London: DSS/Stationery Office.

Earls, F., McGuire, J. and Shay, S. (1994) 'Evaluating a community intervention to reduce the risk of child abuse: Methodological strategies in conducting neighborhood surveys.' *Child Abuse and Neglect 15,* 5, 473–486.

Ferri, E. and Smith, K. (1996) *Parenting in the 1990s.* London: Family Policy Studies Centre.

Fieldhouse E.A. and Tye, R. (no date) 'Deprived people or deprived places? Exploring the ecological fallacy in studies of deprivation using the Sample of Anonymised Records.' Unpublished paper Census Microdata Unit, Faculty of Economic and Social Studies, University of Manchester.

Fitzgerald, J. (1998) 'Policy and practice in child protection: Its relationship to dangerousness.' In R. Jeyarajah Dent (ed) *Dangerous Care.* London: Bridge Child Care Development Service.

Foster, K. (1996) 'A comparison of census characteristics of respondents and non-respondents to the 1991 Family Expenditure Survey.' *Survey Methodology Bulletin 38.* London: OPSC.

Fowler, F.J. (1993) *Survey Research Methods.* London: Sage.

Furstenberg, F.F. Jnr (1993) 'How families manage risk and opportunity in dangerous neighbourhoods.' In W. Wilson (ed) *Sociology and the Public Agenda,* 231–258. Newbury Park CA: Sage.

Furstenberg, F.F. Jnr; Cooke T.D., Eccles J., Elder G.H. and Sameroff A. (1999) *Managing to Make It: Urban Families and Adolescent Success.* Chicago: University of Chicago Press.

Garbarino, J. (1977) 'The human ecology of child maltreatment: A conceptual model for research.' *Journal of Marriage and the Family 26,* November, 721–735.

Garbarino, J. and Crouter, A. (1978) 'Defining the community context of parent–child relations: The correlates of child maltreatment.' *Child Development 49,* 604–616.

Garbarino, J. and Ebata, A. (1983) 'The significance of ethnic and cultural differences in child maltreatment.' *Journal of Marriage and the Family 32,* November, 773–783.

Garbarino, J. and Gilliam, G. (1980) *Understanding Abusive Families.* Lexington, MA: Lexington Books.

Garbarino, J. and Kostelny, K. (1992) 'Child maltreatment as a community problem.' *Child Abuse and Neglect 16,* 4, 455–464.

Garbarino, J. and Kostelny, K. (1994) 'Neighborhood-based programmes.' In G.B. Melton and F.D. Barry (eds) *Protecting Children from Child Abuse and Neglect: Foundations for a New National Strategy,* 304–352. New York: Guilford.

Garbarino, J. and Sherman, D. (1980) 'High risk neighbourhoods and high risk families: the human ecology of child maltreatment.' *Child Development 51,* 188–198.

Gaudin, J.M. and Pollane, L. (1983) 'Social networks, stress and child abuse.' *Children and Youth Services Review 5,* 1, 91–102.

Gelles, R.J. (1975) 'The social construction of child abuse.' *American Journal of Orthopsychiatry 45,* 363–71.

Gelles, R.J. (1983) 'An exchange/social control theory.' In D. Finkelhor, R.J. Gelles, G. Hotaling and M.A. Straus *The Dark Side of Families: Current Family Violence Research,* 151–165. California, CA: Sage Publications.

Gelles, R.J. (1987) 'Community agencies and child abuse: Labeling and gatekeeping.' In R.J. Gelles (ed) *Family Violence,* 62–77. California: Sage.

Gelles, R. (1992) 'Poverty and violence towards children.' *American Behavioural Scientist 35,* 3, 258–274.

Ghate, D., Shaw, C. and Hazel, N. (2000a) *Fathers and Family Centres: Engaging Fathers in Preventive Services.* York: JRF and YPS.

Ghate, D., Shaw, C. and Hazel, N. (2000b) *Fathers at the Centre: Family Centres, Fathers and Working with Men.* Internet publication at www.rip.org.uk/reading room

Ghate, D. and Spencer, L. (1995) *The Prevalence of Child Sexual Abuse in Britain: a Feasibility Study for a Large Scale National Survey of the General Population.* London: HMSO.

Gibbons, J., Conroy, S., and Bell, C. (1995) *Operating the Child Protection System: A Study of Child Protection Practices in English Local Authorities.* London: HMSO.

Gil, D.G. (1970) *Violence Against Children – Physical Abuse in the United States.* Cambridge, MA: Harvard University Press.

Gil, D.G. (1973) 'Violence against children.' In H.P. Dreitzel (ed) *Childhood and Socialisation*, 114–32. New York: Macmillan Press.

Giovannoni, J.M. and Becerra, R.M. (1979) *Defining Child Abuse*. New York: Free Press.

Goodman, R. (1994) 'A modified version of the Rutter Parent Questionnaire including extra items on children's strengths: a research note.' *Journal of Child Psychology and Psychiatry 35*, 8, 1483–1494.

Goodman, R. (1997) 'The Strengths and Difficulties Questionnaire: A research note.' *Journal of Child Psychology and Psychiatry 38*, 5, 581–586.

Goodman, R. (1999) 'An extended version of the Strengths and Difficulties Questionnaire as a guide to child psychiatric caseness and consequent burden.' *Journal of Child Psychology and Psychiatry 40*, 5, 791–799.

Gordon, D., Townsend, P., Levitas, R., Pantazis, P., Payne, S., Patsios, D., Middleton, S., Ashworth, K. and Adelman, L., Bradshaw, J., Williams, J. and Bramley, G. (2000) *Poverty and Social Exclusion in Britain*. York: Joseph Rowntree Foundation and YPS.

Graham, H. (1994) 'The changing financial circumstances of families with children.' *Children and Society 8*, 3.

Greenberger, E. and Goldberg, W. (1989) 'Work, parenting and the socialisation of children.' *Developmental Psychology 25*, 22–35.

Gregg, P., Harkness, S., and Machin, S. (1999) *Child Development and Family Income*. York: YPS/Joseph Rowntree Foundation.

Grych, J.H. and Fincham, F.D.(1990) 'Marital conflict and children's adjustment: A cognitive-contextual framework.' *Psychological Bulletin 108*, 267–290.

Gunnarsson, L. and Cochran, M. (1990) 'The support networks of single parents: Sweden and the United States.' In M. Cochran, M. Larner, D. Riley, L. Gunnarsson and C.R. Henderson (eds) *Extending Families; the Social Networks of Parents and their Children*, 105–116. Cambridge: CUP.

Guterman, N.B. (1997) 'Early prevention of physical child abuse and neglect: Existing evidence and future directions.' *Child Maltreatment 2*, 1, 12–34.

Halpern, J. (1990) 'Poverty and early childhood parenting: Toward a framework for intervention.' *American Journal of Orthopsychiatry 60*, 1, 6–18.

Heath, D.H. (1976)'Competent fathers: their personality and marriages.' *Human Development 19*, 26–39.

Helfer, R. (1989) 'The developmental basis of child abuse and neglect.' In R.E. Helfer and R.S. Kempe (eds) *The Battered Child, 4th Edition*, 60–80. Chicago, IL: University of Chicago Press.

Henderson, S. (1981) 'Social relationships, adversity and neurosis: An analysis of prospective observations.' *British Journal of Psychiatry 138*, 391–398.

Hobfall, S.E. (1988) *The Ecology of Stress*. London: Hemisphere Publishing Corporation.

Howard, M., Garnham, A., Fimister, G., and Veit-Wilson, P. (2001) *Poverty: the Facts, 4th edition.* London: Child Poverty Action Group.

Hubert, N.C., Wachs, T.D., Peters-Martin, P., and Gandour, M.J. (1982) 'The study of early temperament: Measurement and conceptual issues.' *Child Development 53*, 571–500.

Jack, G. (1997) 'An ecological approach to social work with children and families.' *Child and Family Social Work 2*, 109–120.

Jarman, B. (1983) 'Identification of underprivileged areas.' *British Medical Journal 286*, 28th May 1983, 1705–09.

Jones, E.D. and McCurdy, K. (1992) 'The links between types of maltreatment and demographic characteristics of children.' *Child Abuse and Neglect 16*, 2, 201–215.

Kaufman, J. and Zigler, E. (1989) 'The intergenerational transmission of child abuse.' In D. Cicchetti and V. Carlson (eds) *Child Maltreatment: Theory and Research on the Causes and Consequences of Child Abuse and Neglect*, 129–150. Cambridge: Cambridge University Press.

Kempe, C.H. and Kempe, R.S. (1978) *Child Abuse.* London: Fontana.

Kempson, E. (1996) *Life on low income.* York: YPS/Joseph Rowntree Foundation.

Kiernan, K. and Estaugh, V. (1993) *Cohabitation: Extra-marital child bearing and social policy.* London: FPSC.

Kolko, D. (1996) 'Child physical abuse.' In J. Briere, L. Berliner, J.A. Bulkley, C. Jenny, and T. Reid (eds) *The APSAC Handbook on Child Maltreatment.* Thousand Oaks, CA: Sage.

Kotch, J.B., Browne, D.C., Ringwalt, C.L., Stewart, P.W., Ruina, E., Holt, K., Lowman, B. and Jung, J.W. (1995) 'Risk of child abuse and neglect in a cohort of low-income children.' *Child Abuse and Neglect 19*, 9, 1115–1130.

Krugman, R., Lenherr, M., Betz, L. and Fryer, G. (1986) 'The relationship between unemployment and physical abuse of children.' *Child Abuse and Neglect 10*, 415–418.

Larner, M. (1990) 'Changes in network resources and relationships over time.' In M. Cochran, M. Larner, D. Riley, L. Gunnarsson and C.R. Henderson (eds) *Extending Families; the Social Networks of Parents and their Children*, 181–204. Cambridge: Cambridge University Press.

Lazarus, R. and Folkman, S. (1984) *Stress, Appraisal and Coping.* New York: Springer.

Little, M. and Mount, K. (1999) *Prevention and Early Intervention with Children in Need.* Aldershot: Ashgate.

Louis, A., Condon, J., Shute, R. and Elzinga, R. (1997) 'The development of the Louis MACRO (Mother and Child Risk Observation) forms: assessing parent-child-infant risk in the presence of maternal mental illness.' *Child Abuse and Neglect 21*, 7, 589–606.

Luthar, S. S., Cicchetti, D. and Becker, B. (2000) 'The construct of resilience: A critical evaluation and guidelines for future work.' *Child Development 71*, 3, 543–562.

Lynn. P. and Lievesley, D. (1991) *Drawing General Population Samples in Great Britain.* London: SCPR.

McCormick, J. and Philo, C. (1995) 'Where is poverty? The hidden geography of poverty in the United Kingdom.' In C. Philo (ed) *The Social Geography of Poverty in the UK,* 1–22. London: CPAG.

McLeod, J.D. and Shanahan, M.J. (1993) 'Poverty, parenting and children's mental health.' *American Sociological Review 58,* 351–366.

Madge, N. (ed) (1983) *Families at Risk.* London: Heinemann.

Margolin, L. (1992) 'Child abuse by mothers' boyfriends: Why the over representation?' *Child Abuse and Neglect 16,* 4, 541–551.

Mayall. B. (1990) 'Childcare and childhood.' *Children and Society 4,* 4, 374–385.

Meltzer, H., Gatward, R., Goodman, R. and Ford, T. (2000) *The Mental Health of Children and Adolescents in Great Britain.* London: Office for National Statistics.

Middleton, S., Ashworth, K., and Braithwaite, I. (1998) *Small Fortunes: Spending on Children, Childhood Poverty and Parental Sacrifice.* York: Joseph Rowntree Foundation.

Middleton, S., Ashworth, K., and Walker, R. (1994) *Family Fortunes: Pressures on Children and Parents in the 1990s.* London: Child Poverty Action Group.

Milner, J. and Chilamkurti, C. (1991) 'Physical child abuse perpetrator characteristics: a review of the literature.' *Journal of Interpersonal Violence 6,* 3, 345–366.

Milner, J.S. and Robertson, K.R. (1988) 'Inconsistent response patterns and the prediction of child maltreatment.' *Child Abuse and Neglect 13,* 1, 59–64.

Mirlees-Black, C. (1999) *Domestic Violence: Findings from a New British Crime Survey Self-completion Questionnaire.* London: Home Office.

Mitchell, S.K., Magyary, D.L., Barnard, K.E., Sumner, G.A. and Booth, C.L. (1998) 'A comparison of home-based prevention programs for families of newborns.' In L.A. Bond and B.M. Wagner (eds) *Families in Transition: Primary Prevention Programs that Work.* Beverly Hills, CA: Sage.

National Family and Parenting Institute (1999) *Launch Pack.* London: NFPI.

ONS (Office of National Statistics) (1999) *Social Trends 29.* London: The Stationery Office.

ONS (Office of National Statistics) (2001) *Social Trends 31.* London: The Stationery Office.

Page, D. (2000) *Communities in the Balance: The Reality of Social Exclusion on Housing Estates.* York: Joseph Rowntree Foundation, York Publishing Services.

Parton, N. (1985) *The Politics of Child Abuse.* London: Macmillan.

Parton, N., Thorpe, D. and Wattam, C. (1997) *Child Protection: Risk and the Moral Order.* Basingstoke: Macmillan.

Parke, R. and Collmer, C. (1975) 'Child abuse: An interdisciplinary review.' In E.M. Hetherington (ed) *Review of Child Development Research* (Vol. 5). Chicago, IL: University of Chicago Press.

Pascoe, J.M. and French, J. (1990) 'The reliability and validity of the Maternal Social Support Index for primiparous mothers: A brief report.' *Family Medicine 22*, 228–230.

Pelton, L.H. (1978) 'Child abuse and neglect: The myth of classlessness.' *American Journal of Orthopsychiatry 48*, 4, 608–617.

Pelton, L.H. (1981) *The Social Context of Child Abuse and Neglect.* New York: Human Sciences Press.

Pelton, L.H. (1994) 'The role of material factors in child abuse and neglect.' In G.B. Melton and F.D. Berry (eds) *Protecting Children from Child Abuse and Neglect: Foundations for a New National Strategy*, 131–181. New York: Guilford.

Phelps, J.L., Belsky, J. and Crnic, K. (1998) 'Earned security, daily stress, and parenting: A comparison of five alternative models.' *Development and Psychopathology 10*, 21–38.

Pianta, R., Egeland, B. and Erikson, M.F. (1989) 'Results of the mother–child interaction research project.' In D. Cicchetti and V. Carlson (1989) *Child Maltreatment: Theory and Research on the Causes and Consequences of Child Abuse and Neglect*, 203–252. Cambridge: Cambridge University Press.

Pithouse, A. and Holland, S. (1999) 'Open access family centres and their users: Positive results, some doubts, and new departures.' *Children and Society 13*, 3, 167–178.

Polansky, N.A., Chalmers, M.A., Williams, D.P. and Werthan Buttenweisen, E. (1981) *Damaged Parents: An Anatomy of Child Neglect.* Chicago, IL: University of Chicago Press.

Polansky, N.A., Gaudin, J.M., Ammons, P.W. and Davis, K.B. (1985) 'The psychological ecology of the neglectful mother.' *Child Abuse and Neglect 9*, 265–275.

Pugh, G., De'Ath, E. and Smith, C. (1994) *Confident Parents, Confident Children: Policy and Practice in Parent Education and Support.* London: National Children's Bureau.

Quinton, D. and Rutter, M. (1988) *Parenting Breakdown: The Making and Breaking of Intergenerational Links.* Aldershot: Avebury.

Quittner, A.L., Glueckauf, R.L. and Jackson, D.N. (1990) 'Chronic parenting stress: moderating versus mediating effects of social support.' *Journal of Personality and Social Psychology 59*, 6, 1266–1278.

Rahman, M., Palmer, G., Kenway, P. and Howarth, C. (2000) *Monitoring Poverty and Social Exclusion 2000.* York: Joseph Rowntree Foundation.

Reder, P., Duncan, S. and Gray, M. (1993) *Beyond Blame: Child Abuse Tragedies Revisited.* London: Routledge.

Richman, N., Stevenson, J., and Graham, P. (1982) *Preschool to School: A Behavioural Study.* London: Academic Press.

Roberts, C., Cronin, N., Dodd, T., and Kelly, M. (1995) *National Study of Parents and Parenting Problems.* London: FPSC.

Roberts, H. (1997) 'Children, inequalities and health.' *British Medical Journal 314,* 1122–5.

Roberts, I. and Power, C. (1996) 'Does the decline in child injury mortality vary by social class? A comparison of class-specific mortality in 1981 and 1991.' *British Medical Journal 313,* 784–6.

Robertson, E.B., Elder, G.H., Skinner, M.L. and Conger, R.D. (1991) 'The costs and benefits of social support in families.' *Journal of Marriage and the Family 53,* 403–416.

Robinson, W.S. (1950) 'Ecological correlations and the behaviour of individuals.' *American Sociological Review 15,* 351–357.

Rodgers, B. and Pryor, J. (1998) *Divorce and Separation: The Outcomes for Children.* York: Joseph Rowntree Foundation and YPS.

Rodwell, M.K. and Chambers, D.E. (1992) 'Primary prevention of child abuse: Is it really possible?' *Journal of Sociology and Social Welfare 19,* 3, 159–176.

Rosenberg, M.S. and Reppucci, N.D. (1983) 'Abusive mothers: Perceptions of their own and their children's behaviour.' *Journal of Consulting and Clinical Psychology 51,* 5, 674–682.

Rutter, M., Giller, H. and Hagell, A. (1998) *Antisocial Behavior by Young People.* Cambridge: Cambridge University Press.

Rutter, M., Tizard, B. and Whitmore, W. (1970) *Education, Health and Behaviour.* London: Longman.

Sampson, R.J. (1992) 'Family management and child development: insights from social disorganization theory.' In J. McCord (ed) *Advances in Criminological Theory Vol. 3. Facts, Frameworks and Forecasts,* 63–83. New Brunswisk NJ: Transaction Books.

Seagull, E. (1987) 'Social support and child maltreatment: A review of the evidence.' *Child Abuse and Neglect 11,* 41–52.

Sefi, S. (1988) 'Health Visitors talking to mothers.' *Health Visitor 61,* January.

Simcha-Fagan, O. and Schwarz, J.E. (1986) 'Neighbourhood and delinquency: An assessment of contextual effects.' *Criminology 24,* 667–703.

Simons, R.L., Beaman, J., Conger, R.D. and Chao, W. (1993) 'Stress, support, and anti-social behaviour trait as determinants of emotional well-being and parenting practices in single mothers.' *Journal of Marriage and the Family 55,* 385–398.

Simons, R.L., Whitbeck, L.B., Conger, R.D. and Chyi-In, W. (1991) 'Intergenerational transmission of harsh parenting.' *Developmental Psychology 27,* 1, 159–171.

Skogan, W.G. (1990) *Disorder and Decline: Crime and the Spiral of Decay in American Neighborhoods.* New York: Free Press.

Smith, T. (1996) *Family Centres and Bringing Up Young Children.* London: HMSO.

Social Exclusion Unit (2000) *Report of Policy Action Team 12: Young People*. London: SEU/Stationery Office.

Steele, B.F., and Pollock, C.B. (1968) 'A psychiatric study of parents who abuse infants and small children.' In R. Helfer and C.H. Kempe (eds) *The Battered Child*. Chicago, IL: University of Chicago Press.

Straus, M.A., Gelles, R.J. and Steinmetz, S.K. (1980) *Behind Closed Doors: Violence in the American Family*. California: Sage Publications.

Straus, M. and Kantor, G. (1987) 'Stress and child abuse.' In R.E. Helfer and R.S. Kempe (eds) *The Battered Child 4th Edition*, 42–59. University of Chicago Press.

Straus, M.A. and Smith, C. (1995) 'Family patterns and child abuse.' In M.A. Straus and R.J. Gelles *Physical Violence in American Families: Risk Factors and Adaptations to Violence in 8,145 Families*. 245–261. New Brunswick, NJ: Transaction Publishers.

Telleen, S. (1990) 'Parental beliefs and help seeking in mothers' use of a community support programme.' *Journal of Community Psychology 18*, 3, 264–276.

Thompson, R. (1995) *Preventing Child Maltreatment through Social Support: A Critical Analysis*. Beverly Hill, CA: Sage.

Tracy, E.M. (1990) 'Identifying social support resources of at-risk families.' *Social Work 35*, 252–258.

Vaux, A. (1988) *Social Support: Theory, Research and Intervention*. New York: Praeger.

Vondra, J. (1990) 'The community context of child abuse and neglect.' *Marriage and Family Review 15*, (1/2), 19–39.

Warr, P. (1997) *Work, Unemployment and Mental Health*. Oxford: Clarendon.

Wolfner, G.D. and Gelles, R.J. (1993) 'A profile of violence towards children: a national study.' *Child Abuse and Neglect 17*, 2, 197–212.

Woodroffe, C., Glickman, M., Barker, M. and Power, C. (1993) *Children, Teenagers and Health: the Key Data*. Buckingham: Open University Press.

Zuravin, S. (1988) 'Child Maltreatment and teenage first birth: A relationship mediated by chronic socio-demographic stress?' *American Journal of Orthopsychiatry 58*, 91–103.

Zuravin, S. (1989) 'The ecology of child abuse and neglect: Review of the literature and presentation of data.' *Violence and Victims 4*, 101–120.

Subject index

Author index